ONE

ONE

the gospel according to Mike

MICHAEL WILLIAMS

To order additional copies of this book, contact:
Xlibris Corporation
1-888-795-4274
www.Xlibris.com
Orders@Xlibris.com
116962

Contents

The decision concerning this book's dedication has been settled in my heart and mind for decades.

It may sound strange for a man to dedicate his life's work to a woman he has been divorced from for over 12 years. However, without Hazel Ruth Thomas Williams this book would not have been written or published.

Suffice it to say, no one comes close in my 60 years to Hazel in consideration for this dedication.

Thank you, Hazel, for loving me, caring about me, and being my best friend.

Michael Williams

In Loving Memory Of Ruth Gustafson
1955 - 2010

When I first met Ruth, I was struck by two things. Her touching honesty and the deep wounds in her soul from being told she was not in the will of God. Misguided doctrines have their deepest impact on those most honest in this life.

Instead of explaining my conversations with Ruth at the meetings and over the phone, let me just encourage you to pay very close attention to Chapter 10 in this book. As you do, think of the multiple millions who suffer from not knowing the will of God for their life. You will read how important it is to know the will of God and the joy and peace Ruth found when she too understood the will of God for her life.

My thoughts go back to when Ruth came to me. Several months before her death, Ruth said she had spent her whole life trying to figure out what the will of God was for her. She attended one of my meetings in Calgary. She said she heard the gospel as I presented it and was afraid it was too easy and too simple. However, she wanted me to tell her in my own words what I thought the will of God was for her life because, as far as she could figure out, God had failed her and was angry with her.

As carefully and lovingly as I could, I told her that the will of God for her was Jesus, and he had already fulfilled that will for everyone. Somehow she understood it almost immediately and accepted it. Her days from then on were much more peaceful and relaxed as witnessed by her care givers and family.

Ruth loved the gospel and wanted as many people as possible to hear the same good news and experience the joy and peace it brought to her. In loving memory of Ruth, I share in that same desire.

Preface

Most of us unknowingly quote or reference the King James Version of the Bible in most of what we say, even if we don't know the source. In fact, some scholars believe that as much as 64% of modern American English can be in some way seen as being rooted in the KJV. This is as much as to say that just about everyone, know it or not, loves the "Good News."

What is often neglected in our inadvertently quoting the Bible is a full reference, with what we often think of as the address of those specific verses we are quoting or paraphrasing. And many fewer times do we relate those verses to their chapters or even fully point out the context of the entire book from which those verses are being extracted; nevertheless, this is exactly how Mike Williams teaches, whole books at a time and in context.

To this end, ONE does not cite verse numbers, but they or their paraphrases can easily be looked up in the King James Version, because part of the intention here is to help the modern Bible user become as responsible for his or her own Bible understanding as is humanly possible. The Bible, fully read in context, is self-explanatory, and it would work against that message to quote or paraphrase without giving the need to see those verses in context. Don't just take anyone's word for what a verse says; read it for yourself and read it in context, what comes before it and after it!

While paraphrasing is a quick tool for getting a huge swatch of material out, a method that Mike often uses to restate an entire chapter or book in a single sentence or two, it should not be seen as a substitute for reading the context for yourself. The version used here is the King James since it is the one most often cited by most scholars; be aware that there are many ways of looking at Bible scholarship and some authors will accept any verse from any version as having equal authority, and rather than getting into a mudslinging contest over that end of scholarship, the mission of this book is to present a technology for reading and a thematic approach that may allow readers to see a comprehensive way to study the Bible as a document that we can absorb year after year as the definitive source of our own "Good News."

One of the major themes of Mike's work is to allow the Bible to speak for itself; this is something that we seldom do since we are often encouraged to memorize and stand on specific verses, many of which may only be partial sentences in and of themselves. This is easily seen when we pick up the Bible, open it anywhere and read a single verse, looking for the periods at the end of the verses. Sometimes we may see as many as 8 verses or more making up a single sentence, and so it is very easy to see how a single verse alone may be misconstrued or misapprehended.

Isn't studying the Bible all about coming to a clearer understanding of what God's Word has to say to us? Doesn't it then make good sense to read every verse as part of a whole sentence, every sentence as a part of a paragraph, every paragraph as a part of a chapter, and therefore every chapter as part of a book? When we really think about it, this makes so much sense, we wonder why we didn't think of it sooner!

Another thought along this line is that the entire book, the entire Bible, needs to have an overall method for its being understood. This really begins with our seeing the individual books as having a cogent and continuous theme and message. If we read individual verses without their context, without reading them in light of the book they are embedded in, it is very easy to start to think of each disconnected verse as being separate and unto itself.

This may make it very difficult to reconcile various verses, and it opens up a pattern of simply relating words from not only a book-to-book but an author-to-author point of view, which is not really something that can be rationally accomplished because we as individuals use words our own way. Paul and James and John and Peter may all use the same words, but they often see their own pattern or use for those same words. Different authors have their own slant or method of relating the Gospel.

We need to understand the context for each individual author and not simply use an outside resource to try to align all the verses that have a same certain word. The only tricky part about this open source reading concept is that we have often in times past depended on the work of others to network these resources and tell us what they mean and how they tie together. We have in fact been given book report after book report, year after year, but often times we cannot totally say that our own understanding is rooted wholly in the entire context specific verses came from. Therefore, over-riding our pre-conditioned way of reading certain verses out of context can be a jolt sometimes because they have literally been not only taken but ripped out of context.

Reading one book at a time on his audio and video recordings, Mike is able to help us learn to read for ourselves and see that there is a cogent and continuous message in each book. Reading in this way, we might find ourselves seeing a whole new world in the Word. Mike's work here, and herein revealing the path he took to learn this method of Bible study, presents the content that he believes is that continuous story line, the story of that One Man.

Chris Herrington, MISD
Linguistics, Art & Reading

Artwork

The artwork provided for the cover was the gracious contribution of Mural Mosaic. When Lewis Lavoie and his brother Paul heard about *One* while it was still being written, they decided to offer the use of their mural, entitled *Adam*, for the cover. Individual tiles from the mural were used to start each chapter. The video of the actual painting of *Adam* can be viewed on their website at MuralMosaic.com.

Acknowledgments

I would like to thank the many people who contributed to and collaborated on the production of *One*. Their role was significant in making this book a reality. Special thanks goes to Richard Mull for having been my confidant, advisor—my sounding board and dear friend over the course of this process and the course of this gospel journey. I am grateful to the following people who contributed their time and labor:

Lewis Lavoie
Paul Lavoie
Kate Benham
Jeff Robertson
Glenn Klein
Robert Hines
James Washburn
Joshua Tennie
Beres Bartlett
Vic d'Obrenan
Suzanne Johnson
Chris Herrington

Introduction

I recently had a wonderful lunch with a dear friend.

After my attempt to describe the "One" dynamic that God and humanity finds itself in all its potential, she took my cell phone and covered it with the plastic take-home box on the table which had my leftover sandwich in it. As she placed the box on top of my cell phone, she said, "So, it's like that!"

I replied, "Almost!" Then I took my cell phone and dropped it in *with* my sandwich and closed the lid! Her eyes grew wide and so did her smile! "Oh my, I get it!" she exclaimed. "It's just one thing, not two!!!"

Exactly, it really is just that simple while at the same time, in all perceivable applications and purposes, so profound.

YES, this is indeed a whole new creation! Yet, what can cause a cell phone and a Styrofoam box to act as one? What can cause the "new device" to function to its full potential? They need a gospel so profound that it reveals that there is no such thing as a Styrofoam box AND cell phone any longer! They are now entirely one. "One New Man"—that was the result of the all-encompassing, victorious, completely successful mission of Jesus Christ at the cross in Jerusalem 2,000 years ago.

It always was just about One Man. And it still is.

The One New Man is a fully new creation who had never been seen before on planet Earth. Never will any single human or group of humans in any generation exhaust the meaning, reality, and enormity of this new creation. Nor shall any human discover the end of the gospel's effect on the soul, which was awarded to that new creation.

This new creature, as foretold by the Holy Scriptures and through Paul's teachings, is as undiscovered and misunderstood at this point in history as the Internet was in the 1950s. The gospel and its biblically defined purpose is currently as understated today in its power and potential, as the understanding of how important satellites were when being placed in orbit over half a century ago and their role in making the Internet possible.

Is this an exaggeration or overstatement? I think not!

When we first accept this new creation as a present reality, instead of a future hope—that God and the entire human race are now literally ONE—it can be the most startling revelation of our lives.

Still, if we *are* ONE, we are ONE! If we are not ONE, then we are not. It cannot be both or any mixture of the two. The fact that we are ONE is absolute truth or it is an unmitigated devilish lie.

ONE is not TWO! Any first grader can tell you that.

Here is what my life's experience and work has uncovered: Since the death, burial, and resurrection of Jesus Christ, the human race is no longer separate from God in any way. We are no longer "in his image." And neither is God separate from humanity.

Was Jesus' prayer to the Father answered in the affirmative when he asked the Father that we would be one as he and the Father were one? I believe through the work of Christ and his cross, it was.

If you are unsure, please read further. If you are sure, please read further and be continually encouraged by the faith *of* Christ.

If our oneness with God is true, then no longer can it be said that man is dealing with sin. For God himself would be "in" sin if mankind was still a sinner because God cannot commune with sin. Never can there be another judgment after the cross. If there was, would God not be judging himself and his lack of success at Golgotha?

Could it be that whatever God's creative nature was or is now lives, dwells, and moves and has its being collectively in the hearts of the human race? Could it be that creativity and untapped genius is waiting to be unleashed? Could it be that we have just begun to scratch the surface in medicine, scientific research, communication, the arts, etc.?

And if so, what is the source of that genius, what is its power, and how will it be released? Could it be released through the receiving of the message of the gospel of God's peace and grace for all people?

Once that truth is fixed in our minds, and continually accessed, then and only then can the "new creature" reach its intended and full potential.

The union of God and humankind through Christ produced a species that never existed before. Only the gospel is designed to bring a vital, logical, rational, mental disposition to that new creature and give it the ability to release it to its full potential, whatever that may be.

We communicate like we are new creatures with cell phones, video conferencing, the Internet, and with ways to come not yet known. We travel like a new creation in cars, planes, trains and space shuttles. Is it possible in the midst of all these expanded ways of living, traveling, and communicating, is it possible we are still thinking like the "Old Creation," like those who were created in the image of God but were *not* ONE with God? Do we still perceive ourselves as those who had been imputed with sin from birth? This would be in stark contrast to the reality of a new creation, born in righteousness at birth, God and Humanity, ONE in truth, would it not?

No wonder the human race is breaking down mentally and emotionally under the burden of thinking we are condemned by God, yet communicating and traveling as though we are free!

I have come to believe that only the gospel can bring sanity to our situation.

If the cell phone and the Styrofoam box became one, as unlikely a combination as that may have been, how can we see God and humanity as One? Only a new way of thinking will cause this new way to ever be realized in its full power.

How does a phone and box now function as one? How can the God of the universe and humans function as One? Only a gospel of good news can enable something so amazing.

"For He is our peace, who hath made both one, and hath broken down the middle wall of partition between us. Having abolished in his flesh the enmity, even the law of commandments contained in ordinances; for to make in himself of twain one new man, so making peace." Ephesians 2:14-15

Enjoy the journey.

Much Love,
Mike

Chapter 1

The Pursuit of Righteousness

I was raised in a dry-cleaning plant, literally.

My father owned a dry cleaning business and, like so many people who were raised in a family business, I got stuck working there. My dad purchased the store after I was 10. Immediately, I started helping out. But mostly I just got in the way at first. By that day's standards, our shop was antiquated and struggled to remain open. At the age of 15, I quit school to help out, to the tune of about 10 hours a day. I learned the business inside and out. Whether it was shoveling coal to make steam, sorting clothes, checking, tagging, bagging, pressing, or getting orders out, I did it all. In spite of our efforts, Dad was going broke. To make matters worse, our relationship was not a good one. The long work days and strained relationship were too much for a 15 year old to take and I ended up leaving home before my 16th birthday. Around the time I turned 18 I headed for Florida.

When I got to Florida, I found my way to a job (you guessed it) in a dry-cleaning plant. At least I had a trade at my age so I could get a job anywhere. Nobody could believe that I could walk in their dry-cleaning place and be able to run any part of it they wanted me to. Most of them did not have coal-fired boilers, praise the Lord. Most cleaners were at least oil-fired or some other automatic system. I was a presser at one plant, and it was my pride and joy to press and do it more accurately than anybody else. I loved being able to put a crease in a pair of pants that was absolutely perfect with no double creases.

I went down to the beach one day and some people came and sat down on the blanket with us. They were with a group called "The Children of God." It's now known as a cult group. These were the type of people that required you to prove you were committed. You had to sell all your possessions and goods and provisions. The proceeds from the sale would be parted to every man as they had need. I thought, "*Finally* somebody who really, really does this. Somebody who *truly* obeys the Bible! They live according to the New Testament." I say "finally" because I had been a Christian all my life and hadn't seen this level of commitment. So, I joined the Children of God and dropped out of society all together. I started witnessing (preaching) to people 8 hours a day. Not long after, I left the country because our *prophet,* David Brandt Berg, who was called "Moses" amongst the Children of God, had prophesied the judgment of God was coming down on America just like Egypt in the book of Exodus. All of us *had* to get out of the United States before it was too late.

The furthest away I could get was Puerto Rico. I guess somebody failed to point out that I was still in the United States, but I couldn't afford to go any further. I raised $72 for a one way flight from Miami with no intentions of ever coming back. I walked up to the counter and bought a ticket. I got on the plane with my duffle bag and they started playing music. As the plane was starting to taxi out, the song *Exodus* began to play on the speaker system. I just knew it was God himself validating my own personal exodus because that's what we were taught—this is how God confirmed his "will" through a song coming on and other "confirmation" moments. It was a really wild experience actually. I certainly was persuaded that I *was* in the perfect will of God on that flight.

Shortly thereafter, through a series of events, I realized there was something wrong with the Children of God. We got a letter from our prophet instructing us kids that any time we were in a store we should wear a *bulky coat!* He explained there was a difference between "stealing" and "spoiling Egypt." He explained that all of the stores were Egypt, and that God told the Children of Israel to take the silver, gold and all the spoils of Egypt. He said that was not stealing. If we took something from *each other,* that would be stealing because if you took something from a brother or a sister in the Lord, *that* was the definition of stealing. Even though I had swallowed "hook, line, and sinker" pretty much everything this guy had said, my momma had taught me better than that.

From that time on, I began planning another exodus . . . my escape from the "Children of God"!

There were strict rules in the group. We could not go anywhere without someone with us. That was justified because Jesus sent his disciples out two by two. Plotting my escape was made more difficult because of this requirement. In addition, I was hungry. I'd been hungry for 3 months that summer in Puerto Rico. Fortunately, I was on trash detail. For some reason taking out the trash could be done alone. So, I gathered up some news pamphlets we would sell to bring in funding which barely fed us. Well, they fed *me* one day! I took out the trash, sold my pamphlets and fled to a McDonalds where I devoured two Big Macs, two chocolate milk shakes and two large fries. And from there, believe me when I say it was a real crazy trip. I hitchhiked all the way back to Tennessee from the airport in Miami.

After I arrived back in Tennessee, I was still practicing my "soul-winning" crusade and was trying to get my father saved. I think it shocked him that I was so brazenly preaching to him to accept Jesus into his life. My father was never in church anytime while we were growing up. We heard stories about his father, my grandfather, teaching music and singing in the choir. The family was a singing family. They were like the Cumberland Mountain Von Trapp Family Singers.

So I knew about that, but when it came to anything spiritual, my dad really never had anything to say. If he did, it was always negative except this one time. He told me about an experience he had as a boy. He said he was sitting under a tree. "I could still take you right to the tree where I was when I was just a young boy," he said. He was sitting there under a tree, just minding his own business, and suddenly the presence of God was just *on* him. My dad said he got saved that day. I don't know if I actually pressed him with questions like "Did you actually pray the prayer and ask Jesus to come into your heart?" I was in such shock my dad had said anything like this at all!

My dad and I still had a rocky relationship. I think all of us kids did with him. One day he wanted me to go for a ride with him, which was not a usual thing. You did what was necessary. But I never heard "let's go talk," or "let's do *anything!*" It just never happened except this once. I remember exactly where we were on the road near the Brushy Mountain Prison in Petros, Tennessee. We were on a road outside the prison just before you go up the mountain. My dad pulled over and started talking. He was glad I had gotten out of the Children of God and said "Mike, you just go ahead now and find you a good job." It was hard for my dad to directly talk about things. "You just go on now and kind of let that other go," he said. During my whole Christian experience I didn't realize how wise my dad was at the time. I didn't know back then that the wisest thing anybody would ever tell me about my Christianity would be "get a job and kind of let that other go!" But he said it to me. Then he told me, "After I had that experience when I was sitting under the tree, I started getting into that Bible. I started reading it and I came across a part that said that you're responsible for what you know, and that was the day I closed the book and I never read it again."

I thought my dad was about the most spiritually ignorant man that I ever knew. Now in retrospect, he was probably one of the most spiritually wise men I ever knew.

It's true. There is a place in the Bible where it speaks about being responsible for what you know. When he read that, he realized it was time to close the book because he knew he couldn't keep up with what he had already read, so why read more and be more responsible? He was spiritually mature enough even at that time to know that. I really appreciate my dad now after all these years, having tried to speak wisdom from his heart to me. He may not have understood the ins and outs of spirituality or the gospel, but he knew there was something wrong with Christianity.

"Mike, just go get yourself a job and kind of let that other go."

I sometimes stop and think what life would have been like if I had been able to "let that other go." Although I regret nothing because it all has led to where I am now, it is still true the things that took place in my life after that time certainly were things I could have avoided if I followed my dad's advice. It would have made my life better, that's for sure. Unfortunately for me, the Children of God experience was not my only hopeless pursuit of righteousness in the Christian religion.

It's been a six decade journey for me so far. I've learned some important lessons.

Of all the things that could lead to complete freedom from ALL religion around the planet, it is the truth in the scriptures that I like to call the "One Man Doctrine."

The reason that people become self-righteous and get in bondage to religion is because they have deduced that there is something in the scriptures about *them*. But what if there was a doctrine that from the very onset would remove us from the picture? Think of it. In this entire story of sin, righteousness, judgment, and redemption . . . what would it be like if we could view all scripture through the experience of one individual person, instead of it's being about us? This is how Paul understood scriptures, contrasting the First Adam with the Last Adam. It is crucial to come into this understanding. This literally by itself, has the power to obliterate every religion on the face of the Earth.

The biggest problem in the world, according to the teachings of Paul, wasn't sex, drugs, and rock 'n roll. It was self-righteousness. Paul's own conversion was from self-righteousness. It was not from Paul's murderous past. His conversion was from believing that keeping or not keeping laws could have an impact on his relationship with God.

If we accept that there was indeed only one Redeemer, isn't it strange that we cannot accept that this Redeemer redeemed all even though we teach that one condemner (Adam) condemned all? Isn't that the comparison? Sure, we teach there is one Redeemer (Jesus), but somehow we have to get ourselves involved in the story? Give me a break! Moreover, if there is any one doctrine that all Christian denominations teach, this is the one: everyone is a sinner because of the one man Adam. The Catholics teach it. All Protestant Churches teach it. Yet, none of them will accept the comparison and teach one man's obedience, Jesus' obedience, made all righteous.

This "One Man Doctrine," first seen in the Genesis, became a foundational center-point of Paul's teachings.

What I do not want to do is to try to help people figure out whether or not the book of Genesis is historical fact or spiritual truth presented in a way that we could understand it. I am not smart enough to figure that out. What we have to do, if we are going to have a belief in the Redeemer, is accept the analogies given. Then we can actually find out what exactly is being taught. We can discover what this Redeemer came to do. Very simply, there was a problem that developed in the garden between God and this "first Adam." We need to discover exactly *who* had the problem, what that problem was, and *who* redeemed the situation. You will see how it has *always* been about One Man.

I am completely convinced of the truth and reality of the redemptive work of the cross through the One Man Jesus Christ. To see the extent of the redemptive work of one man, you have to see the extent of the condemning work of one man. The problem promoted by religion is that it adds *us* into the equation. This creates self-righteousness when we actually think this is somehow about us. That we could have displeased or pleased God, this is the very definition of self-righteousness.

There are millions of people who say, "We don't believe everyone became sinners because of one man." They also say, "We don't really believe Jesus was the *only way.*" You can say anything you want, but to resolve this *scripturally*, you have to stick to the story that is provided about the subject in the body document, the scriptures.

There aren't several versions about the fall of man. There are not several versions about a redeemer coming to this planet. There's only one. There is only one place that talks about a fallen condition of mankind. There is only one source of material for the foretelling and the fulfillment of the redemption of that fallen world, and that's within the context of *scripture.*

The story told right from the outset in Genesis is the basis for redemption. It is also the basis for understanding the gospel. It is the basis for understanding the work of Christ. Without it, there is no need for the work of Christ, because we could become knowledgeable about spiritual things through our own conceptions. And that, my friends, can get into a really weird zone. I'm sure most everybody has experienced the weirdness of trying to come up with one's own individual spirituality. Still, when spirituality is allocated to the reality of only *one man's* experience, freedom begins to dawn upon the soul. Anytime any of this becomes about *you*, the light begins to go out. You do not become enlightened. Blinders begin to cover your eyes, opening the door of your thinking to shame and guilt.

When God spoke through the prophet Isaiah, he was talking about the light that was coming through the Redeemer and said, "I would give you sight, but it wouldn't do you any good because you are in complete darkness. And I would take away the darkness, but it wouldn't do any good because you are totally blind." It's irrelevant whether or not you have sight if you are in complete darkness. It's also irrelevant to have light if you're blind! And here we see this incredible struggle in the religious world. People claiming to be "in the light" yet can't see. People who claim to see, yet in complete darkness.

The first time I understood what Jesus meant by "being in darkness," it was really funny because I had previously accepted a totally different teaching about what darkness meant. Being in darkness was about my sin. My life simply did not measure up. Sex, drugs, and rock 'n roll—that was darkness. However, in John's gospel, Jesus told the disciples directly that they were in darkness. He said they were in darkness because they didn't know where they were going. The light went on for me! Being in "darkness" doesn't mean you are in sin. It doesn't mean you have done something wrong. Being in darkness means . . . you don't know where you're going.

We have an entire world that is "in darkness" because they don't know where they're going. So, let's shed some light on the subject.

Our destiny is to be in God's presence for eternity. Paul said, "to be absent from the body is to be present with the Lord." It doesn't make any difference who you are, what you've believed, what you have *not* believed, what you've done, what you have not done. To be absent from the body is to be present with the Lord. Paul was persuaded of that. I agree.

The story in Genesis could be broken down into a verse-by-verse understanding, but let's just look at what we all know about Genesis and "The fall of man."

God put Adam and Eve in the Garden of Eden.

This is about only one man. When we say "Adam," we have to understand that it refers to "Adam and Eve." Adam and Eve were "Adam." We are not leaving the female out of this because Genesis says that God created Adam and Eve, "male and female created he *them* and *their* name was called *Adam.*" It uses the singular term "Adam" for male and female. It makes no difference if it was the male or the female! In God's eyes they were one because Eve was in Adam.

From there on, it was realized and has been taught from the scriptures by Paul, that because Adam sinned, because Adam transgressed, because Adam partook of the Tree of the Knowledge of Good and Evil, God imputed Adam's transgression to the entire planet. Paul makes this very clear in his writings. Because of "*one* man's transgression," *all* were declared to be in sin.

Paul uses the term "imputed." God *imputed* sin. The term "imputed" is interesting. It means to *have charged to or against one's account*. It is to assign liability to someone making them responsible for the act of another. God literally rendered a class-action verdict in the charge of Adam's sin against all humanity.

In the exact same way, whenever we're talking about God's imputing righteousness, God is crediting righteousness to our account, even as he imputed sin to our account. This *is* the good news. Your account and everyone else's have been eternally credited with righteousness! The good news is the most wonderful thing to know and be aware of on a constant basis. It is to the on-going saving of your soul (which is different than being made righteous. Later, we'll examine this much more).

Let's return to that first man. We know the truth that it was one man who transgressed. What was his transgression? We must look at the temptation to see the transgression. We've already read that God created man in his own likeness, in the very image of God. The temptation that came from the serpent was for a specific purpose—to undermine the knowledge of that creation. God did say, "Do not eat from the Tree of the Knowledge of Good and Evil." Yet, it was the serpent who said "The moment that you do, you will be like God."

Sin did not start on this planet. Sin started in heaven. *The* sin was the attempt and desire to be "like God." And it was not started by your own efforts.

It all started with Lucifer in heaven through *his* effort to be like God and even to supplant God. So, God cast Lucifer out of heaven for breaching the trust that God had bestowed upon this now fallen angel.

Where was Lucifer cast out of heaven to? Right here on Earth. And we see him early in the book of Genesis interacting with God's creation. And what does he do? He tries to "infect" the humans that were present with the same condition that he found himself in. He tempted Adam to become like God. The moment Adam partook of the tree does not just represent disobedience to God's direct command. The real issue was that Adam was subtly manipulated into disagreeing with God by his wanting to become like God rather than accepting he was already like God.

How ironic! Man (Adam and Eve) was attempting to be something he already was.

In all of man's dealings with God, from when Adam first bit into that fruit and all the way up to Moses, every time man tried to relate to God based on some law man failed. So, when Moses came along, God decided to give man "the law." I see this as God saying "OK, so you want relationship with me based on law? Then I will be the one who determines what those laws are," because God wanted to ultimately free man from the bondage which man had *bitten into*. He wanted to free his creation from it, but the only way he could do it was to choke humanity on that fruit of self-righteousness first. It's as if God was saying, "If you want to take a bite, here's the whole thing, the whole knowledge of both good *and* evil. Now chew on that awhile!"

It was for man's benefit to show him he cannot ever relate to God based on performance. Here is why it is so deadly to attempt to do so. When every thought and intricacy of your life is tied up, even your every thought regarding rules and regulations in relating to God brings you right back to the mindset that resulted in the consumption of the fruit in the Garden of Eden. Talk about rotten fruit!

One of the most common definitions of "The Original Sin / The First Transgression" is *unbelief*. Unbelief was the problem.

In Chapter 1 of Isaiah's prophecy it states, "My people don't know who they belong to, or where they go. The ox has its home, and the ass has its crib. He says "even donkeys know who they are, and even donkeys know who they belong to, but my people—they don't know." So, even in Isaiah, when God was trying to resolve the problem, he didn't say, "My people don't belong to me." He was saying "The problem is my people don't *know* they belong to me."

The entire tragedy with the first Adam was his unbelief. So, let's accept that at face value. Adam's unbelief was "the sin." What did God impute to them? Did God impute the eating of that fruit to everyone? The true transgression has to be seen in light of the true temptation, and the temptation was to "become like God." The actual eating of the fruit is not what was imputed. Yes, it was the direct disobedience to God. But as Paul tells us, we did not "sin" in the same way Adam did. What was imputed to all was this condition of unbelief and ignorance about who we are. Adam was "deceived" by the serpent into doubt and disbelief.

Religion is always trying to get us to become something, to effect change in us, to cause us to be more holy and righteous. What a travesty that religion's whole focus is to get us to be something we already are. So, what is the evil in that? Institutions trying to get people to become believers are actually getting people to become *unbelievers*. Religion reinforces the same unbelief of Adam. It is trying to get us to *be* righteous before God when we already are.

Christianity, like most religions, is all about trying to make points with someone who is no longer keeping score.

The most hideous thing that ever happened pertaining to the law was not that men broke the law, because ALL men broke the law. The conclusion of the psalmist was "There is none righteous; no, not one." And this was the conclusion of all the prophets—there is nobody righteous. Nobody could become righteous through the law. I will bring up this point again later about how Jesus was righteous. Was Jesus righteous because He kept the law? Or was Jesus righteous because of his spiritual birth and lineage?

The real problem in the pursuit of righteousness was not the breaking of the law. The real problem was trying to keep the law so that man could *attain* righteousness. Read Deuteronomy. After God gave the law, man looked at it and said, "Wow, this is good! This shall be our righteousness: to keep all that God has commanded." Do you see? The first time the idea of righteousness coming from doing everything God said came from man! It did not come from God. This was man's idea. And they were off to the races pursuing something they could never attain.

Now the law was given *after* the fall of Adam. In fact, it was some 2,600 years after. A reprobate mind is the condition of man that senses disapproval and rejection from God. The law only intensifies this mindset. As Paul understood, "the law is the strength of sin (or unbelief)." Make no mistake. Unbelief was the original problem.

Amazingly, it hasn't changed, folks!

The law, as Paul speaks of it so clearly in Romans, was given to reveal the condition that existed before the law was ever given. Paul is telling us that the law never made a man a sinner. It was God who made the human race sinners by imputing Adam's transgression. Only by imputed righteousness without works can God be a just God by his own determination for it was God who imputed sin to the whole world by the deed of one man. Makes you wonder doesn't it? Why are we so obsessed with doing right when doing wrong was never the issue in the first place? There must be something fundamental we are missing. We must keep in mind both sides of the coin here. Just as the law never made man a sinner; it also never made man righteous. People can expand the law out in so many different ways. We hear "The law is a pattern. The law is a blueprint for how we *should* live." But the law was not given to take care of the problem. The law was given to reveal *what the problem was*. The problem was with *one man*.

The ultimate conclusion of this, even as the prophets foretold, was that one man—who Paul referred to as the Last Adam—was going to come and resolve the problem that one man, the First Adam created for all. By doing so, he would completely vindicate the human race from this imputed sin. Please understand, no one has ever been a sinner because of what they did. It is not possible. Sin *existed*. Note: that word is in the past-tense. (We'll delve into that later.) Sin existed at one time because of what *one man* did, one man's transgression. One man's unbelief was imputed to all people. And it was not man's choice. It was God's choice to impute.

So, the law was given. Why was the law given in such expansive detail? In its absolute condemnation of all, right down to what you eat, what you drink, who you sleep with, when you worship, how to rest. You name it, it's condemned. It became illegal to be a human! We would all be guilty *of that*, right? Whether you're heterosexual, homosexual, whether you are right or left-handed—all condemned. It may sound funny, but the law is not funny. It very seriously condemns ALL to the point of even a blemish on your skin would keep you out of the Temple.

It was a big deal to be left out of the Temple. The Temple is a type and shadow of the Kingdom of God. So, even a blemish on the skin, a *mole* would keep you out of the Kingdom of God. However, had they actually kept the rules of the law about who could go into the Temple, *nobody* could have entered into the Temple, ever. This is even true of the High Priest who went in to the Holy of Holies once a year to offer the sacrifice for the transgressions of the law for all of Israel. The Holy of Holies was the inner sanctuary of the Jewish Temple where the priests offered animal blood sacrifices for sin. The sacrifices were not being offered because they took away sin, because animal blood cannot take away sin. The law was given and these sacrifices were offered to manifest to the human race how *the* sin would ultimately be dealt with. Not how *sins* are to be dealt with, but how *the sin* of unbelief would be dealt with at the ultimate altar of sacrifice, the cross. The shedding of the blood of animals was used strictly for the covering of the transgressions of the law. The shedding of the blood of Christ took away the sin of unbelief and only *it* could.

This incredibly brilliant story evolves and takes place over the long history of Israel and all of mankind building to a climactic finish. Just like any great story, this one has a climax, the cross. But unlike any other story, this one has an eternal conclusion for all humanity. One man brought complete and total resolution forever. Once I realized that we are instructed by Jesus to go back and search through the scripture, it was a wonderful revelation to know that Jesus said the Holy Scriptures were all about *him!* That should pique your interest. At the very least it ought to give you some pause to stop and think and study these ancient writings and their prophecies in their full context with a fresh eye for what they actually are *all* about.

One thing that stands out about all of the prophets was their emphatic predictions about the punishment and judgment coming upon ALL flesh. No flesh would escape this wrath, anger, and judgment of God. This was going to culminate on one day, which was called—"The Day of Judgment" or "The Day of the Lord." Especially in Isaiah's writings, the Day of the Lord and the Lord's Day are very prominent. And it is used *only* in reference to one thing. This is of crucial importance. Throughout the references to The Day of the Lord, Isaiah is exclusively talking about the Day of the Cross, the day that Jesus would die for the sin of the entire world.

This detail is pivotal because it's the very thing that has been so horribly lost in the religious pursuit of righteousness.

The reason I'm going into these details is not to teach you how to *live* righteously. I am stressing this so much because you ARE righteous in the eyes of God. You ARE holy. You ARE perfect. Therefore, this ends ALL religious struggles between you and God. It ends the need to attempt to resolve a problem already resolved for you and for all people. This has been imputed to us. The resolution has been imputed. And this resolution does not involve you. Just like the characters in a story that have gone through the climax, we are now experiencing the wonderful catharsis of its conclusion! Just as God never asked us to participate in being made a sinner, he also never asked us to participate in this "New Covenant." He asked *no other person* to become a *participant*. Your involvement was prohibited and it never required your agreement or involved your will. You didn't have to "believe" in Adam. You didn't have to "know" about Adam. It didn't make any difference if you knew about Adam or not—God imputed the sin of unbelief to ALL. If God imputed sin to all, not only would it have to be God who imputes righteousness, he would have to impute it to *all*. If righteousness is imputed *at* all, it must be imputed *to* all.

Humanity was literally *one* in its sin, the sin of the First Adam. And now what are we? We are literally *one* in his righteousness, the righteousness of the Last Adam. Can you see the comparison Paul is trying to communicate?

As this story progressed through the prophets, the entire revelation of the gospel can be seen. It's important to note that all of the books of prophecies came *after* the law was given. All prophecy was influenced by God's law. That's why Jesus said that not one jot or tittle shall pass from the law until *all* prophecy is fulfilled. You cannot separate the two. Prophets prophesied according to the law. If it didn't match up, they were to be stoned to death.

You might say, "Well see Mike, that's where I disagree with you. I don't believe that all of God's law and all the prophets were fulfilled at the cross. What did Jesus say in Matthew 5? "For verily I say unto you, till heaven and earth pass, one jot or one tittle shall in no wise pass from the law, till all be fulfilled." But you and I both know every Christian denomination believes that *some* of the law was changed, right? At least a jot or a tittle had to be changed, correct? If you are a believer in Jesus, you know the laws of sacrifice have been changed—they are just not there anymore. Why? Jesus fulfilled them! Accept the fact that Jesus said "Not one jot or tittle of the law." A jot and a tittle are Greek terms. A jot or a tittle is something that would change the meaning of something just a little bit. Jesus said, "Not one jot or tittle shall pass from the law until all prophecy is fulfilled." You cannot separate the two.

Christianity will agree immediately with the fact that the law has been altered to some degree. But they haven't really grasped the magnitude of what Jesus declared here in Matthew 5. Simply put, if all prophecy is *not* fulfilled, why are we not still sacrificing animals? The law is still in effect if all prophecy is not fulfilled. There is no "gradual fulfillment." The Jews know this, but Christians don't. God spoke of a "*day,*" not thousands of years. We are very quick to judge the Jewish people for "missing their Messiah." But I think it would be wise for us to consider what kind of kingdom we are looking for and examine what exactly we are expecting.

Just because we do not "see" what we think we should see, it doesn't mean that we can twist the words of Jesus himself about the fulfillment of scripture. We all must come to this revelation on our own, so I'll encourage you to study this for yourself.

Throughout all prophecy, the prophets foretold of the judgment coming upon the whole human race. Why was it coming upon the whole human race? God had given the law. And what was the judgment for breaking the law, any law? Death. Therefore, the prophets had to prophesy according to the law. Their prophecies were restricted, guided, designed, molded, and shaped by the law. Each and every one of these prophets foretold of a cataclysmic, catastrophic end to the human race through the judgment, punishment, anger, and wrath of God. However, within the next breath you will find each of these prophets following with a big old "BUT!" At that moment, "God will raise up a standard." I never will forget seeing those verses in context, "When the enemy comes in like a flood, God would raise up a standard." Do you know that "a standard" is actually what the cross is called by Paul? He spoke of God raising-up a standard, the cross of Christ.

Judgment was *coming*! Like it or not. Judgment was on its way. But remember, the same prophets also said "Yes, this is going to happen, *but* something is going to intervene." That's what the term "savior" or "redeemer" indicates.

Jesus saved us from God.

He saved us from God's anger. He saved us from God's wrath concerning sin.

I understand the wish to believe that God was never really angry. But you see if we rely on the validity of scriptures for the truth of this marvelous story, then we have to receive the *entire* content of it. The cross brought a resolution. It resolved God's enmity with man. It may have been a symbolic anger or division. I don't know *how* you want to take it, but the one thing you can't do is *take it out*. The prophets were only too aware of the one time God had wiped out the entire human race, except for one extended family. They remembered how God had wanted to wipe out Israel altogether and start over with Moses in Exodus 32. The prophets were in no way ignorant of God's anger with sin. I know a lot of people want to think "Well, I don't believe God was ever angry." Well, that's fine—that's like saying "Well, I don't believe that just one man threw us into sin." But you see, if you don't believe *that* then your mind is going to become self-righteous, and *you* are going to place yourself in and as part of this redemption story. But you and I are NOT part of it. Our names are not in the redemption story. Your life *was redeemed* by the one man and HIS redemption story. But your name is not in the plot or the plan of redemption.

What a movie this story would make!

Can you imagine all the religious concepts about judgment, punishment, and wrath, and actually accepting what the book of Revelation said and what all of the prophets said, and letting this whole movie be built on these pre-conceived ideas? Then the realities—not just pre-conceived notions—that REAL anger of God is coming! Wrath is coming! Punishment is coming! Judgment is coming!

Then all of a sudden the reality of the cross appears at Golgotha, and the four winds of the Earth gather all of this judgment up—all the prophecies culminating in "the great and terrible Day of the Lord."

Imagine the reality hitting every person who views this movie—that literally all that anger, all that wrath, all that judgment coming, all of the madness we read of in the book of Revelation, those things flying out of the heavens, aiming at the human race, and all of this judgment that was foretold, and all of them getting caught up in this whirlwind that is swirling around the planet, and pulling every bit of it together, at the very moment that the cross goes into the ground, and seeing these winds of the world gathering . . .

ALL wrath,
ALL anger,
ALL judgment,
ALL prophecy into a whirlwind—
ALL being funneled, not into the human race, but into the body of ONE.
ALL into the body of the last man, the last Adam, *Yeshua*—"the anointed one."

Now that would be a blockbuster. Imagine what Steven Spielberg or George Lucas could do with that?

Just briefly recounting the story here is enough to give you a complete understanding of what redemption really is, that we have been redeemed from the sin of unbelief and its corresponding consequence which God had imputed to the lineage of Adam.

Let's look at the origin of this story again. When God was "looking" for Adam in the garden, he asked, "Adam, where art thou?" So, check it out. Here is God, the creator of all things, having lost the only man he had ever made. And he didn't know where he was? God, the "Omniscient, Omnipresent One," who knows the very hairs of your head, lost the only man he ever made?

This is ridiculous and sad at the same time. When God was asking, "Adam, where are you?" what was he really asking? Do you really believe God lost Adam and was trying to find him? Well, I think that God was asking *where Adam's head* was at. Because it wasn't *God* who didn't know where he was, it was Adam who didn't know where he was. In his unbelief, Adam didn't know what God had said about man. God was asking, "Do you *know* you are in unbelief?" Sadly, Adam did *not* know he was in unbelief.

We must emphasize over and over the reason God gave the law. David said that he loved God's law. I'm here to tell you that, like David, I love God's law, too. I love it because I understand and so appreciate the reason God gave it. Institutionalized Christianity says it loves the law for the same reason that ancient Israel openly stated that they loved it. Israel claimed that the law would be their righteousness. David, however, claimed that God would be his righteousness.

The reason you ought to love God's law is because it has that wonderful revelation in it. All those laws were given for the revelation of unbelief as THE sin. The real problem was imputed unbelief, not the transgression of the law. The law was designed to create hopelessness, revealing the unbelief of ALL. And it worked real good!

It is only through the hopelessness of self-righteousness that we can fully understand the hope that is realized in his righteousness.

In Romans 7, Paul taught about things before and after the cross. Because Christianity has yet to grasp the enormity of the cross, people think Paul is talking about life after his conversion. But he is not. He's comparing being under the law *before and after* the cross. If you are under the law now, after the cross, there is immediate deliverance available from that mindset. Paul's teaching in Romans 7 is not about *before* he got saved, and *after* he got saved. It's about what life was like under the law.

Paul no longer struggled and warred against "sin" as Christians hopelessly do in their religion. They think it is normal because that's what Paul did, they reason. However, Paul was indeed delivered from this never-ending battle. He realized Jesus had set him free from the law of sin and death, finally and forever, at the cross. There was no more "law of sin" working in his members." Paul is describing the liberating power of the gospel in his life, not the current battle for morality he was fighting. Our battle is to keep this revelation! This is particularly good news for Christians! Paul *did* get his revelation after his road-to-Damascus experience. But Paul was not talking about his "daily Christian experience" even though this is what is taught by Christianity.

Really, this is just so sick

Paul was actually teaching how wonderful the law is. Within the context of our current unconditional love relationship with God, Paul's talking about how wonderful and perfect the law is—for it had accomplished its purpose to perfection. Paul, being a "Hebrew of the Hebrews" and the only scholar among the apostles, understood the law's designated purpose. He says, "Therefore, I find a real battle going on. When I *try* to do good (trying to keep the law), I don't find the ability to do it. And when I try not to do wrong (to not break the law), I don't find the ability to do *that. So,* then woe is me! Who shall deliver me from this?" Then he makes it very clear that Jesus himself is the *one* who delivers Paul, and also us! Jesus is our Deliverer! Paul is really teaching about his deliverance from this struggle under the law and how it all ended with the sacrifice of Jesus.

We do not wrestle with good and evil anymore.

It is Christianity that continues to implore every person to war over good and evil within themselves and within society. And it is Christianity that is constantly reviving the old battle of self-righteousness.

We need to tell them the battle is over. The battle has been won by . . . ONE!

Chapter 2

The Gospel of Peace

If I had understood earlier in my life what Paul's term "Gospel of Peace" actually meant—that all hostilities between God and humanity had ceased—things may have been very different for me.

While I do not regret my journey in any way, because that is the path that delivered me to where I am today, the reality is that since I was a child there was a war waging on the inside of me. In fact, I struggled desperately well into my adult life.

Married just after I turned 21, my bride Hazel was 23. Hazel is very special to me. I do love her, but it is not in a classic romantic or sexual way. Hazel came into my life in the middle of my earnest attempt to break free from homosexuality. I was engaged in what seemed to be a make-or-break effort to resolve the raging internal conflict over my spirituality and my sexuality. If there was to be a resolve to my sexuality with what I saw as my spirituality, then only one of them could survive. This is a major reason why I am so grateful for the gospel, not only for my life but for every human being. The gospel allows your "humanity" and your spirituality to co-exist.

What seems like such contradictory, conflicting aspects of each person—their humanness and the holiness of God which resides inside each are at perfect peace with each other if we would only realize it. This is what the scripture means when it speaks of the lion and the lamb being able to lie down together. Spiritually speaking the lion and the lamb of your soul—in your mind—have found such peace that you can come to accept both your perfection in God and your need to grow as a person.

Although the scriptures actually say "the wolf lies down with the lamb" in what Bible scholars call a "type or shadow" of Jesus and his effect on humans and their respective souls—that reference is commonly known as "the lion lies down with the lamb." For our purpose here, I will stick with the common understanding.

There's a part in each of us that is a lion, that is aggressive, that has a predatory nature. Everyone has this very aggressive part, and then everyone has a very passive part—the lamb. But there's reconciliation for these seemingly warring factions in each heart. I recall so well trying to choose which one in my own soul that I would side with. Was I going to be one of those people who are really aggressive and demanding or am I going to be one of those people who are really submissive and nice? It appeared they could not exist together. But they did indeed find peace with each other.

I now know I have both these aspects in my heart and personality, and I'm more than good with it. Anybody who's ever spent time around me knows these two parts are both alive and well in me, that they co-exist peacefully with each other and within me. This "internal peace treaty" is a major deal. Before the gospel came into my life, nothing would co-exist in me. Nothing could lie down.

Nothing could be at peace. There was just a constant conflict in my heart and mind and soul, a conflict that manifested itself in mental illness in a very profound way culminating with six terms in mental institutions and lock-up wards and three attempts at suicide.

The battle over my sexuality and my religion had reached a fevered-pitch. It was unbearable. This was a major driving force behind my desperate need to get married. I needed to force myself to be heterosexual. I didn't mind forcing myself to do it, but it just did not work no matter what I did. Within this struggle came an attempt at suicide. It was not a cry for help; it was a very real attempt to kill myself. I had survived, but it was that suicide attempt that actually persuaded my brother to become a believer. My brother became a very religious man. He had never been to church a day in his life before that as far as I could remember.

It's really strange. My brother, who has found it very difficult to accept me and who I am, was driven to the "altar of God" as his gay brother lay in a bed having almost died from suicide. Please don't get me wrong, my brother is a very good man. However, his stance against my sexuality has persisted to this day.

This journey of life gives us all kinds of things that we'll never be able to explain.

Soon after this episode in my life, I was introduced to Norvel Hayes through a man who lived in the town where I was from. A man, whom I found out later, had actually fasted and prayed for me for 40 days. No one knew why he was fasting and praying, but he *fasted*. He had nothing but water for 40 days and went from a very large, strapping man to just a little frail guy in 40 days. It was amazing. So, I agreed then to go visit with Norvel.

Norvel Hayes was becoming a popular speaker in some fringe Evangelical/Pentacostal groups known as "Full Gospel" and later, the "Word of Faith" movements. He was a good story teller and made a name for himself as someone who cast out demons and laid hands on the sick to be healed. Teaching the so-called "Prosperity Gospel" was also high on his list of "specialties."

During my time with Norvel, the conflict between my sexual orientation and my religious persuasion became magnified. Far from finding resolution, it just added fuel to the fire. The desperate need to come to some resolve led to a lot of things that just were not true. Norvel helped me construct a "testimony" that I had been "delivered" from homosexuality. It's remarkable that when we become so desirous for truth that we will tell a lie to try to get there. Simply said, truth arrived at through a lie is never the *truth*.

By 1979, I was pastor of a church in Illinois. After being pastor at that church for close to a year, I was offered a pastor position at a larger church. We left the first church and had to move because the new church was in a town about an hour away. So, I had actually been the pastor of two churches from 1979-1983. Right after that is when everything really took off for me "professionally." I hit the speaking circuit full-bore by sharing my "testimony," which turned out to be quite lucrative. At that same time the knowledge of the real gospel was growing in me.

I first shared the Gospel of Peace in 1982. I discovered that the Gospel of Peace literally meant the good news of the cessation of hostilities—the end of the hostile relationship between God and man. And now I went public with it.

Realizing through the gospel that God was at peace with me, it was troubling that I was not at peace with myself—especially about my sexuality. This contradiction needed to be resolved. The tough thing was that I was trying to resolve it on stage in front of people while all of this turmoil was taking place within me. I didn't have the luxury of finding somewhere to go away to, to take care of all of this. It was all dealt with on stage and in public in front of everyone.

The first major departure from Evangelical Christianity that the gospel presented me was what Paul called "the Gospel of Peace." I studied for five years before I ever spoke a word of it. I had been with Norvel Hayes Ministries since August 15, 1974.

The first time I spoke of the Gospel of Peace was 1982 after having delved into it for those five years prior. So, it was four years with Norvel before I even ever started entertaining the gospel at all. Then in 1978, I commenced contemplating this wonderful reality. Still, it took me FIVE years to get up the gumption to go public with it in 1982. The only thing I was focused on was the Gospel of Peace. It was such an immense issue in and of itself. It was such a radical change from everything I had ever been taught or had taught myself while in Evangelical Christianity.

I searched everywhere to find someone who understood the Gospel of Peace. It wasn't as though I was coming up with terminology that was not in the Bible. Still, it seemed that no one, *no one* believed that there was a Gospel of Peace. The search was really amazing. The very first time that I taught on it in public was when I was the pastor of the church in Southern Illinois. There were a couple hundred people in the congregation before we built a new facility, and it was full. It was always fun to have a full service. Those things meant a lot to me. It could affect me one way or the other, as to whether or not I felt *anointed* or not! If the crowds were good—I was anointed. If the crowds weren't good—I didn't feel anointed. It was great to get past that to where it really didn't make any difference what the size of the crowd was. I stood and preached the Gospel of Peace, declaring that God is not angry with anyone and had not been for 2,000 years. I was so emotionally spent when I finished that session. The message was greeted with great joy. No one tried to take me aside afterward and contradict me. That particular congregation of people certainly never did hesitate to voice their opinions in the past. So, if they did have reservations, they really didn't know how to express them or where to start. It impacted people's lives profoundly, mine included.

As I looked for someone who seemed to "get it," I remember thinking it sounded like a popular Word of Faith preacher believed the Gospel of Peace. As I listened to him, I hoped and prayed that really was the truth. Then I heard him say, "God is not going to put up with that anymore. God may have winked at sin once or twice, but He's not going to wink again, and God's ready to bring judgment because of sin." My other hero was a patriarch of the modern-day Word of Faith movement. So, I looked to him to see if he was aware of the Gospel of Peace. I then heard him tell a story about how a man tripped over a tape recorder and broke his foot. He said that was God's judgment on that man for some reason. So, I realized I had another hero who did not know the Gospel of Peace. I listened to every well-known and minimally known speaker—at least in my religious world. I listened to a famous respected evangelist, who without a "coming judgment," would have to find another line of business. And then there was a world-renowned evangelist with a major television ministry in many countries. Oh, my goodness! There was no need to check his message out twice! According to him, everything that was moving and breathing was the target of God's anger and vengeance. So, for me to teach this was a step into the unknown. I can't say that *no one* that I knew had believed or taught the Gospel of Peace. However, I can say I searched for five years for one person who did. I *can* tell you that in the circles that I knew of within Evangelical Christianity in the United States, every minister and ministry that I was aware of, not one of *them* preached the Gospel of Peace. *None* of them. I resorted to book stores to find books written on the subject, but I could not find a book on the Gospel of Peace anywhere.

The Gospel of Peace is the foundation for understanding the entire implication of the work of the cross, of all scripture and why they were given to us. It all hinges on this one marvelous subject—which is way more than a subject—The Gospel of Peace. This is the good news—there has been a cessation of all hostilities between God and his creation.

Taking this dramatic first step, that God is at peace with everyone, was just the initial one for me. Many other subjects and topics came up over time, because if God is at peace with everyone it begs an awful lot of questions. If he *is* at peace, *why* is he at peace? If he's at peace, *was* he angry? *If* he was angry, and *if* he's not now, then why would he not still be angry if there's still sin in the world? If God is not angry *but* he hates sin, then is man still a sinner? How can there be anything but righteousness if God is not angry? Contemplating these questions was a watershed moment for me. The tone of everything I believe to be the gospel is rooted in the Gospel of Peace. From there, it has been a wild ride, an amazing journey.

Over these years, both my life and my message have been totally transformed because of the grace and peace of God. When we read Paul's letters, his greetings and his salutations are almost without exception "grace and peace be unto you all" in some form or another. These two terms of God's perspective toward us, unconditional acceptance (grace) and a halt to hostilities (peace) are the basis of Paul's ministry. However, for the rest of the disciples, this was not their approach.

When I first started contemplating the Gospel of Peace; the cross became something different to me. It became a *world event* that I couldn't really explain. I pictured a people living on the planet knowing there was an angry God, having witnessed and experienced his anger, and then having a peace treaty being declared at the cross. In my mind's eye, I saw at the cross this raging, violent storm with all the lightning, thunder, and vengeance in all its demonstration. And then, just like a storm that passes, the air feels different, it smells different—it's the smell of ozone being released. It is the aroma of new life. Contextually, everything is completely different. I tried to imagine the world we now live in, which has been in effect ever since the cross, even though people have perverted that reality ever since. I knew that the very existence of mankind had changed, and this transformation via the Gospel of Peace had been instituted 2,000 years ago at the cross. This was a monumental paradigm shift to say the least.

As I attempted to present this most significant change in thinking in my ministry, one of the number-one arguments I always got was the verse that says "I am the Lord God. I change not." I was bugged with that question enough times that I finally thought, "You know . . . I've got to figure this out!" I went back to the Bible and read it in context. It didn't seem to be saying that at all because it says "I am the Lord God. I change not. Therefore you sons of Jacob are not consumed." So, it sounds like there *was* a change instead of something that never changes. To my great shock, I went back and looked at that particular verse and there's nothing about that word that should have been translated as "change"—it is the word "duplicate." It means *to fold.* It means *to do over again a second time.* It means everything *but* "I never change." It means: "*I never do the same thing twice.*" When God does it, it never has to be done twice. The Gospel of Peace doesn't have to be done twice. The Gospel of Grace does not have to be done twice. The giving of the law did not have to happen twice. Nothing that God has ever done has needed to be done a second time. So, this evolution of God's relationship with man has been real, and the reason it has been real is that God never does anything the same way twice.

The Gospel of Peace has so changed everything that in reality we now live in a world, whether anyone knows it or not, where there is no such thing as an angry God anymore. The reality of the impact of the cross is to the transforming of the human mind and soul—the way we think.

The way we think is so powerful. Several times as a young man, in my years from age 15-21, I spent time in a mental institution. Many of the people there, as well as I, talked about the reason our lives were so messed up. It was because they *knew* God was angry with them. One young girl, having been raised amongst ignorance and a whole heap of religion, was there just based on her illiteracy. One of the elderly gentlemen in the hospital could barely scoot his feet to get around. He was in massive depression, but he really was a sweet old guy. One day the girl was in a group session and this elderly gentleman came shuffling into the room with the help of someone else, and this girl just went crazy. She started yelling "It's the old devil! It's the old devil! It's the old devil!" She was absolutely terrified because something about him caused her to think, from the doctrines and things she had learned in some backwoods church, that this man was the devil. I never will forget the look in his eyes when he realized that somebody actually thought he was the devil. He was just a sad, elderly man in the grip of depression.

Can you see how the Gospel of Peace, when one is made aware of it, is the most life-changing event that can possibly happen to anyone—especially someone who has been dominated by guilt, fear, and condemnation? It will not change the things that do or don't happen to you, but it will certainly change every perspective you have as to *why* it has happened to you. You'll be able to eliminate so many possibilities—not the least of which is God is punishing me or trying to teach me a lesson.

In my Word of Faith days, I simply never considered *anything* that ever happened to me to be anything other than "spiritual." If I had a flat tire, God flattened my tire because he was trying to do something or say something to me. Years later I got so frustrated with that kind of thinking that I just thought, "If you've got something to say God, . . . *just say it!!* And if you're mute, then fine you're mute but don't try to talk to me through flat tires and accidents! I beg to hear from you all the time. Is this what you are reduced to, to speaking to me in ways so that I can't even decipher what it is that you're trying to say?"

When I left Norvel Hayes Ministries, I was pulling my travel trailer with my wife and my two kids at the time, and one of the wheels burned up. The whole apparatus almost caught fire. We wound up staying with some wonderful Christians which led to me speaking at their church. However, Norvel made it clear to me that the tire going bad and burning up was God trying to show me that I had made the wrong decision. And of course by the time it got through Norvel's story-telling ability, my whole family "almost getting killed" . . . well, suffice it to say, sometime later, I even succumbed to that theory, too.

There are not enough words in the English language to describe the positive, powerful impact on my life having then studied the Gospel of Peace for five years. But the waiting, and waiting, and waiting to hear someone else teach it in public was torturous. So, I prayed. I begged God to show it to Billy Graham. I begged God to show it to Kenneth Copeland. I begged God to show it to anybody who had a voice. I added to my plea "I don't have a voice! Why in the world would you allow me to see something so wonderful as this when I have no voice? I'm not someone that people see when they turn on the TV. Why?" It made no sense to me whatsoever. I eventually had to give up on all of that, all of the *whys,* and just accept the fact that I did understand it and whether by default or design, it was irrelevant because the glorious thing was that *I* had understood the Gospel of Peace! From that day to this, it has remained in my heart and my mind has not changed.

As people I shared with started learning more about the Gospel of Peace and the grace of God, some folks started entertaining the possibility that God had never been angry with humanity. I accepted it was their prerogative to think that and that it was quite possibly true though I didn't put much effort into studying it. However, recently this issue has come into clarity for me. I don't think I ever agreed with God having never been angry, although I'm always open. It is important to me when contemplating anything that my conclusions need to be logical and they need to give me the ability to reply to people's honest inquiries.

A few months before the writing of this book, Jeff Robertson had just started working for the ministry and we were talking about the issue of God's anger and whether God was ever really angry. Jeff said to me, "Michael, God's anger was real and it was born out of his love." That really clicked in my heart, because I so understand that kind of anger. This cleared up the one and only hurdle I had to making this declaration again. Not only of the Gospel of Peace but of the *anger* of God, because without that anger, how can you accurately present the scriptures? Yes, God's anger was born out of his love and his response to the unrequited love of his human creation.

The words anger, wrath, vengeance, and many more show up throughout the scriptures. The prophets spoke a lot about a God who described himself as angry in so many different ways. It is replete throughout the scriptures. The whole issue of the need for redemption was first to resolve this issue of anger.

In Chapter 12 of John's gospel, Jesus explains that he was here to *see* the judgment of the world, the entire world. The moment the cross would go in the air, that would be the moment that all of God's wrath, all of God's anger, all of God's judgment would be completely satisfied. Isaiah speaks of it in so many different ways, that "God would see the suffering of his soul and be satisfied."

I never will forget reading that blessed chapter. In context it's even more powerful. God watched the suffering of Jesus' soul *and was satisfied!* Religion may not be satisfied with the suffering of the soul of Jesus at the cross, but God is completely satisfied with that cataclysmic, earth-shattering event. It was where and how God's own anger and wrath was resolved for all eternity. The validity of this issue is brought out not only in those verses in Isaiah but also in the scriptures speaking about the result of how many people would benefit in righteousness from that suffering—the entirety of humanity—the whole world.

Isaiah Chapter 54 is just mind-blowing. The prophet Isaiah compares the cross to the waters of Noah. This comparison between the waters of Noah and the cross impacted me so deeply that it sealed the Gospel of Peace in my heart forever. He said that "even as the waters of Noah" and then describes a promise that comes out of the cross. He said that even as God judged the entire world through the flood of Noah and then said "but a promise came out of it." God set a rainbow in the sky and by that promise the entire human race would know that God had promised He would never flood the Earth again. The big deal here was that there was a promise.

The chilling and stark reality that became blatantly apparent was that nobody had to believe *anything*—even atheists benefited! I started going through my mind and asking, "every time there's a rainbow it's supposed to remind us of this promise according to Genesis, so how many people benefit from that promise?" I realized it didn't make any difference whether you were a Hindu, a Buddhist, an atheist, a murderer, a rapist, a believer, a non-believer, or which one of the tens of thousands of Christian denominations you belong to. Everyone benefitted, and continues to benefit, from God's promise in Noah's day. By comparison, Isaiah then gives us the reality of the cross and gives us this powerful picture that once this takes place, humanity would never see God's anger again. Jesus bore the suffering of his soul for the sin of the world, and that sin, being touched by God's fiery judgments of anger and wrath, would be burned up in the Body of Christ at the cross. That's the other thing about the anger and the wrath of God that the scriptures state so clearly—there is NO sin, *there is NO sin* that would not be visited by the wrath of God.

Every sin would have to be visited by the wrath of God.

Every sin would have to be touched by God's anger.

Every sin would have to be judged by God.

So if there is now a Gospel of Peace, what does *that* portend? A cascading effect takes place from the beginning of the understanding of the Gospel of Peace. It begs so many questions, and it contains so many answers. The Gospel of Peace truly is the foundation for our understanding of this glorious gospel that has been given to us to share with the entire human race. When the same prophet spoke of the reality that came out of the flood, the reality that would come out of the cross would be similarly definitive. It would and has forever "flooded" the entire Earth. "*And I will never be angry again saith the Lord.*" Wow!

Isn't it strange? Christian doctrine will accept forever and a day that the Earth will never be subject to another flood. I don't care what church they are a part of—Pentecostals who handle snakes or Presbyterians who just go in, sing a verse, have a 10-minute sermon and walk out—they ALL believe that the rainbow signifies that God would never judge the Earth again with water. How could they *all* believe that? *How* then, can they come up with a God that is still angry? The description by Isaiah himself, who is using the flood and the promise that came out of it as the direct "type" or comparison to God's promise to never be angry again, says "I will not be wroth with thee, nor rebuke thee." Isaiah said "the mountains and hills may depart" and indicates that a lot of destruction is going to happen, and then says "but *not by me* saith God." Then he says, "and the covenant of peace, my covenant of peace will not be removed off the Earth forever." *Forever!* The covenant of peace would not be removed ever! It is certainly *as* sure as the covenant of the rainbow that signifies that God would never flood the Earth again. You know the whole world is absolutely confident that this planet is never going to be destroyed again with water. But why do so many people believe *another* judgment resulting out of God's anger is coming? Because holding on to God's anger is a tool continued to be used in order to manipulate people and their behavior.

We should be celebrating the Gospel of Peace!

Remember the angels at *Christmas?*

What was it exactly that the angels got all excited about? I went back and read the "Christmas story" in the book of Luke and the Gospel of Peace is even in there!

There's a verse in Luke Chapter 2 that is rarely quoted properly. There is no place where it says "Peace on Earth and goodwill toward men." That's what you see on all the Christmas cards. However, it does not say "Peace on Earth." Of course, I wish for peace on Earth just as every sane person does. But the power of the gospel is not based on how well *men* do this. The gospel is based on how well *God* did it. Sometimes we *do* have peace as individual nations. We stop warfare for a moment. We'll even have ceasefire during a war. Over the decades and the world wars, mainly involving European nations, on Christmas Eve they would briefly stop fighting. There would be an absolute cessation of hostilities for a day or so. Why? Because even they hoped for peace on Earth as they continued planning on killing each other. Well, a day later the killing resumed. So much for the hope of peace on Earth, but that is not what it says in Luke. The angels *did* get excited about something. The Bible says "and on Earth peace and goodwill toward men." You just have to read what it says *in context*. This is not an issue of coming up with your own new doctrine. It's simply an issue of reading something the way it is written, and *this* is what the angels were excited about. God was introducing on Earth the process of peace between himself and humanity! Now that is something to get excited about AND something DID happen!

In the Word of Faith movement, we talked about healing all the time. We talked about deliverance all the time. We talked about how Jesus brought us prosperity. We talked about all of these external or material things. But logical thinking began to take over my thoughts and this came to me: "*Why* did the angels get excited about *peace*? Why didn't the angels say "Glory to God in the highest, and on Earth *prosperity* toward men?" Why didn't they proclaim "Glory to God in the highest, and on Earth *healing* toward the human race?" Because the angels had already seen all of this! I realized that the greatest miracles and the greatest wealth ever seen took place in the "Old Testament." To this day I don't care how many Bill Gates types you stack up next to each other, there's still no one as wealthy as Solomon or David were. Just the gifts that David gave to build the Temple are off the charts compared to any man's possessions today. So, the angels are not going to get excited about prosperity. They've seen all that before. They're not going to get excited about healing. They've seen the greatest healings ever seen. They had seen the creation take place for goodness sakes. They had seen it all! But what did the angels get excited about? They got excited about the only thing they had never, ever seen. They had seen the anger of God against the human race, but they had *never* seen God declare peace with the human race. That is what the angels were excited about. I don't know if the angels were *told* what to get excited about, but if they were that's even more confirmation! What if the angels got excited because they knew what was about to happen? This was the redemption and salvation of the world they were about to witness. This was the declaration of peace between God and man that they had never seen before.

At least the angels were smart enough to see the power and the impact of this declaration of peace!

"So then faith comes by hearing and hearing by the word," as the author of Hebrews puts it. Show me somebody who says they no longer believe in God. Show me somebody who no longer believes in the God of Abraham, Isaac, and Jacob. Show me somebody who no longer believes that the sacrifice of Jesus is valid for today, and I will show you someone who does not believe the Gospel of Peace. Perhaps they don't believe it because they don't believe there is a need for it. The Gospel of Peace is the only way of understanding the Bible both simply *and* honestly.

Please make no mistake about that. Without the Gospel of Peace, we are left making excuses for, or inventing weird theology to explain the gaps we can't explain. When we accept that God resolved all his anger at the cross, that he will never be angry with anyone again, you'll believe in God more than you've ever believed in him before. When you resolve that God saw the suffering of Jesus' soul and was satisfied, you'll believe in Jesus more than you ever believed in Jesus in your life.

This is the stuff that brings stability to one's heart. It brings the ability to contemplate with an open mind all the aspects of the gospel. These are the thoughts of great spiritual importance—all rooted in the Gospel of Peace which relieved God of all his anger.

How did God spell relief? T-h-e C-r-o-s-s. "It is finished."

Chapter 3

A Scriptural Heritage

I was watching the news and a story came on about a man from my old "stomping grounds" in Tennessee. I laughed so hard at what I saw I had to call my friends and family about it.

There was a storm that went through Nashville. A huge church steeple there was blown over and fell across an intersection crushing a car being driven by a man named Michael Williams. Many people in my former religious circles assumed it was me. You just would not believe what some of the people who've opposed me and the message I've been sharing in recent years were saying . . .

"God finally got him! . . . with the church steeple even!

Of course, they eventually found out it wasn't me. Also, that particular Michael Williams actually *did* survive just by inches. The massive steeple did crush his car, but it hit it far enough towards the front that it missed him. If his car had been a few inches forward, it would have definitely killed Mr. Williams.

The mindset prevalent in the world of an angry God looking to judge us at any time, which so many religious leaders propagate, *must* be addressed and focused on. My hope is to completely destroy the notion of an angry God which permeates the whole world. Whether they believed it was because of the cross, or by what event, or no event at all, makes no difference. If the notion of an angry God full of wrath and judgment was eliminated off the face of the Earth, can you imagine what a different world this would be?

The Bible translation I use to study and teach is the King James Version. One day, reading the Gospel of John, I saw where Jesus said "Now is the judgment of this world. And I, if I be lifted up from the earth, will draw all *men* unto me." Perhaps by pure happenstance, I noticed that the word *men* is italicized, which the King James translators used to denote that the word was not in the original text. I read it without the added word "men" realizing the subject of the statement was *judgment*. I had to read it this way. "Now is the judgment of this world. And if *I* be lifted up from the earth, I will draw all *judgment* unto me." The prophets spoke of the Day of Judgment, the Day of the Lord, the Day of Mercy. Isaiah spoke of the Day of Mercy and the Day of Judgment being the exact same day that would occur; the Day of Judgment and the Day of Mercies of our God would all happen on the *same day*.

I have to take you back to my thought processes at the time. One thing I discovered is that consistent, persistent, and repetitive exposure to the Gospel of Peace will cause you to think logically about spiritual things.

It was around this time that a large portion of Universal Studios in Hollywood had been burned to the ground. Roughly a year earlier, the movie "The Last Temptation of Christ" had been produced by Universal Studios. So, when such a massive part of these studios burned to the ground, the U.S. Christian media machine—a prominent Evangelical leader and television personality, a pastor of a mega-church in the South and so many of their ilk—went to the airwaves saying it was the judgment of God on Universal Studios for producing the movie. Churches boycotted and protested this "B movie," which would have never ever made it into a large theatre had the Christian community not protested it. Their loud objections were its greatest advertisement. The protests that spread around the country were about this horrific *"anti-Christ"* movie portraying Jesus being tempted in a relationship with Mary Magdalene. It was the best free publicity the film producers could have hoped for. By this time I was thinking logically about these kinds of crazy statements and actions that were coming out of Evangelicalism.

I thought through that situation logically. If this was God's judgment on Universal Studios for producing that movie: 1 - They did find that an arsonist had set the fire. In all of the annals of God's relationship with man, it would have been the first time God hired an arsonist to carry out his judgment. For some reason, the Christian community didn't stand up and say this man should not be punished for his crime—that he was simply being used of God to accomplish his purpose. The man went to prison for it. There was not one Christian minister at his trial saying that the man was used as an instrument in the hand of God. But you see, they do *not* think logically. They didn't think this thing through at all or they would have realized they had a modern-day Moses or a 20th century Elijah on their hands. If they really thought this was the work of God, shouldn't they have defended him to the hilt? They did not. Their inconsistent thinking is obviously so far from anything logical that it's scary. 2 - It occurred to me that only about a quarter of Universal Studios burned down. It was a huge fire no doubt, but still it didn't consume the entire complex. Then I started thinking about insurance, and I thought, "You know what, this was all an older part of Universal Studios, and if it was the judgment of God, then half the corporations in America, if not more, are going to be praying for the judgment of God to hit *their* place!" Because with insurance, you get all you had invested back and a brand new place! And Universal did. The insurance companies fully re-built Universal

Studios with better, state-of-the-art equipment than they had when it burned to the ground.

I continued applying logic to these types of cases where people were saying, "this was the judgment of God," and I began using the next major example of this idiocy . . .

I don't think they had ever declared a Gay Day in Orlando, Florida, but they did agree to put up gay pride flags one particular day some years ago. It may have been a gay pride event, and the city agreed to put up the flags. There were *fires* that year running rampant around Florida and they hit everywhere . . . everywhere, that is, except for Orlando! But the response in the media of those Christian "leaders" was that, without a shadow of a doubt, those fires were the judgment of God. So, my logical application to this was—"well we've got to understand that God's a little older now. His eyesight can't be as good as it was for Sodom and Gomorrah, and he can't see that well anymore, but at least he got *close* to Orlando!"

The Evangelical "talking heads" on television and in the pulpits preaching sin and judgment would have us accept that this was God's judgment because it was somewhere *close to* Orlando. More recent events of course bring these declarations of God's judgment on a specific people. However, that so-called judgment is causing the suffering of believers *and* non-believers alike. Some churches love it so much that when something happens to someone or something, and it obviously does not involve the church or a Christian person, they just don't tell the stories to the *other side*. They don't tell the same story when something does happen to the church or a Christian. But of course if something does happen to Christians, then it's an attack from the devil. It's the *devil* who is attacking God's people. These "celebrity" Christian preachers and others like them will blame it on the devil, or persecution, or the immorality of the nation. What a joke they instantly become. Because of our modern ability to communicate instantly and accurately, it's on display for the whole world to witness and reject out of hand.

What hasn't changed with all our increased knowledge and technological advancements is that we still have religious groups of all kinds that oppose all the others. Most terrorist groups justify their actions by pointing to an angry God. However, the only way to truly resolve a God of anger is with the solution he himself provided, the cross. Even people who don't believe in Jesus can still believe in an angry God. Still, there is only one way to resolve and explain the reality of the Gospel of Peace and that is through the cross which manifestly assuaged an angry God. It is the reality of the most profound historical event in human history—the death, burial, and resurrection of Jesus—that brought peace. God came to peace in Christ's work. It is an accomplished fact. An individual's own "faith" has *nothing* to do with God's judgment being effectively dealt with.

So, I read that Jesus said he would bear ALL of God's judgment. He said also in the book of John "It is for judgment I have come into the world." However, he also said in John Chapter 3 that "he didn't come to judge anybody." So, which was it? What does that *mean*? He didn't come to judge anybody, but it's for judgment that "he is here."

People need to understand that the cross is *the* declaration of peace! Please, please consider this truth. The perilous position of multiple millions of your fellow human beings hangs in the balance at the hands of those other human beings who believe in an angry God and are willing to take actions on those beliefs, and who believe that God's anger justifies the slaughter of thousands of their fellows or even more.

Talk about a peace sign. The cross is *the* peace symbol! It was where peace between God and humanity was declared and sealed. And it was at the cross that all judgment ended once and for all time.

Isaiah 54 describes this peace in so many beautiful terms. It will benefit you immensely to read all of Isaiah Chapter 54 because it is very self-explanatory. He then concludes this particular chapter with "For this is the heritage of the servants of the Lord and their righteousness is of me."

What is the heritage of the servants of the Lord?

Well, the verse begins with "And every tongue that rises in judgment thou shalt condemn." There's no place else in all the scriptures where this verse would fit other than after the absolute declaration of peace—the Covenant of Peace. *The Covenant of Peace* that God established at the cross—this incredible covenant has been finalized by the Almighty himself. Then he says that, "every tongue that rises in judgment, thou shalt condemn." I don't think we've come even close to condemning this religious, legalistic, judgmental garbage enough. We need to be much more vocal. Everyone who believes the gospel should be speaking up *every time* they hear somebody talking about or even implying that something was left undone at the cross which leaves open the possibility of judgment of an angry God. Whether it's a car wreck or something on a much larger scale like a tsunami, or someone tripping on something, that it is the judgment of God? WRONG! And it is our heritage, privilege, and honor to speak-up and condemn that nonsense.

Just the other day, I saw one of the members of the Westboro Baptist Church on TV talking about how angry God is. They were protesting the funeral of a soldier. They were praising God, saying, "Oh thank God for their death,"—that this was the judgment of God. They carried signs reading "God hates fags" and "Thank God for Dead Soldiers." This may sound really weird, but although I don't respect what they say *I respect them* because at least they are honest and say it fully and totally as it should be said IF there is indeed still an angry God. If God is still ticked-off, then those protesters are *correct* not only in what they are saying but how they are saying it! At least it's not this mealy-mouthed, made-for-Christian-TV brand of wimpy, slithering, spineless, subjective teachings that God's happy with this and he's mad about that. Of course, God's never mad about what *they* do. God is only mad about what *they* don't like! At least these folks that are protesting have the transparent integrity to condemn everybody. Now I agree that they do not condemn themselves, but they do condemn EVERYBODY else. They leave nobody off the list. And people are appalled by this.

Even other Christians are appalled!

It's good that Westboro Baptist Church says it bold, brazen, and loudly. I would rather people hear their voice than the mediocre, vacillating, convenient and self-serving empty declaration of God's wrath that most of religion puts out, whether it's a televangelist, the Pope or Ahmadinijad.

When an earthquake leads to a tsunami and kills hundreds of thousands of innocent (and redeemed) people, it is a natural disaster of tragic proportions. It's a tectonic plate, folks—not the anger or wrath of God! The natural shifting of tectonic plates causes the motion of the ocean. It is an action and a reaction to cataclysmic movements of the Earth. That's what it said in Isaiah—these great tragedies will happen—but why can't we understand? He said these things would happen "But not by me saith God." It will never happen by his hand ever again. And since the cross it never has.

Are there places where people misinterpreted things that happened as a result of God's anger and wrath before? No doubt about it. They, too, were probably even selective in their belief about the anger of God. However, make no mistake, the scriptures verify that God was indeed angry and was full of wrath, judgment and punishment. If you take those terms and concepts out of the scriptures, you literally would have no scriptures at all!

There would be no reason for a cross, there would be no reason for a redeemer, there would be no reason for any of this—we all would just be blowing a lot of hot air—if God had never been angry.

And the scriptures, the actual scriptures, verify this in no uncertain terms. But we are not blowing hot air. I believe we have a heritage as those who have been made righteous by the blood of Jesus Christ (and know it) to speak up about these things. I am so glad that the prophet said we should "condemn every tongue that rises in judgment" because I cannot condemn the parishioners of Westboro Baptist for what they're doing. They are the redeemed of God who are deemed holy and righteous and perfect by the God who declared peace with them along with the rest of the human race. However, they are ignorant of the gospel. For those who know *how* they are righteous, and *why* they are righteous, it is their *heritage* to speak up and to condemn these judgments that come out of people's mouths. It's the people of Westboro Baptist Church's heritage too, but as long as they remain ignorant, they'll not understand their heritage.

The questions I always got from people who challenged the reality of this great peace were about two events in the book of Acts: The deaths of Ananias and Sapphira and the death of King Herod.

In answering, you have to take into consideration how removed from the gospel the disciples were. They did not believe the Gospel of Peace. We've got to be honest and face up to it. According to Acts 21, they were still offering sacrifices for goodness' sake. They still were putting gentiles under the law even though they said "we know they're not under the law, but here we go, we're going to give them four laws just to satisfy our structure and our religious conscience." They also thought (in the same way the leadership of Westboro Baptist Church thinks about God's judgment) that what happened to Ananias and Sapphira was the punishment of God or that Herod was stricken with worms because he didn't give God praise for a great speech. Under that criteria President Barack Obama would have been struck dead many times by now. Because if Luke's conclusions were true (Luke, the writer of Acts), the President would have to stand there and say in public, "I just want to give God thanks for doing what he just did through this speech." He's *never* done it. Accordingly, he would have been struck dead many times over. And not just him but anyone, anywhere that gave a wonderful speech and did not immediately give God credit. Winston Churchill, Abraham Lincoln, Franklin Roosevelt, Ronald Reagan should have dropped dead hundreds of times each. It never happened, not once.

I am going to say something here that should be self evident, but has been obscured by twenty centuries of religion, some of which were so worthy of contempt as to have been historically termed "The Dark Ages."

The only thing that qualifies as "scripture" is what *Jesus said*, and the apostles confirmed, was scripture. So, what *did* Jesus and the apostles call scripture? In Luke 24, it is stated as clearly as anything could be. To repeat the words of Jesus, "scripture" consists of and *only* of: the law—the first five books of the Bible called the Pentateuch, the psalms and also the prophets. None of the rest of the Bible qualifies as scripture. It doesn't mean they don't have good insight or contain useful teachings. However, when we do not accept the authority of the Redeemer's own words who said what the scriptures were, we're lost. This is even confirmed by those whom he chose as disciples—and those guys agreed on almost nothing else. All their quotations in their letters included in the New Testament writing were only from scripture—the law, the psalms and the prophets. Saul, who was converted on the road to Damascus by an incredible intervention and became Paul the Apostle, knew what the scriptures were. He was a scriptural scholar. When we don't accept what both Jesus *and* his disciples said are scripture, we are lost in a world of religion trying to make this work and that work and choosing on our own what is and what is not holy writ.

Please do not be lost in a religious world without the compass of knowing what the scriptures are *and* what their purpose was for.

I teach a lot out of the New Testament writings. I am glad to do so. Why reinvent the wheel when there is so much commentary on the scriptures there? The writers of the New Testament and the debates that took place there have a *lot* to offer us. In fact, there's a lot of *truth* that resides within them. But the fact of the matter is that we all have the ability to go back and look at the scriptures: the *context* of the story—and we should. That is where the story was told. It's all there. The fall of man is told in detail. And, of course, there is the detailed foretelling of the story about the redemption from that condition in the prophecies.

We *have* to rely on the scriptures. Why? Because it was these specific and unique texts that Jesus said spoke of *him*. So, if we want to understand what's up with Jesus, we must adhere to the scriptures as our source AND understand the reason for their existence. Not only do the scriptures clearly detail the anger and the wrath of God, but they also declare the Gospel of Peace. When we accept this as reality, it is to the saving of our souls. This is when you are able to begin to think logically. Before you receive the clarity of the Gospel of Peace, there is no such thing as logical thought. None. It does not exist. Logic goes out the door completely.

We can see how important it is to grasp the Gospel of Peace in Paul's letter to the Romans. As we saw earlier, Paul was able to articulate from the scriptures this doctrine of the One Man. One Man's unbelief and unrighteousness was imputed to all, but then One Man's belief and righteousness was imputed to all. Obviously this "all" includes Israel as well. This is important to remember, for when we get to Chapter 10 of Romans, Paul is talking about his desire for the salvation of Israel. It is important to realize that Israel is righteous in the sight of God, but they were ignorant of that righteousness. Here he's saying that his heart's prayer and desire for Israel is that they might be saved. He very clearly states what they need to be saved *from*. It is their ignorance that they need to be saved from. He wrote they have zeal for God but not according to *knowledge*.

Being zealous for God is dangerous territory. That's why it's vital that we speak up, condemn teachings and statements of judgment AND therefore participate in our heritage. We need to speak up when we hear these damnable prophecies of future judgment and wrath whether it is about an oil spill in the Gulf of Mexico or whatever bizarre interpretation of some current event they like to make. While those strange claims may never end, in the same vein it should also never end that we raise our collective voice against such ignorance and such insults to the work of Christ's cross. It should not just be atheists like the comedian Bill Maher and others of his persuasion who raise their voices against this stupidity. It needs to come from those who *know* their heritage. "The Redeemed of the Lord" should say so, too.

Paul in Hebrews 10 stated that Israel needed salvation because of their lack of knowledge. It was not because they were going to hell. They needed to be saved simply because they did not understand their real heritage. They didn't get it. They needed salvation from their ignorance. Then of course, later in that chapter as he's describing this salvation, he seems to say out of the blue, "How beautiful are the feet of them who preach the Gospel of Peace and bring glad tidings of good things." However, he's not saying it suddenly *out of nowhere* because he is talking about the ignorance that is in Israel's thinking. Israel did not know that God had declared peace. This was the issue. This is what was preventing the saving of their collective soul. They did not know that the cross, the Roman mode of execution, had become the symbol of peace. They did not know the cross was where a covenant of peace had consumed all of God's judgment and anger for eternity!

Following that is the well-known verse almost *never* quoted correctly: "Faith comes by hearing and hearing by the word." I never will forget reading it in context! It doesn't say "Faith comes by hearing and hearing by the word." It says, "So then." *So then* faith comes by hearing and hearing by the word. *So then*—what? After he says "Who hath believed our report" and speaks of the Gospel of Peace and says "how beautiful are the feet of them who preach the Gospel of Peace." *So then*, this *is* the salvation, this is the salvation of Israel, the Gospel of Peace. It is the salvation of the modern state of Israel. The only reason Israel is in the situation they are in today, or any other nation on the planet, is because they (and their neighbor countries) do not know the Gospel of Peace. Do you see? The Gospel of Peace is the end to this entire Middle Eastern conflict.

Can you imagine what it would do to this planet for there to be the same universal acceptance of the Gospel of Peace in the same way as we have all come to accept that the Earth is actually round and never was flat? God is at peace and has been ever since Golgotha.

We should be speaking up folks. This is your heritage. Can you hear what God is saying? *This is the heritage of the servants of the Lord and their righteousness is of ME . . . saith God.*

If you know where your righteousness comes from, then you should be speaking up against *every* prophecy of judgment. I don't care *whose* mouth it comes out of. It doesn't make any difference, because there is something defined by Jesus himself as "the scriptures" and I believe the scriptures (the law, the psalms, and the prophets) are true. I believe the same scriptures that said there was an angry God are the same inspired writings that declare that anger and wrath has been satisfied.

The elimination from the planet of the concept of a still seething, wrathful, angry God from the human consciousness is our ONLY hope for a better future. Either Jesus satisfied the demands of the Father and pleased him or he didn't.

Chapter 4

Definitions

The insidious influence of religion and legalism can be felt and seen throughout our society. It's on display on an almost 24/7 basis through our cable news channels. I find myself talking back to the TV—as if that does any good! Christianity's impact is experienced in many ways not the least of which are in the many misconstrued and mistranslated definitions of terms and concepts taught from their pulpits and media. They are so entrenched in our minds that we just take most of them for granted. And, furthermore, this is not just a matter of semantics, far from it. Our perception of "the truth" is reinforced by "the church" and even the world around us. Recently I saw the son of world-famous evangelist Billy Graham, Franklin Graham, on television speaking about Christianity. He offered his very own definition of Christianity which many of his colleagues would likely concur with.

Graham said Christianity is not something you are born into. Christianity is rather a means by which you, through your own belief, faith, trust, and obedience towards God *gains* you redemption. In other words, you change the course of your journey towards *hell.* He said from the moment you are born, you're on your way to hell.

Now even Franklin's doctrine, as well as most of Christianity, will usually find some loophole for children, who are exempted from hell should they die sometime before puberty. They call it the "age of accountability"—which is absolutely nowhere in the Bible!

So, obviously, the gospel is "a Christianity-Free gospel" because the gospel does *not* support Christianity in any way, shape or form. Christianity, as Franklin Graham described it in no uncertain terms is *not* validated by the gospel. Jesus is not the protagonist of Christianity. He is *not* its main player. He is not its centerpiece, and he did not start the religion as many if not all encyclopedias would have you believe.

The term "Christian" was something that was imposed upon people in the first century who were believers in Christ. The gospel is very clearly the good news about the redemption of the entire planet without need of man's works, efforts or beliefs in God. It is not about changing your destiny from hell to heaven. You were born into an eternal destiny in the presence of God and that without need for your belief and without your involvement whatsoever. So, that in and of itself makes it a gospel that is free from Christianity.

Believing the gospel does NOT make you a Christian.

One of the most tragic things happening to the mind of the Evangelical Christian is that they learn Bible verses out of context. Reading and understanding in context when examining the Bible is pivotal, crucial, and revealing.

The chapters and verse numbers were added to the Bible a few hundred years ago. They may have been added for a noble purpose to help people find what they wanted more easily. In fact, we used to call them "the addresses." We'd say, "This is the address of this particular verse." The benefit of the Bible being laid out in chapter and verse was when people began to become students or read the Bible on their own, it was a helpful tool to say "yes, this was over here in this chapter and in this verse." But there has been a serious downside. We began to think in terms of chapter and verse rather than the concepts outlined in their proper context. Reading the content of the whole chapter in context is the only way to do the subject justice.

The most critical thing in understanding what the writer wants to communicate is by reading in context. It seems kind of strange to even have to say that. It's strange because if we got a letter from anyone or read anything in a book, if we took one line out of a book and tried to determine what that book was about because of one line, we would all know that would be an extremely foolish thing to attempt. We would at least need to read some of the paragraphs around the sentence.

Before I started teaching in context I could "cut and paste" together a message with the best of them in a successful attempt to draw a lot of people. We used to fill buildings with hundreds of people, thousands of people, but we also had the ability to manipulate the things that we were teaching. Did I do it consciously? No. That's just how I was taught to do it. And I was a good pupil. We had certain doctrines that we were promoting because they were promoted to us and we believed them. I did like everybody else and I'd pick a verse in Timothy and one from the psalms and one out of Isaiah and one out of Revelation. I'd put it all together and find a Greek word that made it all fit and teach on it. You can come up with some really strange doctrines that way. We certainly did.

However, when I started teaching more in context, I strayed from the party line.

In the Word of Faith movement, I was introduced as "America's foremost authority on demonology." When I started unraveling the demonology doctrines, I realized that they were built together on a bunch of different statements that had absolutely nothing to do with each other. Each one of them in context explained themselves in their own right. They in truth had nothing to do with demons or demonology. That was quite a wake-up call for me. To be called America's foremost authority on demonology and then take my own doctrine and deconstruct it completely and set it aside—well, it was an interesting trip to say the least. So much for being an authority on demonology!

Time after time I found myself revisiting definitions pertaining to Christianity, the Bible and the scriptures and I had to let them define themselves. The whole process didn't just destroy *my* doctrines; it started uncovering the fallacy of the fundamental doctrines in Christianity.

I didn't set out to expose Christianity as a fraud. That was never my goal. I was a Christian, for goodness sakes! I was trying to prove Christianity was real! I was trying to prove that it is true. The more I learned about the gospel the more I realized Christianity was a lie. The more I realized Christianity was a lie, the more I believed the gospel, and the more I understood the gospel, the clearer the gospel became. I was amazed as I saw the issues dealt with so clearly in the scriptures are twisted and repudiated by Christianity. Yet the scriptures completely solidify and proclaim the gospel.

Most fundamental doctrines of Christianity cannot even be found in the Bible at all, especially when you read in context. It truly is remarkable. I could go back and point out so many things that are not even in the Bible which are the fundamental principles of Christianity. One subject in Christianity that has become extremely misleading, misguided and even deceptive is the issue of the free will of mankind.

There was a little argument which took place on a Facebook thread. People were falling on either side of the issue of whether we have free will or not. Someone who started this conversation wrote, "I threw a coke bottle at somebody and hit them in the head, so obviously I have free will," and extrapolated that all the way back to be proof of free will. This is one of the dangers of thinking backward instead of thinking forward. That person extrapolated it all the way back to draw some spiritual relevance to it. There's nothing spiritual about picking up a bottle and throwing it at somebody's head. That may very well be something that is *illegal*, but there's certainly nothing spiritual about it!

There are things spiritual and there are things temporal. The confusion that has come in Christianity comes from their belief that free will is involved in redemption and things of *eternal* consequences—what our position with God is and will be. Then they turn around and surrender temporal things, that which happens to us in this natural life, to the will of God. These are things like looking to God for answers to decisions such as where do I go to school? Who am I going to marry? Should I turn right or left at Oak Street? Do I witness to this person and how do I go about it? Do I go into fulltime ministry? What is it that I should do every second of every day? It does get just this extreme and paralyzing.

When the Word of Faith movement was teaching on the will of God, it caused a lot of confusion for many people. They actually gave us a directive about the will of God. It was one of the few things that we didn't have to try to *seek* the will of God about. It was imposed on all of us that it was God's will that everybody be in fulltime ministry. So, nobody had to pray about whether or not they were going to be in fulltime ministry. They just had to figure out *which* fulltime ministry they were going to be in because God's perfect will was to be in the ministry full time. So, as a result of that, we had a lot of people that surrendered their lives, forfeited their careers, and forsook and even renounced their educations, because "the will of God" was already known—that everybody should be in fulltime ministry. I know that sounds weird to a lot of people and it should. But that is what we were taught.

A lot of pastors left the ministry after I started sharing the gospel with them because they never wanted to be there in the first place. They were so glad to go back to their homes, back to their jobs, back to their careers. Their wives became nurses or went into some other profession. Some took up investing. Many of them have developed financially prosperous lives knowing they are in the will of God at all times regardless of what their daily choices are.

So what was it that I shared with them to release them in their freedom? Today, and since the cross, free will pertains to things that are temporal—not nor *ever* is it for things of eternal consequences (the way we relate to God). When we begin to try to include free will into things which are eternal, that's where religion begins to really show its true colors—not a pretty picture to say the least. Religion begins where man's free will is taught to be responsible for eternal things. Even *stranger* religion begins when you apply the will of God to temporal things. These two things should be maintained in their proper understanding and application. If we don't try to combine these two, but understand them as intended, sanity ensues. That's where the saving of the soul (meaning a person's mind or the way he or she thinks and relates) actually begins for many people. In both temporal and spiritual matters, free will is meant to be alive and well. In spiritual matters, the free will is God's. In temporal matters, the free will is humankind's.

The most tormented people I have met in Evangelical Christianity are those who anguish over figuring out God's will for their lives. I've seen people try to figure out what the will of God is and then be tormented about eternal things because they don't know whether they really believe well enough for themselves and for those they love. They don't know about the proper application of their personal wills. They don't know whether they are committed enough, or dedicated enough, or have obeyed enough. On both sides of this issue, it seems to lead one on a path of extreme mental and emotional turmoil, if not debilitating mental and emotional illness.

People sometimes wonder why I have such passion for these things. Why do I speak about them with such intensity? There is not a thing that I teach that was not borne out of seeing the pain and the sorrow that came out of the doctrines that I once believed and taught. When you observe these things, something has to give inside you emotionally. Either that, or you harden your heart to the suffering of the human race at the hands of religion altogether.

One of the clearest illustrations of the torment of these issues comes from the experience of a personal friend, a young man who attended the Bible School I used to teach at in Cleveland, Tennessee. He was a very tender-hearted, sharp young man. He was attempting to make it through New Life Bible College founded by Norvel Hayes in Cleveland, Tennessee. He had been taught about the will of God. One of the things you are taught excessively at New Life Bible College is the will of God, finding the will of God, obeying God, doing what God says, listening to the voice of God. The craziness just goes on and on. This young man took it to heart. When you have any issues with guilt and you are desperately trying to find the will of God but you don't know that the will of God has been settled for everyone forever, then you are definitely in the "spin-cycle." I don't know of anything that I could tell you that would bring this out any more than this story.

As I traveled the country speaking, I often returned to New Life to teach seminars. I had developed a friendship with this young man and we would talk each time I visited there. He was free as anybody else was to call me on the phone or to ask questions, and he was interested in working for me and travelling with me. When he left New Life Bible School, there were already signs that there were some things troubling him. He was trying to make it to his family's home several hundred miles away. He started calling me from the road because he was trying so hard to figure out what he was supposed to do, which way he was supposed to go, what route was God's will for him, literally.

About an hour into the drive, he had reached a stretch of interstate. It was about 10 miles long. He had spent hours covering just those 10 miles, going back and forth, over and over. He would drive down to an exit and then be persuaded it was the will of God that he go back. So, he would drive back and be convinced it was the will of God that he return on his journey. He would drive back 10 miles then go back the 10 miles, and do it again. He was stuck, quite literally! For the better part of the day he was yo-yoing on these 10-miles. In those hours going back and forth, his mind and emotions were paralyzed because he doubted himself and therefore he couldn't figure out what the will of God was. This young man needed so desperately to know that he *did* have free will, and that God's will was not involved in whether he went home or not or whether he got involved in ministry or not. It absolutely did not make a difference at all as to what he did whether or not his actions were in the will of God. Man's actions simply do not determine the will of God.

I often think about the many people I was involved with. I am grateful for the little that I did know at the time. Sometimes I think of how *little* I knew to try to help someone in that position. I tried to convince my friend that whatever he decided was going to be fine. However, when one sits in Bible School and has it drilled into your head day after day, week after week, that if you get out of God's will you are subject to attack from the devil, and you trust your teacher and what they're saying, you can go crazy.

"If you're out of God's will, when you die you're going to hell." We were taught this as children! The last verse of "Jesus Loves Me" from the Baptist hymnal of the 1950's reads, "Jesus loves me he will stay, close beside me all the way. If I love him when I die, he will take me home on high. Yes, Jesus loves me."

If you get out of God's will, your family will be in jeopardy. If you get out of God's will, your finances will be in jeopardy. *Everything* is jeopardized when you're out of the will of God according to Christian teaching.

Do you see the insanity of that doctrine? People actually believe it and are psychologically and emotionally damaged for life by it.

Thankfully most people are just playing games with their religion or our mental institutions would be over-flowing. In the final analysis, the only people that survive Christianity with some semblance of sanity are the ones who don't take it very seriously.

For most involved with Evangelical Christianity it is just a game. They hear these sermons, exactly like my young friend did. However, thankfully, most dismiss it within hours of hearing it. They may talk about it while they're having lunch after church or after a service, but it's rarely applied to their lives.

However, there are some very tender hearts who do take this *into* their soul and it will destroy their lives. In fact, in this young man's life, *it did* destroy his life eventually. He jumped to his death from the roof of a 31-story hotel.

People concerned about what the will of God is for their life would do well to understand what the phrase "will of God" actually means. In the scriptures, the book of Amos says that God would not do anything unless he first revealed it to his holy prophets. We must recognize that God's will is never negotiated. God's will is only revealed. God's will is revealed to man. God doesn't need a revelation of man's will. God already knows man's will. In fact, he knew man's will so well that he exhausted every possible means of it in his covenants with man. Read through every one of the covenants in the scriptures. Every one of them included man's will. They included these statements to some degree or another: "I will if you will." "I will do this if you will do that." "I will bless you if you do this. If you don't do that, then I will curse you." "We'll be in covenant if you keep this." "If you follow through with these commandments or keep this commitment then we will be in covenant together."

Man broke every one of those covenants.

God was not surprised that man broke those covenants, but *man* needed to know he could not keep covenant with God. This was a revelation that man needed, not God.

Man was led through this phase of human history for many centuries to establish that he could not keep a covenant with God as the law was established. It should have made us understand that no one can keep the law, and that no one can keep a covenant.

If no one can keep the law, how in the world could we think someone could keep covenant with God? The prophets themselves declared "there's none righteous, no not one." There's no one that's ever kept the law of God. *No one* has ever done that! And now that we are under grace, the power of God's grace is not to give you the ability to keep God's law; it is to give you the freedom to live life. Why this gets so confusing is amazing, but the confusion emanates from our misunderstanding and confusion about free will and God's will. Religion, and in this case specifically, Christianity, is responsible for this confusion.

The will of man has never stopped and will never stop the will of God from taking place. God does not stop and consult with man. God does not stop and ask man for his opinion. There are no negotiations. There's none of this except where God wanted to be in covenant and asked man that if *he would* be in a covenant relationship then *God would.* Obviously God's will is never carried out in conjunction with man's will. In fact, God's will is totally independent from man's will. Man's free will needs to be carried out in this life based on an understanding that God's will has already been accomplished.

The moment you believe that your will is involved with God's will you are trapped in religion. You will go through an emotional cyclone until you get spat out on the other side. That's the best one caught in this stormy process can hope for. Most people never come out of it and go to their grave trapped in this horrible whirlwind of confusion. The proponents of free will in Evangelical Christianity make this statement: "God will not do anything outside of man's will." However, like so many other maxims in Christianity, that is not found anywhere in the Bible, much less the scriptures. In fact, God has been imposing his will over mankind's will since the beginning of time. What else was getting kicked out of the Garden of Eden about? What else was the confounding of the languages of man at the tower of Babel about?

The fact of the matter is that God's will is not a violation of man's will no matter what God does. Also, humanity's will can never violate God's will. These two have been mutually exclusive from each other since the cross. God separated the issue of his will and man's will right then and there—forever. God's and man's respective wills, like so many other things, had to be delineated at the cross to bring clarity to the issue.

The purpose and application of both God's and man's wills become crystal clear through the work of the cross because it is there that we all are set free. Always rehearse, "it was for freedom that Christ set us free."

We now do have free will. We have been set free from having to try to make the will of God work for us. Man does not and cannot make the will of God work. God did not consult man when God put the stars in the sky. God did not consult with man when he put the sun and the moon in the sky. God did not consult with man through any creation (and perhaps most importantly his new creation). God did not even consult with man about whether or not he wanted a helpmeet or not. God just said, "This is not good for man to be alone; this is what I am going to do." He didn't turn around and ask Adam, "Do you want a helpmeet? What do you think about it? Let's come to an agreement here and once we're through conferencing I'll decide because I am the decider." No, he didn't confer with Adam at all. He didn't discuss the situation with the human race when he declared the entire human race to be sinners because of the sin of one man. Where was human free will, when they were all declared to be sinners at birth because of the sin of one man? These are eternal issues. Man's will never was, never is, and never will be relevant to eternal issues.

The giving of the law was where the muddling of man's will and God's will began to be stirred together in the same pot. It's like man's will and God's will and man's righteousness and God's righteousness got all mixed up. Everything was thrown together hodge-podge like. At the cross EVERYTHING was brought to light and placed in its accurate and precise meaning, relevancy, and ability.

God, in redeeming the human race, was never hindered by the will of man. The will of man, when rejecting the will of God, likewise cannot hinder the will of God. God's will is always completed regardless of man's free will choices. God's will does not interfere with man's free will regarding temporal choices, but neither does the free will of man on earthly matters affect God's will regarding eternal things.

We were taught in Christianity regarding our will that by that free will we must make Jesus our personal Lord and Savior. It more than implies that if you have to make Jesus your personal Lord and

Savior then obviously your will is to be involved with eternal issues. Here again, Evangelicalism has come up with a statement which is not in the Bible. There is no place that has anything to do with the will of man declaring that Jesus is Lord. The only one who was to make and declare Jesus as Lord was God himself.

There is just no room to credit man's will with making Jesus Lord.

God's will was designed to redeem man in spite of man's will and without man's involvement because if our fickle and inconsistent will were involved, all humanity would fail. The reason why we have an unfailing redemption is because we are not involved. We are the recipients of the most magnificent event that has ever happened to the human race carried out by the will of God.

We and God are One!

Period.

End of story.

Another very misconstrued concept Christianity has come up with is a participation of man's will being involved is in the requirement Jesus gave to be "born again." A man named Nicodemus came to Jesus by night and said, "How can I enter into the kingdom of God?" Jesus said, "Except a man be born again, he cannot see the kingdom of God." Then Nicodemus asked the question, "How can a man be born again?"

First off, we don't have to try to define whether or not it is a demand or a requirement. We know that it *is* a requirement. "Ye *must* be born again." Nicodemus was a devout religious man in Jerusalem who was attracted to what Jesus was preaching. Because of the problems it could cause him if he were seen actually showing an interest in what Jesus was teaching, he came to Jesus by night.

The conversation that took place sparked a world-wide, history-altering religion. At least this concept is in the Bible. The "born-again" discussion is not nearly as absurd as the "You *must* make Jesus your personal Lord and Savior" one. There's no way to really approach the "You *must* make Jesus your personal Lord and Savior" discussion in context because it *ain't* in the Bible! The only way you can address that is to show that no man can make Jesus *Lord.* It's obvious someone greater has to make someone lesser into Lord, someone higher than the individual being made "Lord." It would be absolutely unprecedented for a lesser to make a greater "Lord." It makes perfect sense when you realize that the actual teaching about the Lordship of Jesus is that *God has made him Lord,* and that the Father made him Lord over ALL. It's incredible how these subjects get tied together. The term "born again" gets tied together with "saved." Then the term "make Jesus your personal Lord and Savior" gets lobbed in there all together. Some of them aren't even Bible subjects. Others are simply taken out of context. This is one of the biggest factors in breaking down a lot of this misunderstanding and to unraveling some of the assumed traditional doctrines and definitions.

Concerning "being born again," let us *let it* define itself first.

It is vital to know that when you hear "you *must* be born again" and then you hear the church's doctrine as to *how* to be "born again" that there is a chasm of a difference. What *is* in the Bible is that "you must be born again." There is no *how to* be "born again" in the Bible. It does not exist there. So, here is a combining of statements and doctrines to try to weave together something that has evolved into a *patchwork* gospel, which in fact, fully opposes and negates the original intention behind the statement. It has, in fact, become "another gospel."

You can pick up little tracts here and there which read on the cover "How to be born again." They first quote that Jesus said "You must be born again." It is the height of bizarre that people who say they adhere to the word of God or the scriptures or the Bible or what they believe comes right out of the Bible and then have an entire doctrine that is not even spoken of AT ALL in the Bible. Still, if you're going to have a requirement that you must be born again, somebody had to figure out what that would mean.

Wouldn't it have been much more logical to accept what the scriptures had already foretold about this amazing event—this most amazing *single event* ever on planet Earth?

Evangelical Christianity again makes this eternal truth—something that equally affects all (being born again)—a *personal* experience. While I take it very personally that I have been born again, being born again is not an individual *personal* experience. As a personal experience, it just does not exist in the scriptures *or* the Bible. Now, one can continue to believe that being born again is an individual, *personal* experience just like you *can* believe that Jesus is your *personal* Lord and Savior. However, there's nothing personal about what God did at the cross through Jesus, nor through his death, burial, and resurrection. In fact, it is the opposite of *personal.* No one was *singled out* and no one was *left out. That*, ladies and gentlemen, is the power of the gospel! No one was singled out AND no one was left out. If we could only remember that statement, in everything we contemplate about the gospel, it would always lead us and guide us in a direction that would cause us to understand what it is that we're actually studying. No one was singled out! No one was left out! *That* is the gospel truth. You hear a lot of things called "the gospel truth." But there is only ONE gospel truth, and that is it!

By using this guideline, we can see how that applies to the subject of "you must be born again." One of the things we have to look at in this brief conversation that Jesus had with Nicodemus is the statement that "a *man*" must be born again. He said *a man,* singular, must be born again to enter into the kingdom of God.

Now the first concept you should be introduced to was that "a man" *was* born again. So, we are back to the singular "one man" being involved. It was not *a multitude* that had to be born again. It was just "a man" who had to be born again (in its accurate translation and definition, to be born *by the Spirit*). Later in his exchange with Nicodemus Jesus did indeed say "ye must be born again." However, in light of Paul's teaching on this subject in I Corinthians 15, when "a man" (Jesus) was born from the dead (born again or raised *by the Spirit*) *ye* also were born again.

At this point, please get this: everything Jesus required (and that God the Father required) of all mankind—whether it be "being born again," "be ye holy," "obeying the Lord," "you must believe"—all these and ALL requirements were ALL fulfilled by the One Man for the whole human race forever.

With that settled and us understanding exactly what Jesus said to Nicodemus, we see that it is an absolute requirement for existing in the kingdom of God. Paul's use of the terms "being *in* the kingdom" or Jesus' "the kingdom of God being *within*" seems to be interchangeable. I won't challenge that at all at this point, but it seems that the terms were interchangeable to "being in the kingdom of God" and "the kingdom of God is in us." This is paramount in understanding the teaching of "being *in* Christ" and "Christ being *in* us."

Again, the only *teaching* on being born again is by Paul and that teaching concerns Jesus being raised from the dead. Paul states that Jesus was the "first born" from the dead and everyone else came after Jesus because of Jesus. For "in Christ, if one is dead, all are dead, and if one is alive then all are alive." That term "alive" is extrapolated from the born again teaching. That's what the subject is. So, if one is dead then all are dead, and if one is born from the dead then all are born again. That is what the story is telling us in its context and its content.

These doctrines in Christianity begin to multiply and pile up upon each other like a massive accident on a turnpike. They need to keep inventing doctrines to explain the gaps in earlier invented doctrines. And it never ends.

So all we are doing here is attempting to take all these things a little at a time. It is important that we are addressing this, because whether we resolve this or not; it's really not going to change anything. If we come out of this today and we say man's will is involved or man's will is not involved, or it's all man's will, or it's all God's will, it's not going to change what it is. It is better to find out what really exists scripturally and biblically than to have an opinion about it that you probably learned in church and/or through Christian media. You cannot find anything eternal that has been left to man's will. So, by knowing this and having these two clearly defined in their own right, man is now truly free to live his life and is empowered to live his life through the power of the truth of the gospel, a gospel eternally established for every person as much as gravity was established for every person. ALL are affected equally.

This is so very conclusive in Romans which, oddly enough, is where everybody goes to try to teach what they call "the four spiritual laws" to support this hideous doctrine. In fact, it is in Romans Chapter 10 where we find the subject about believing in your heart and confessing with your mouth. But please understand that redemption is *eternal* and an established fact while salvation is *temporal* and is ongoing. That one bit of knowledge will make you free for the rest of your life. Redemption is eternal. Salvation is temporal but *is* impacted by the eternal truth of redemption of ALL.

Salvation means to be saved from something whether it's sickness or disease or poverty. But in Paul's context of salvation, he speaks of the saving of the soul. Your soul or mind will be impacted dramatically through the power of eternal truth. However, we must acknowledge that this can be temporal because this change can go right back to where you started if that truth is not maintained in the meditation and contemplation in the minds or souls of people.

One needs to keep an eternal reality of redemption active in your thinking in order to "cleanse one's soul and renew one's mind" (salvation). You have got to be able to separate these two, redemption and salvation, and be able to see them and respect them for what they truly are.

Christianity uses this one verse that says: "Whosoever shall call upon the name of the Lord shall be saved." That sure sounds like it's all up to (and involves) the will of man, doesn't it? We have to decide. We have to call upon the name. We have to do all these things, but then Paul brings all of that into question and says who could possibly do that? Who would call upon the name of the Lord? He says, "Who can call on him whom they've not believed?" "How can they believe in whom they have not heard?" "How can they hear without a preacher?" Then he continues on and he begins to speak about the Gospel of Peace in that section of the New Testament writing. He is NOT talking about our need to believe!

Paul concludes the matter in this chapter in Romans with this: "But Isaiah was very bold and saith "I was found of them that sought me not. I was made manifest to them *that asked not* after me. "This is ALL in the same chapter. Earlier Paul says that the Lord would be available to anybody that asked for him. Then Paul turns around and quotes Isaiah and says that none of that worked. Man doesn't have sense enough to ask for what he needs. Our will is pivotal in redemption? Really? We don't even have the ability to ask for what we need! Paul first quotes Isaiah saying, "whosoever shall call upon the name of the Lord, shall be saved." Then seven verses later says, "But Isaiah was very bold and saith, I was found of them who sought me not. I was made manifest unto them *that asked not* after me." Now, that is the power of God's will! This is a great example of Paul's style of comparative teaching.

Man's will is so unstable it doesn't even know what to ask for. We didn't know what we needed. Man had no understanding what he needed from God. God knew what man needed, so he carried this whole incredible thing out all by himself. Therefore, HE gets all the glory. HE gets ALL the credit. You've heard Christians say they give God ALL the glory? What a crock!

Paul was quoting from Isaiah. That's what makes this sensible, understandable, and do-able. What makes it do-able is so important. The only thing that makes redemption do-able is that it was God's will accomplishing it. God is the ONE who does the eternal stuff, not us!

The only factor that makes man's will absolutely do-able is that it at all pertains strictly to temporal things, things in our lives in the here and now. Christ set you free to be free, to do what? What do you want to do? God respects your autonomy. In fact, he provided for it. If he respects our freedom, and paid such a high price for it, should not we honor the freedom we have been given? Should we not revel in it as opposed to fretting about something that God has nothing to do with anymore?

One of the most liberating and empowering things you will ever understand about free will is that it truly is now *free* will. It is free of having to measure up to any qualifications or to be measured by God or to be measured by his law. Your free will is not a measure of your righteousness in any way. Look at the term "free will" and emphasize the term "free."

You ARE free!

Yet, the only way you will exercise your free will in a healthy way is when you know that God's will has already been finished in Christ once and for ALL!

Chapter 5

You Have a Future

Several years ago I was speaking in Canada and unbeknownst to me a family was there who had a son that was about 14 years old. A friend of his was visiting with them and brought him. I don't remember what I was speaking about, but evidently it was something pertaining to the last and final judgment of the world having been accomplished at the cross.

The following year I went back and held a convention in Canada. There were quite a few people in attendance including a father and his son.

At first I didn't recognize the boy sitting there with his father as having been the one in the meeting the year before. I spoke three sessions a day. It was quite exhausting. As I was walking back to my room to get some rest in between sessions, the father came up to me in the hallway. He stopped me and said, "Excuse me, Mr. Williams, I would like to speak to you just a moment if I may," and I said, "Sure."

As he started to open his mouth, he began to get emotional. He couldn't say what he wanted to say. He finally got it out between absolutely choking on tears and said, "Last year my son was visiting friends of ours, and they brought him to your meeting. Quite honestly, had we known that they were going to bring him to your meeting; we would have forbidden him from coming. I've raised my children in a very strong Christian environment and thought I was doing everything right to raise a healthy family. But over the last few years my son, as he got into his teenage years, began to become unstable, mentally and emotionally." He said, "My son would walk through the house wringing his hands, pacing back and forth, and couldn't sleep at night at all." He told me the rest of the story. He said, "We were actually at the point of considering taking him for professional help, which was against all of our Christian beliefs. That was how he was when he left to spend the night with our friends, until he came back the next day." He said, "Mr. Williams, I have to thank you because after listening to you for 45 minutes, my son no longer walked the floors and he has stopped wringing his hands. From that night forward, for this last year, he has slept peacefully in his own bed with no signs of any mental or emotional disturbance whatsoever."

When we finished that particular seminar, my heart broke for that father. I know what it is to raise children with all of the best intentions in the world, being taught by pastors to spank your children and to make sure it hurts, and make sure they believe in Jesus, and make sure they are warned about hell. You think you are doing exactly the right thing to prepare them and protect them. I didn't know that I was abusing my children by doing these things, even as this parent did not know the child abuse that was taking place in his son's Sunday school classes. It was taking place in his church, and it was, by any definition, child abuse. At the end of our conversation, I thanked him. It was very difficult to listen to his story, but I was grateful to know that my words had been of some help.

We finished up that seminar and, as my custom is, I took the lapel microphone that I had on, and we started passing it through the crowd that remained. Each and every one of the people that took the microphone had something positive to say. It really touched my heart. Finally, there was only one person who had not made a comment of some kind, which was the 15 year old boy. So, I asked him, "Son, can you tell me what you got out of the teachings in this seminar?" His simple reply stunned me. He said, "I have a future."

It still makes my heart ache to know the pain and the suffering that children are going through because of Sunday schools across the world. I know that it just doesn't seem possible that the worst abuse in a child's life is happening in Sunday school, but it is. A child can get bruises and wounds to some degree from a sibling or even a parent in a moment of rage. However, when you believe that for the rest of your life that you're under an angry wrathful God who absolutely cannot be satisfied and believing that your future is being terminated by teachings such as "The End of the World is near because the Judgment of God is coming"—now that IS child abuse. That's why I'm so compelled to speak out. Whether it's a teaching from Peter or anybody else that teaches there is a judgment left to come, I cite my heritage according to Isaiah and condemn those teachings and those words of judgment and proclaim as emphatically as I can: "They are just not true!"

"I have a future." Isn't that an amazing statement? You wouldn't think that this would be the plague that hangs over not just my country but over countries like Iran and other religiously strict regions and cultures throughout the world. There are few places in the world where children don't grow up with the threat that they may never even become adults and that if they *do* become adults, they may never become parents, and if they *do* become parents, they may never see their children grow up, and if they *do* see their children grow up, they may never see their grandchildren. Not because of natural disaster, or a disease, or some other possible early exit, but because of an absolutely sure and pre-determined judgment that is coming to the world. And they're taught it is going to be in their lifetime. Soon and very soon!

Scores of generations have come and gone since the actual and prophesied judgment of this world took place over 50 generations ago.

Over fifty generations have been taught this horrendous, hideous doctrine.

Over fifty generations have come and gone.

Over fifty generations have been told theirs would be the last generation.

Even as this book is being written, we stand in this 51st generation, another generation that is ready to face a termination of life and living on this planet by an angry wrathful God who must satisfy his vengeance against sin. Even thinking about it at this moment is difficult for me, to know that this debilitating view of the future is still out there.

At times, I feel incredibly inadequate at what I do because the pain and the suffering are so prolific. This pain can run so deep that it sometimes leads to mental and emotional disorders of which suicide is just the tip of the iceberg. The ones who end up taking their lives conclude it's all going to end anyway. Then why not just go ahead and take matters into their own hands and end their own personal fear and misery? If that doesn't get them, the impending sense of doom that comes from teaching God is angry at people does.

I was told as a young man that every time I sinned that I was crucifying Jesus over and over again. So, rather than continue offending Jesus, I decided that I would commit suicide. My reason for attempting suicide was not because I didn't know God and didn't love God. But rather, it was BECAUSE I loved Jesus with all my heart. It is a profane and vicious thing to teach a child to fear the very same God that you then tell them they must love. The mental conflict brought about by this irrational love/fear mindset is there for all to see in failed individual, national and international relationships.

It is now approximately the 51st generation since the cross, figuring about 40 years for a generation, according to a Biblical generation. We're talking about fifty-one generations of misconceptions, torture, manipulation, domination, and control. Some wonder why we haven't made more progress than we have. I honestly believe that it borders on the miraculous that we have made as much progress as we have given the dominant role of religion in the last couple thousand years.

The gospel must be understood in the context of THE One Man, Jesus, and this One Man's judgment. The only alternative is the failures of the human race just described.

The first thing we have to remember about judgment is that it was for *the sin*, not the *sins*—it was not plural—it was for *the sin* of the whole world. We also have to remember that *the sin* of the whole world was one man's sin—the sin of one man—Adam. As the story continues, it would become more apparent why the one sin is what it is, but for now suffice it to say that it was *one man's* sin—the initial sin committed by Adam.

Paul explains in detail that the law never made a man a sinner. Breaking a law never made a man a sinner. Man (the first Adam) was a sinner long before the law was given. The revelation of sin is what was in the law. It is the revelation of the one transgression. The law was given 2,600 years after Adam and 1,400 years before Jesus was born. One sin—the sin of Adam's unbelief—was what was needed to be dealt with.

It is an amazing privilege to point out the wonderful and profound truth that our actions and our deeds did not send Jesus to the cross. Jesus died for one man's transgression. He died to remove the law which had imposed the curse. He died to remove the law that imposed the revelation of sin because, remember, the law *never* made anybody a sinner. We were transgressors of God's law, but by transgressing God's law we were supposed to get the revelation that Paul got. And it truly *is* Paul's revelation in Romans Chapter 7. A lot of people try to teach Paul's teaching in Romans Chapter 7 as being "this is what a normal Christian life is all about." Paul said, "When I want to do good, I can't and when I try not to do evil, I do it. This is the conflict that is in me." But Paul was not talking about the current Christian life. That *may* be the way traditional Christians live, yes, but that is not the crisis. The crisis he was speaking of was what the crisis was all about *before* the cross. It was this conflict and this struggle under *the law* that could not produce righteousness. That's all he was saying; that the law could not produce righteousness. Then he says "Oh wretched man! Who will deliver me from this body of death?" And then he goes on to say "Thanks be to God through our Lord Jesus Christ!" It's Jesus who delivers us from this body of death, from this body of conflict, this body of contradiction and delivers us to his peace. Now that's a Redeemer!

Just think if all people were taught this when they were growing up! On the contrary, the amount of guilt that is placed in a child's mind because his or her parents were taught the darkness and ignorance of Christian doctrine when they were children, and so on and so on, for fifty-one generations—that everyone that is born is born a sinner—is unfathomable. As with so much abuse, the abused become the next generation of abusers.

That we were born sinners is simply not true.

For 2,000 years it has not been true because God imputed righteousness from the cross for every human being. It's because of the same logic and reason that everyone was a sinner, because of imputed sin—not because of what anybody did but because of what *God* did. God imputed sin to the entire world.

This begs the question, "Why did God impute one man's transgression, one man's sin, to the entire world?" It is a very important question. The resolution of this question is quite revealing.

If God took the transgression of one man and made everyone guilty for that *one* transgression, how many redeemers do we have to have for all of those people? That's an interesting equation. Even though multitudes of millions of people had come and gone from Adam to Christ, in God's eyes this was all still *just one man*, and that's why God only sent *one man* in response. God sent one man because there was only *one* problem with *one* man. Through the process of eternal sacrifice, Jesus redeemed the entire world. To deny Jesus the credit for redeeming the entire world is to place sin squarely on each and every individual. Sin was *not* an individual issue. Sin was a *one man* issue, and God himself imputed that sin, even as Paul said unto them who had *not* sinned after the "similitude" of Adam's transgression. Even those who didn't do what Adam did were still guilty.

Jesus' redemption removes not just guilt. Christianity offers the removal of guilt, and people go through this tremendous salvation experience by being told that, "At the moment of conversion, your sins are all going to be washed away." I know what that feels like, but you see, we got shorted a bit. No, let me take that back; we got shorted a LOT, because we traded a total redemption for a partial salvation. That's not fair! Instead of accepting that the work of the cross is what God said it was, religion seeks to redefine it altogether. It becomes nothing. It is vapid. It is empty. It voids the whole purpose of the cross to reduce it to being something that only relieves us of the issue of sin and guilt upon our confession, our belief, our faith; and that's why it is only partial.

Paul ascribed to Jesus the title of: *The Last Adam*. That is pure genius!

There was a First Adam, and there was a Last Adam, but it all was still just Adam. The Last Adam *was* "Adam." We still aren't dealing with anything more than just one man in this equation: that out of one *all* are condemned and out of ONE *all* are redeemed. This is the gospel mystery that has been passed over because of legalistic teachings and the lack of understanding of the most simple and yet the most profound thing that has ever happened on this Earth and that is the redemption of the world through One Man because of one man.

It is vital to look at this *One Man's* judgment.

The book of Revelation, this single New Testament letter, has been the source of a great deal of the confusion and heartache. Just take it at its face value and understand that John is quoting scripture throughout this entire vision that he had. It wasn't *just* a vision; it was a rehearsal in which he was quoting scripture to paint a picture that we would understand. With a large percentage of Revelation being direct quotes from the scriptures contained in Isaiah, Ezekiel, and Daniel, John wants us to understand clearly what he was seeing.

It is a wonderful revelation the Apostle John got when he said that "the word was made flesh." I would love to go into the book of Revelation like everybody else does and put a private interpretation on it and say, "Let ME figure it out! Let ME try to tell you what he's talking about. Let ME try to tell you where this is going to happen, when it's going to happen, where in history it's going to be placed." However, I DO NOT have a right to do that. No one does. No one does because the scriptures that are being quoted are the prophets Isaiah, Ezekiel, Daniel, etc., and all of those prophecies were *made flesh* and dwelt among us because the Word of God became flesh and dwelt among us, as John said.

There can be no such thing as the interpretation of a law, or a prophecy, or a psalm for that matter, outside of the life, death, burial, and resurrection of One Man because that would be outside the perimeters of the equation of *ONE*.

None of this is about us.

None of this is about me.

None of this is about the people that I think should be punished.

None of this is about the people I think should be rewarded.

None of this is about me or you!

The prophets said God would give *him* the heathen as an inheritance. This is about the One Man and *his* reward. WE are HIS reward! How awesome is that?! That's why we are redeemed. God gave us to Jesus as a reward! We are his bounty! We are his spoils of war. We belong to him because he won the battle. He WON! He did not fail. It is foretold in the prophets that Jesus would inherit the heathen for an inheritance. He inherited the entire planet as an inheritance. It couldn't have been said better than how it was said by Paul: All things are of him, by him, through him, and by him all things exist.

So, when we look at the book of Revelation, we must know where John was when he had his vision. It says very clearly where he was when he *got* the vision; he was "in the spirit on the Lord's Day." Now this is how bizarre this has all become. The Lord's Day has been presented to be the Sabbath. It has been presented to be Sunday. It has been presented to be any number of holy days but mainly the Sabbath and/or Sunday, and even those two get wrongfully mixed together as though they are one thing.

The Lord's Day, according to the prophets that John himself is quoting, is the day of the cross, the Day of Judgment.

The importance of knowing this cannot be overstated.

The Lord's Day is the day that judgment would come to this planet.

The Lord's Day is the day that God would judge ALL sin.

The Lord's Day is the day that God would bestow ALL mercy.

The very same day that was prophesied to be the Day of Judgment was also prophesied to be the Day of Mercy—all on the SAME, "One" day, which the psalmist saw from afar and said, "Truth and mercy have met together, righteousness and peace have kissed."

How in the world could the Day of Judgment be the Day of Mercy?

Well, we see there is only one way that the Day of Judgment could be the Day of Mercy and that is because this is all about just One Man. And in this One Man, we see the divine "meeting" and the divine "kiss" of seeming opposites.

Let's look again at what Jesus had to say about what would happen when that cross would go up in the air. He is quoted in the book of John as saying, "Now is the judgment of this world"—Now—"and I, if I be lifted up from the earth, I will draw ALL . . ." Now, remember we've already seen in the King James Version of the Bible the word "men" is italicized, which means it was not in the original text, which says "I will draw all *men* unto me." It was inserted by the translators. Without that italicized word, we're left to read it as "I will draw all unto me." Now, the word "all" has powerful significance, because that is a powerful, all-encompassing word that means literally "everything." Jesus believed that he was about to draw all judgment, all wrath, all sin, all of the scriptures—the law, the psalms and the prophets—all of creation—heaven and Earth themselves—EVERYTHING unto himself. To get an even clearer picture, the word "unto" means "within." So, literally everything was fulfilled—ALL RIGHTEOUSNESS was fulfilled within the body of this One Man. Remember, Jesus not only took all judgment "within" him. He took the judgment, the judged, the judge, the law by which we were judged, the prophecies that foretold our judgment. It all went to the grave inside of Christ—and died. It was raised again an entirely new creature, which will NEVER be destroyed! Ergo, as Paul so eloquently talked about, "So when this corruptible shall have put on incorruption, and this mortal shall have put on immortality, then shall be brought to pass the saying that is written, Death is swallowed up in victory."

I personally believe John may very well have been imprisoned on the Isle of Patmos because of this vision—because this man was declaring that *all* scripture—all of these prophecies had been fulfilled. Imagine John standing there. The only disciple reported to be present at the crucifixion of Jesus, John is standing at the foot of the cross, and he gets this wild vision, this incredible revelation.

Now look at this vision. He sees all of these prophecies becoming reality in front of him. He is seeing all of these prophecies of judgment, and wrath, and anger, and the end of the world even as Jesus himself spoke of it taking place in front of his very eyes. Even Matthew tells us much of the things that Jesus talked about when he spoke of the "end of the world" himself. Jesus told of the things that would happen. And indeed, the things that are spoken of in Matthew did take place. The Sun was darkened. The Earth shook. The mountain split in two.

When the prophet said that "his feet would touch the Mount of Olives and the mountain would cleave in two," I believe with all my heart that he was talking about Jesus as he was crucified on the Mount of Olives. There is a lot of speculation about this. If we go on a tour of Israel, they're going to take us and show us rocks where, if we look at it at the right angle and the right time of day with the sun shining on it, it looks like a skull, and they say that that is where Jesus was crucified. But it's really very clear in the New Testament and I think in the scriptures also, that Jesus was crucified on the Mount of Olives, and that being just outside the Eastern Gate.

According to my very dear friend Glenn Klein, who is Jewish and has visited Israel many times, as you tour Israel you will look directly toward the Eastern Gate. When he was there, the tour guide told him and his tour group that somewhere in the ages of history there was a massive earthquake that split the Mount of Olives down the middle. There's actually a road that runs in the valley that goes between the mountains where the prophet said that this mountain would cleave in two, and part would go to the north and part would go to the south. Do you know that was the great earthquake that was spoken of when Jesus died at the cross? From where Jesus was crucified, he would have been facing the Eastern Gate. He was crucified outside the Eastern Gate. When the cross went in the air and the judgment of God came down upon One Man, for one man's receipt of ALL sin, he redeemed the entire planet. And the mountain split in two.

I'm going to paint the picture for you that I get when I read the entirety of the description of the crucifixion in John. Try to conceptualize this awesome moment when *all* the law, *all* the psalms, *all* the prophets, and *all* the redemption the world would ever need was meeting in *one place,* and there John is standing and facing the cross as this happened in real time.

One of the most important thoroughfares to Jerusalem was the road that led to the Eastern Gate, because this is where the Jewish people would have travelled coming into the city. It was important to the Romans to demonstrate their authority when people came into their city. The Bible places the crucifixion at Golgotha or the Place of Skull. A friend of mine who is a scholar of ancient Greek explained to me that the actual translation of the word "skull" means "the place of *skulls*," multiple. The place of skulls was this entrance into Jerusalem and according to scripture Jesus was crucified on the Mount of Olives. With that being the case, the road that came into the Eastern Gate came directly across the Mount of Olives, right straight across the Mount of Olives, and then just directly into the Eastern Gate. So, it makes perfect sense that this would have been where they would have crucified Jesus. This is where they would have wanted the Jews to *see* this crucifixion on their way into the Eastern Gate.

I pondered the prophecy that the Mount of Olives would cleave in two for several years. One part would go to the north and one part would go to the south. That's a pretty big cleaving! It was interesting because when I was studying this I had the privilege of talking with Glenn about it. I was just absolutely in shock when he began to explain to me that the tour guides would take them to the Eastern Gate and then turn around and show them the Mount of Olives, where there is *now* a road running between the northern pinnacle and the southern pinnacle. I do believe that verse of scripture *was* fulfilled as I believe *all* scripture was fulfilled at the cross. So, this much-believed futuristic view that somehow at another time yet coming, that Jesus is going to return and his feet are going to touch the Mount of Olives is redundant to say the least—it already happened at the cross. Why would it happen again? At that moment, when the cross went up in the air, something incredibly powerful occurred. The prophecies also describe many of the events that would happen. There would be lightning and the sky would darken. They also describe that there would be a great earthquake and hailstones. All of these things are described. The powerful thing that you see when John is standing there facing the cross is to know the mind-blowing vision he was having—not to mention all the other stuff that was happening all around him.

Then, in his penning of the book of Revelation, John says that he heard a loud voice *behind him* as the voice of a trumpet.

The scriptures teach very clearly that the last trump was blown on "the Day of the Lord" at the cross of Jesus because the trumpet was always sounded when judgment was coming. This, therefore, would be the *last trump* of the Lord; the very last trump that was blown because after it there would be no more judgment to declare.

The Feast of Trumpets that is found in the scriptures was fulfilled on this day. There would be no more trumpets after the day of the cross in Judaism because the trumpets would have been fulfilled.

There are so many things I still don't understand. I know that people will always be learning new things after I depart the scene way beyond what I have learned. Still, right now we can imagine this beautiful picture of John standing there facing the cross. John heard a voice that was like a great trumpet from behind him, and that great trumpet was signifying the end of that age. It was the ushering in of this incredible age, and there is no end to this world that we are now in. It is a world without end.

I have no doubt.

John saw the cross, had this awesome and terrible vision and penned what he experienced in the book of Revelation as it took place—this incredible graphic judgment in the body of One Man. All God's prophecy and judgment swirled over and came crashing down on the body and soul of Jesus. The entire human race, Jew and Gentile, was pulled into his loins, into his very body, and the very destruction of all things that had been created to bring us to this monumental point in the history of humanity.

At the cross, we simply cannot have the survival of a single thing that was designed to bring us to this point. When this point came, there was a cataclysmic failure of all things that were before, of all things that existed prior. There cannot be a mixing of these two. So, this voice that was as a trumpet that came from behind John, which would have been directly toward the Eastern Gate of the Temple, heralded this fact.

The Bible tells us that at the crucifixion there was such a great earthquake and the rocks cleaved in two. To finish the story that Glenn was telling me, the Israeli tour guide told him that out of what is now the Eastern Gate, there's actually a road that goes by *in a valley* between a northern peak and a southern peak.

There is a road that goes between them to this very day.

So, here we have the culmination of all this, the totality of the work of the cross, the absolute necessity of the destruction of all things all at once.

The incredible use of imagery from the law, and the trumpets, and the Temple—what a movie this would be!

The Bible tells us the curtain at the entrance of the Holy of Holies split in two while these events were taking place at the time of the crucifixion. The curtain was the very separation of the inner court and the Holy of Holies. This was not like a curtain that is in your house, but was several inches thick and very tightly woven. It was split in two!

Indeed, this is one of the most beautiful pictures that a person could possibly see. The magnificent story of the event where all of the past and everything that brought us to this point was wiped away and all possibilities of future judgments were completely abolished. You've got to understand this: the *future* was abolished, the *past* was abolished; EVERYTHING was accomplished at the cross! Now there is only the eternal day, today. The future of the human race which would have been destruction and punishment and anger was eliminated as a possibility by the work of Christ—nothing was left except the power of the grace of God and the power of the blood of Jesus Christ.

Everything that you read in the book of Revelation took place and took place in the body of Jesus Christ. That is truly a mind-blowing thought and a place to stop and rejoice.

This was THE day!

We used to sing this song all the time in church. *"This is the day, this is the day, that the Lord hath made, that the Lord hath made. I will rejoice, I will rejoice, and be glad in it, and be glad in it."* Had we listened to the prophet, we would all have known that there is a day that the Lord made that we can all rejoice in regardless of what happens *today*. THIS is the day: The day the Lord made—it is the Day of the Cross! It was the day that John spoke of when he said he was "in the spirit on the Lord's Day" and *the* Day that John had his vision and penned it years later. It is forever sealed in the annals of history. And it is time that it be understood in its magnificent context.

Not only was it the Day of the Judgment, it was also what Jesus spoke of as "The End of the World." It is important that we understand the significance of what Jesus was telling the disciples on the day when they were leaving the Temple.

In Matthew Chapter 24, they had just walked out of the Temple and the glorious Temple grounds. They turned back to look at the buildings and spoke to Jesus and said, "Look how magnificent these buildings are, Jesus!" Then Jesus turned to them and said, "It's all coming down." It is ALL coming down. His disciples were shocked and asked him when this would be. Jesus was speaking of the time when this would all be destroyed.

Please note here that he's talking about it being destroyed physically. However, the simple beauty of this statement is that what we're looking for is not a physical destruction, but the spiritual destruction of the Temple. Jesus even referred to his own body as the Temple when he told the priests "destroy *this* Temple and I will raise it back up in three days." So, here we see in this type and foreshadowing that even the *Temple* was Jesus. Not only was Jesus the Prophet, the Sacrifice, the High Priest, but Jesus was the entire Temple!

There is a school of thought known as Preterism which believes scriptural prophecy was fulfilled with the destruction of the Temple in Jerusalem in 70 A.D. But we did not have to wait until 70 AD to see the fulfillment of the prophecies about the Temple. We don't even have to wait until 70 AD to see the fulfillment of what Jesus had to say; even though in 70 AD the Temple was destroyed. Consider the precision of the term "not one stone would be left upon another." There *are* stones left upon another, even to this day. However, spiritually speaking, there was not one stone left upon another. All of the blocks and the building of *the Temple* had been torn completely away. They were torn away through the death of Jesus Christ on the cross. Every stone was dismantled, and the stone which the builders rejected has become now the Chief Cornerstone of the Kingdom of God!

Jesus had already told them, "Destroy this Temple and I will raise it back up in three days." They were looking at a massive structure; but when Jesus said "this is all going to be destroyed, and not one stone would be left upon the other," He wasn't talking about that building. He was talking about his own existence. Not one stone would be left upon the other because *he* was the manifestation of the Word of God. He was *all* the law, *all* the psalms, *all* the prophets.

All of this was coming completely apart and being completely fulfilled and done away with in the body of One Man for the redemption of the whole world because of the transgression of one single man named Adam!

So there they are standing outside the Temple. Jesus said it's all coming down. Then they asked him, "When will these things be? What shall be the sign of thy coming?"

How can it be that religious men take this question and cause these people who are talking about the Temple and about Jesus—who *know* he *is* the Temple, and then argue that this is referring to some place thousands of years later? It is beyond me.

It is the very same reason they have to redefine the entire prophecy of Daniel when the 70th week of Daniel *was also,* of course, fulfilled at the cross like everything else. The 70th week of Daniel is not a futuristic prophecy. There were *not* 69 weeks that brought us up to the cross. The cross *IS* the 70th week of Daniel! The cross—the 70th week of Daniel—is when sin was done away with! It was when everlasting righteousness was ushered in. It's when Jesus was crowned Lord of All. It/he was Daniel's prophecy coming to fruition!

So here we have this horrible, futuristic terminology being spread around the planet like "The End of the World." Practically every religious sect teaches "The End of the World." Yet, Jesus made it clear as to when the end of the world would be

I was handed another flyer the other day that "The End of the World" was supposed to have taken place 5 days ago. I guess I missed that one, too. I've missed every one of them. So have you!

They all talk about "The End of the World" and when it will be and what will precede it, but Jesus went through a list of things that were NOT signs of the end of the world, and everybody quotes them *as signs* that "The End of the World" is near: earthquakes, wars, rumors of wars . . . after every one of them Jesus said, "But the end is not yet." All of these things have happened and they will happen, and in fact I just turned on the TV and they're advertising "The Prophecy School" here in Houston Texas, where everybody is to come because there are wars and rumors of wars, and there's famine and pestilence in diverse places and everybody's supposed to come and learn about when these prophecies are going to be fulfilled.

How long will this planet suffer under this misrepresentation of the finished, complete, and successful work of Jesus Christ?

We in the Gospel Revolution are doing our level best to bring an end to all of this insane teaching because Jesus already brought an end to it 2,000 years ago and it has been so damaging to the psyches and emotions of countless generations. How many more generations need to suffer under this ignorance and strategy of controlling people's lives, money, minds, and futures?

In Matthew, Jesus is asked what shall be the sign of his coming, "and of the end of the world." The interesting thing is the term *world* there is not the same as in the term "End of the *World.*" That term "world" is not *kosmos*—the end of the *planet*; it is the end of the *aion,* which is the Greek word which means the end of the *age.* Jesus was bringing about an end of an *age*, literally dismantling it stone by stone and leveling it, leaving it without remedy. There was no need for a remedy. The remedy was already there to replace it.

Later in that very same chapter, Jesus says "These are not signs. But if you want a sign, here's the real one." He said "This gospel." (He is talking about what *he* was preaching) "This gospel of the kingdom will be preached in all the world, and then the end will come." That term *world* does not mean *kosmos* either. It is a third Greek word *oikoumenē,* which means *a region*—specifically—the Roman Empire. And do you know that throughout all four Gospels in the New Testament we're told that Jesus' fame spread throughout that region, throughout the Roman Empire? The gospel that Jesus preached over the course of his three-year ministry was spread—*preached*—throughout the world! In Romans Chapter 10, even Paul says the gospel *was* preached throughout the world. Paul said the *whole world* heard the gospel. Sometimes these things are maddening; that the most brilliant minds on the face of the Earth will not stop and look at the simplicity of these statements. They are not complicated. But humans, in their ignorance, promote religion and fear and control over others—not the gospel. What better way to do it than say and teach that the "End of the World" is just around the corner. However, the good news is that the true gospel is self-revealing. Still, if a person is determined to stay in religion, to control others and be controlled by others, he or she will be blinded to the gospel until the day they choose to allow the gospel to reveal its beautiful, simple-yet-profound reality to their soul.

The gospel *was* preached throughout the world and the end of the age—the end of their world—*did* come. It came in a very violent way at the cross at Golgotha on the Mount of Olives. This is where the mountain split in two, the curtain was rent in two, enormous hailstones fell, the sun was darkened—these things are all reported in ancient writings of the gospels predicted by Jesus himself prior to his sacrifice on the cross—all witnessed by John and interpreted in his visionary revelation on "the Day of the Lord."

There is no greater pleasure I have in sharing and teaching this wonderful gospel than uncovering for folks that they and their loved ones and that all generations to come have a future—that "The End of the World" already was fulfilled.

The evidence is simple, direct, and concrete in its conclusion. It's found in the book of Romans and in Corinthians. Paul speaks of the judgment seat of Christ—and when his words are read in context it is clear this all occurred 2,000 years ago. The last verse in that chapter in Romans speaks of the judgment seat of Christ. It is the verse that says, "For he that knew no sin was made sin, that we might be made the righteousness of God in Christ." This is so glorious! This is where we get the term "new creature." This glory also shines through in Corinthians—that if any man be in Christ he is a new creature—a new creation—a new species that literally never existed on this planet before the day of the resurrection of Jesus Christ.

And the very good news is that this new species indeed has a future and will continue forever as sure as Christ will continue forever.

Chapter 6

The Fulfillment of All

It was at the Vacation Bible School in the basement of the Southern Baptist Church in Harriman, Tennessee. This is where, for the very first time in my life, I believed on the Lord Jesus Christ.

My memory of it is clear as day.

The teachers held up a red piece of construction paper and said, "Though your sins be as scarlet," and then slid a black one over it and said, "This is how God sees your heart." Then they took a white piece of the construction paper and slid it over the front of the red and black ones and said, "They shall be made white as snow." They began to tell me how that this process of having my sins washed away took place. And if I didn't walk down that aisle and confess my sins that I would burn in hell forever.

I was five years old.

So, of course, I walked down that aisle. I walked fast. I cried. One of the most moving reasons that I was crying was because Jesus loved me and that he was willing to save me from hell.

I prayed what is called "The Sinner's Prayer," confessing my sins and accepting Jesus as my personal Lord and Savior. Years later I began to understand that I really hadn't been given an option as to whether I believed in Jesus. I had believed under duress.

This was a pivotal and dramatic event in my young life and would shape the way I viewed the world, myself, and God for decades. I cannot overstate its import. It was so clearly impactful and tangible. But at the same time it bothered my mother so much that it happened at a vacation Bible school. So, she immediately called the church and asked the teachers to come to our home. She wanted to get to the bottom of this with them and with me because I came home claiming to have gotten *saved* at the ripe old age of five.

My mother's concern was that I was too young to know what I was doing. She was very direct in dealing with things. At least that's how she was with things when I was involved. I was the youngest of six children. I don't have a clue how she dealt with the rest of the kids. But I knew I didn't have a whole lot of wiggle room!

So, the vacation Bible school teachers came to our house. We all sat down together. The teachers told my mother what had happened. Then my mother wanted to hear from me. She asked me what I had done and asked me if I understood what I had done. I said, "Yes, I understand what I did. I got saved." Then she asked, "What does that mean?" And I said, "I got saved from hell." Then I explained to her that if I believed in Jesus that I would not go to hell. Well, my mom couldn't refute that I understood their message and had believed according to what I was told, so the issue was dropped.

Decades later I realized under what circumstances that I had come to "believe" that they had put an emotional gun to my five year old head. I went to the Lord and prayed, "I've got to take a break here. I'm not sure. I want to know that I believe in you. I don't know what happened to my mind when I was told that if I didn't believe in you that I was going to burn in hell, but I don't believe that anymore. I do believe that if you have done this work, you did it completely, fully, and I want to decide for myself what I actually believe and what that means to me."

So, I took a vacation from God. However, I did not take a "vacation" from "Bible school."

I poured through the scriptures: the law, the psalms, and the prophets. I studied to discover what it was the scriptures actually said about the work of Christ. It was a beautiful process and for the first time in my life I got to go before the Lord and tell him, "Jesus, I believe that you are the Lord of all. I believe that you are my Redeemer. I believe that you have redeemed me. I believe that you rose from the dead. I believe you were born of a virgin. I believe that you have done the work that you said you did and you fulfilled the scriptures."

A salvation began in my soul that day when I began to believe without being under the duress of spending eternity burning and being tortured by a so-called loving God. After all those years of believing and being afraid I wasn't believing right or I wasn't believing enough, I finally found peace. If you do have to believe, can you trick yourself into believing that you believe enough? How much do you have to believe? How well do you have to believe?

All those questions disappeared and my soul began to be saved.

One series that I have taught that presents my view of end-time doctrines and the fulfillment of all scripture is entitled *The Doctrine of Fulfillment*. The Doctrine of Fulfillment is an attempt to put into proper perspective all concepts about the fallacy of unfulfilled scripture. This series focuses more on fulfillment of prophecy rather than that of the law. I've spent a lot of time covering the territory of fulfillment of the law, but even though you can't separate the two, this is a focus on the fulfillment of prophecy. The prophecies that Christianity says are yet to be fulfilled are undoubtedly one thing that occupies the time and the minds of many people around the world. Whether in Christianity or other faiths, the issue of prophecy and what constitutes the fulfillment of those prophecies is critical.

This part of the religious system—the end-time doctrine teachings in Christianity, seems to have been focused on by the more radical sects and yet it has affected every part of our society. There is even a huge newspaper headline font that is called "Second Coming." Terms like: end of time, end of the world, last days, judgment day, and even resurrection day and Armageddon are replete throughout our lexicon. You'd be hard-pressed to find somebody who couldn't use these terms in a sentence.

How many times have we seen the proverbial guy with the sign hanging over his body "The End is Near"? I've seen up close and personal the last day's doctrine effect on a person. Maybe you have, too. The only way one could describe its impact is to liken it to mental illness. Often people who embrace these things are certainly depicted that way in movies as characters representing the mentally disturbed and for good reason. I certainly had my own experience with that during my stays in mental institutions when I battled such horrible debilitating depression. It seemed that all the people there with me had an opinion about the end of the world if they had any opinion about anything else at all.

The teaching of what the end of the world *actually* is really is a major part of the gospel and the Gospel Revolution. To clarify this issue is a focal point in order to further one's comprehension of the gospel.

What did Jesus have to say about this in Matthew Chapter 5?

"Think not that I have come to destroy the law or the prophets, I am not come to destroy but to fulfill." So, Jesus brings up two subjects here and he wants to make it very clear about what he *has not* come to do and what he *has* come to do. He did not come to destroy the law or the prophets. In the same way that Jesus spoke of the stones of the Temple and surrounding structures in Jerusalem that they would be "all be thrown down" or "destroyed," this is the same term he used when describing the "destruction" of the law.

The actual meaning of the word "destroyed" has been, like so many others by the translators of the Bible, "destroyed" in its application. The true connotation of that particular word would be better articulated as *fragmented*. So, in my opinion it should be more accurately understood as, "I am not come to fragment the law but to fulfill it."

Whenever I have been confronted about this teaching, it's always the same argument. People will come up to me and say, "But Jesus said I have not come to destroy the law!" However, the verse is never quoted in context. What Jesus said was that he had not come to destroy the law *or* the prophets. He said I am not come to *destroy* but to *fulfill*. The defenders of the law leave out the fact that Jesus was not only talking about the law, he was also talking about the prophets. They also leave out the fact that if he didn't come to destroy the law or the prophets, then there is something that he did indeed come to do with the law *and* the prophets. But what is that thing?

Jesus came to *fulfill* the law *and* the prophets

The term "fulfill" is really quite descriptive and actually means something else like so many other Bible words and terms that have not been accurately translated. Among other things it means is to finish, to be complete, to make replete, to diffuse.

Jesus did *not* come to *fragment* the law—which he never did. He presented it in its entirety, never watered it down, and emphasized not just the letter of the law but its spirit, too. He never spoke against the law. Jesus taught and spoke of the law perfectly.

In fact, the first time the law was ever taught accurately was when it was taught by Jesus. It was given by God to Moses, but it was never taught accurately until Jesus stepped on the scene. As Moses said when the law was given, there would come a prophet who would teach on everything that was said. That's when the accuracy of the law was taught because Jesus refused to fragment it. He did not destroy the law, and he did not misconstrue the law. He left the law completely intact. Thus, my response to a lot of Jesus' teaching, "If you want to lose all hope that you are ever going to make it to heaven all you have to do is read the teachings of Jesus." If Jesus' teaching does not take away *all* hope that you have in your heart that you will *ever* possibly be able to qualify yourself for heaven then nothing will take away that self-righteous hope.

Jesus is the one who came to initially make sure that the law was held intact, that it was understood in its complete form and intent. Yes, it's true; Jesus did not come to destroy the law because the law is the foundation by which we now understand the gospel. If the law was fragmented, then the gospel itself would be fragmented.

The reason that people do not understand the gospel today is because they have been taught and embraced a fragmented interpretation of the law. They do what Jesus said he did *not* come to do. Yet they will not accept at the same time, what Jesus said he *did* come to do with the law and the prophets. Jesus did not come to *fragment* the law and he wanted to make sure that no one misunderstood that. He came to teach the law and to teach it accurately, and as Isaiah said, "To make his law honorable," to restore honor to the law by teaching it in its fullness and its complete picture.

Jesus made it very clear that the only ones that were going to get into the Kingdom of God based on the law were those who kept it, who did not destroy the law, but who kept it perfectly. These people would be honored in the Kingdom of God. Jesus said the man who keeps the law and who does not fragment it would be great in the Kingdom of God. The fact is that a man has to keep *all* of God's law to be great in the Kingdom of God. Believe me, there are no *great men* in the Kingdom of God who have kept the law of God. But when the law was in effect, the full picture of the reality of obedience to the law was that it had to be obeyed in its entirety. You could not fragment the law. You could not take away any part of the law whatsoever.

I often make reference to the issue of homosexuality and how most people in the gay, lesbian, bisexual, and transgender community who are Christians or are members of a gay church, make a great attempt through their own ministers to whitewash the scriptures and the law to take homosexuality out of the list of sins or that which was condemned by God. But if you take away that, if you take away that homosexuality was a sin, you are guilty of fragmenting the law. Therefore, and this is critical, there would be no way to come to grips with the full reality that on this side of the cross gay people and God are now one!

The only way you can know you and God are one is to first know that through the law you are totally condemned!

Under the law you must understand that *all* humans were condemned. All people, all sexual orientations, all races, all skin colors, all people of any actions or any deeds or any thoughts at all were condemned. Any words at all, *any words at all,* could and would be judged. Can you imagine?! Jesus taught that any idle word would be judged by God. That's too much for our minds to even conceive of; but that is the fact under the law—even every idle word, every thought is judged by God under the law.

One process that Israel experienced after the giving of the law was that of prophecy. The prophets came after the law chronologically and biblically. The prophets began to foretell what the future held for Israel and the world based on the law they lived under. And they told it well. They predicted judgment was coming. They told it with great accuracy. The reality of this was that not only was all of this prophecy given under the law, but the outcome of the breaking of every law was death. There is no other penalty for the breaking of the law other than death. And as the prophets were very careful to foretell exactly what would come under the law, the prophets also knew that there was a Mediator that was coming, a Redeemer. He would be someone that was going to come and intervene.

In the prophets, the consequences of what the breaking of the law would be for the human race is juxtaposed with the revelation of the eventual Messiah. He would be the one who would come and intervene in all of this. He would stop it all. He would absorb all that the law required. The breaking of the law is not satisfied by obedience. The breaking of God's law is satisfied only by death.

The first way to satisfy the law was through obedience. There was no obedience to the law because not only did you have to obey the law *all* of your life, not just on a good day but all the days of your life—you had to obey all of the law. You also were required to raise children who obeyed the law. And then your children had to raise children who obeyed all the law, and *then* it was all counted back to you. Then, and only then, would you have qualified for keeping the law!

We simply cannot take *anything* away from or fragment the law. If we did, or could, we'd have to take something away or fragment the gospel.

Please do not fragment the law. Please don't make the mistake of trying to water down the law to make you accepted by God and others condemned. The only way we are going to feel accepted by God is to first accept the fulfillment of the law in the body of the One Man, Jesus Christ. And the only thing we can do then is to accept the fulfillment of the scriptures as Jesus defined them regarding their fragmentation: the law and the prophets must remain intact. And the law was indeed fulfilled as the prophets foretold through death, the death of the predicted Anointed One.

Jesus' words "think not" stand out strongly. It's all about thinking. "Think not that I have come to destroy (or to fragment) the law or the prophets."

We have spent a lot of time on just the law, but you see it's not just a single subject that Jesus is speaking about. Jesus has covered all the law and the prophets here. "I have not come to destroy the law or the prophets but to fulfill." Fulfill what? To fulfill the law and the prophets, that's what. "Verily I say unto you, until heaven and earth pass, not one jot or one tittle shall in no wise pass from the law till all be fulfilled." To fully understand this, one must understand that the heaven and earth that Jesus was speaking of did pass away, and a "new heaven and earth, in which dwelleth righteousness" now exists. Now that's a bigger mouthful than most people on any religious level could ever accept, because here we have the revelation of the greatest mystery of all—ALL things being fulfilled—and that is the connectivity between the law and the prophets.

One cannot separate the law from the prophets. Jesus coupled them here which is exactly where they belong: together. Remember, all the books of the prophets came after the law. They prophesied based on the law's existence. You may ask, "Well how did they prophesy about Jesus?" The law required death. So, the prophets had to foretell what the ultimate requirement of the law would be. Paul taught that the law is our schoolmaster to bring us to Christ, to lead us to Christ who has been delivered for us. So, he made it very clear that not one single law is going to pass until *all* are passed away. There's not one jot or tittle going to pass from the law, not one single law can be reduced. It cannot be tampered with. The only thing that can happen to the law is that all of it must be fulfilled. Jesus said the only way all law could be fulfilled is if all prophecy had been fulfilled. You cannot fulfill a prophecy and not have all law fulfilled, too. And likewise you can't fulfill one law without having all prophecy fulfilled. This is a perfect picture. There's no other way of describing this comparison. It is beautiful. And now it is our reality.

Two things that Christianity has done with great skill and bravado through their schools around the world is that they teach how to fragment the law and how to fragment prophecy. That's literally what it does. All monotheistic religions that rely on what is called "the scriptures"—the law, the psalms, and the prophets—it doesn't make any difference which one it is—their schools teach people to fragment the law. They teach people to fragment prophecy. If you fragment the law you will fragment prophecy. If you fragment prophecy you will fragment the law. This is like two eyeballs and a head, in order to get an accurate view you can't just look with one eye. You have got to look with both at the same time. You can't take away one without distorting the view of the other. One of the main benefits of having two eyes is that it gives you depth of vision. So, too, with the law and the prophets, having both you can see the depth of the Redeemer's work and success.

The premise that Jesus presented is this inexorable linking of the law and the prophets. He said that not one jot or tittle shall pass from the law until *all* be fulfilled. Please remember it was Jesus who said that he did not come to destroy the law or the prophets but to fulfill. So, according to Jesus' declaration you cannot have a portion or a fragment of the law that is fulfilled and not have all prophecy fulfilled. There's no such thing as a single law being dealt with out of its context within the entire law. The law is a complete package. The prophets are a complete package, too! There is a complete understanding in each, and we have no right to fragment either one of them. Always remember that a fragmented law and fragmented prophets result in a fragmented gospel.

The impetus for the greatest fragmentation of the prophets by Christianity has happened because religion has never embraced, understood, or taught the true reality or purpose of the law.

The ONLY way that the End of the World, the End of Time, Judgment Day, the Last Days, the Resurrection of the Dead, etc. can be in the future *after* the cross is if we fragment the prophets.

If Jesus came only to fulfill *some* of the prophets, but he's not going to fulfill the rest until some future day, then Jesus fragmented the prophets. And, of course, this would be a contradiction to his statement that he did not come to *fragment* the law or the prophets. Either the law is completely *intact* or it has been completely *fulfilled*. One should not mess with this, because the confusion that has been caused by doing this cannot be overstated. It is immense! Jesus has given us a complete picture of the law and the prophets. However, Christianity has more than distorted it to the detriment of multiple billions of precious people.

If you're going to embrace *any* law, you need to teach *all* of the law. It is only through teaching it all that you come to the clear revelation what the law contains, that man is a sinner in need of a redeemer. But it also reveals who the redeemer is! This is the awesome thing about it. The prophets also reveal who that redeemer is AND tell us what the full consequence of the law is . . . death. There's no other way to fulfill the law than death. The only way to fulfill their prophecy was through death.

The arrogance of Evangelical Christianity to think that we have some hand in obedience to the law or in the fulfillment of some prophecy is the height of self-righteousness.

Jesus didn't say, "I can teach you how to be obedient to the law." Jesus did not say, "I came here to teach you how to fulfill prophecy." Jesus said HE came to fulfill all law and all prophecy! And he did!

This was never a commandment to you or me or to any Christian group or any religious group ever.

Jesus said first that he came to make sure that the law is not fragmented. If you fragment the law you can never understand the prophecies. You must let the law condemn everything and everyone or you will lose your ability to comprehend prophecy and its intent. Prophecy will then become some self-fulfilling, vain, self-righteous inclusion of man's abilities, man's prayers, man's dedication, man's commitment, and man's obedience to God to keep the law and to bring about a prophecy.

We have even gotten to the point in some Christian sects that men and women make a living delivering personal prophesies. What a scam!

There is no prophecy that is about you. There is no prophecy about me. There are prophecies that tell what the fulfilling of prophecy would *do to me* and *you*, but there is no prophecy that *includes* me or you. There is no prophecy that includes any nation, any country, or any city. Bibles are probably flying across rooms right now from those reading this who think they are astute in prophecy. People may be saying, "Wait a minute! You said there is no city involved in prophecy, and no country involved in the prophecy!" You must see that the cities and the countries and the people that were involved were simply actors in the ultimate play. They were demonstrating and playing out on the public stage what Jesus would do—whether it was a country, a nation, a city, or an individual. The scriptures were not about a city. They were not about a country. They were and are about Jesus! That's what Jesus said. Jesus said we need to study the scriptures because we think we had salvation in them. However, he said you need to go back and read them because *these are they which speak of me.*

The scriptures are not about us. They are not about Israel. They are not about Egypt, the United States, Russia, Iran, or China. The "actors" in the scriptures were characters—a play on THE Word, if you will. These are roles that were played out on the human stage. And while they were not about a reconstituted Roman Empire or any other individual or group of individuals, they *were* about ONE individual. Again, they were and are ALL about Jesus!

Even the most mainline Christian might be offended to hear me say that the scriptures are not about Israel. But the scriptures *aren't* about Israel! They're not about Jerusalem. They are not about a war on this planet. It's about a war that took place in the heavens, and that war was completely won and it was about ONE Man that would become one—the Man that was God and the God that was that Man.

That Man took the place of all men and then unified God and man once and for all 2,000 years ago. It is all about that One Man and it is in that understanding where one can find rest and peace.

When one reads the Bible, and takes him or herself out of the equation, his or her own personal life as it plays out in the here and now, the things that begin to open up are amazing! But the problem is most people look at the Bible trying to find *answers* for their current circumstances—and that of the nations. This is not what the Bible is for. The Bible might give you a lot of things: right answers, wrong answers, good insight, bad insight, but the scriptures are all about Jesus and that is what gives us the foundation to have that revelation, that the entire Holy Writ was always only about One Man. There's nothing in the scriptures about you, but the scriptures in their fulfillment become all about you. Not because it applies to something happening to you, but because it was all about Christ, and we were all in Christ!

Wow!

This is the great mystery and the power of the gospel.

It places us all in the same place at the same time. We all had a grand meeting. There was an appointment. It was appointed unto man once to die and after that the judgment. The appointment date came and God himself had arranged that appointment. Man had an appointment, a destiny with death. Man had a judgment coming. We all turned up for the same appointment at the same time and we all went through the same thing in the body of Christ, in the body of One Man. Jesus kept that appointment and hid us all safely in his body. Terms like "hidden in the cleft of the rock" and "under the shadow of the Almighty" come to mind when I think about Paul's description in Ephesians of Jesus taking the human race into his body. I perceive that loving kindness tucking us away in the cleft of the rock and under the shadow of the Almighty.

Then this appointment brings him (us) standing before the judgment of God and that judgment comes down. Even after the resurrection you see Jesus standing before the throne of the Father, standing there with his own blood on our behalf. He stands before God to answer for the deeds of mankind whether they are good or whether they are bad. Even our good deeds were like filthy rags before a Holy God. Jesus offered up his own blood and God said "That's good enough."

Let us review. Jesus' sacrifice ultimately and completely was made to redeem humanity from the *bad* deed, THE sin, of one man's unbelief.

Why does Christianity think Jesus' sacrifice was not good enough, that we must have a role to play in it? The reason is described perfectly by one hyphenated word: self-righteousness.

These appointments were made by God, kept by Jesus, and included every single one of us. We cannot stress this enough. Because the gospel is the truth, and because truth is both finite and infinite, people can hear it regardless of where they're at *and* it's going to impact their heart and mind right where they are at, regardless of their background or biblical literacy.

Everything that you read about Israel is about Jesus. Everything that you read about Jerusalem is about Jesus. Not just some of it. *Everything*. We don't have the right to fragment prophecy. We don't have the right to fragment the law, because to fragment either will reduce our ability to understand both. According to Jesus they are both completely fulfilled or they are completely not fulfilled. This is not my description of the law and the prophets. This is Jesus Christ's description of God's law and his prophets.

The doctrine of fulfillment applies to both the law and the prophets. We must understand that all prophecy has been fulfilled, too. We've talked about the Judgment Day and Resurrection Day as something to come. In reality, they took place at his cross and his resurrection! We talk about the Last Days—the last days were the days leading up to the cross. The End of the World was at the cross, where Jesus put an end to the entire judicial/religious system of Judaism, its structure, all its power and authority. All ranking of mankind on any level was done away with. The Day of Wrath—Jesus made it very clear that he believed that the Day of Wrath was the day that he died on the cross. We have turned it into so many things and defined our categories of the end times into so many doctrines, that we miss the simplicity of such statements like, "I will draw it all (judgment) to myself.

The moment the cross was raised up in the air that was the moment when all prophecy about the law bringing punishment to every individual was funneled into one individual for all men for all time. It brought a complete end to a beautiful story, a story of a love affair—the completion of a love affair; the story of a rocky relationship with all its unrequited love coming to an end.

And then another love affair, the forever love affair, commenced.

When I think of the fulfillment of all things, every nerve and every muscle in my body relaxes. This tumultuous relationship between God and man ended. "It is finished," he said. No more turmoil between God and man. No more turmoil for God or for man because now God and Man are One.

People in cities around this world holding the proverbial "The End Is Near" sign or teaching this in their so-called places of worship are the ultimate insult to the work of Christ on the cross. I have no stomach for it any longer—none at all. They say, "Well, these people deserve to be punished!" I agree! But that's the marvelous thing about the gospel—none of us will ever get what we deserve. Jesus took what we deserved and we got what Jesus deserved. We all get all the benefits of a believer. We get all the benefits of someone who's been obedient unto death. We get all of the benefits of the Son. We get *all* of the benefits as though we had carried out every jot and tittle of the law and had obeyed unto death the satisfaction of the law. For the only satisfaction of the law was death.

It's as though it was we who God spoke of when he proclaimed, "This is my beloved son" to Peter and the others at the transfiguration. As magnificent as those days were when Jesus heard this on two separate occasions, compared to what God says to us now, it pales in comparison. I wilt when I think of the power of such a statement, especially in light of what Christianity has done to the revelation of this relationship which has now been completely satisfied. It is a relationship that is no longer struggling, that no longer has conflict, has no more jealousy, no more anger, no more strife.

The only way that the two could never have *any* more jealousy or *any* more strife, was if the *two* became *one*. This is the concept, the vision fulfilled. This *is* the doctrine of fulfillment; that *all* have become *one*. You cannot be one *in* the presence of God. You are not one if you're *in* the presence of God. You now are simply and profoundly in totality *in* God! And he is in YOU! You can't separate the two. The same as you could not separate the law and the prophets, you now cannot be separated from God. You are *one* and the same.

It is so painful, so sadly clear that Christianity, from its inception through Catholicism and its "reboot" in Protestantism, has never fully embraced the gospel, the cross, Christ, or his redemptive, victorious mission—not even close.

The gospel is the power of God unto salvation. This salvation, of course, is the great and magnificent salvation of the soul. The gospel reveals to the soul that there is nothing to dread between you and God, that there is no space between you and God or anyone else. The gospel teaches the soul there's nothing you have to do to please God. There's nothing you have to do to win God's favor. There's nothing you have to do to satiate his anger. All anger and all wrath has ceased and all struggle is over. In Christ God has gathered all together in *one* body, *the entire* human race, that we are all *one* in Christ.

Jesus prayed that we would be one with him as he and the Father were one.

Jesus' prayer was answered with a resounding "Yes!"

The doctrine of fulfillment is that all things are fulfilled. And I mean ALL things pertaining to God and humanity. The power that this understanding will release to the collective soul of humanity could bring an end to the religious wars that have raged for millennia and which continue to this very day.

Paul said the reason why you are at war is because there is a war going on inside of you. Paul said all war comes from within man. What if Paul is right? What if Paul's right that all war comes from within? If he is, then that war that we are carrying out with God ceased to exist 2,000 years ago. The implications of the power of the gospel are without a doubt beyond anything we can conceive. You might say, "Well, Mike I'm not sure that I believe the gospel can do all of that."

Then you do not believe in the power of God. Let's stop fragmenting the power of God by denying the power of the gospel.

The gospel makes no one righteous. It never has.

The gospel in its infinite and finite nature, profoundly and simply, *reveals* humanity's righteousness. After all, would it not take the power of God for any human to accept all humans as righteous? Yes, even our most infamous historic villains are as equally perfect and righteous in God's sight as you and I are, as righteous as Jesus! Would it not take a divine revelation to see those who inflict such pain and suffering on others to know without a shadow of a doubt that we and they are ALL righteous and completely equal in God?

The gospel has never made a man righteous. The gospel has never made a man holy. The gospel has never brought peace between God and man. The gospel is information, the good news that it has ALL already happened. Your belief in the gospel does not make the gospel true. The power of the gospel is that it is revealed truth, something that already is in existence the same as the power of the law. The law never made a man a sinner. The law revealed the condition that already existed as a result of one man's decision in a garden. The gospel itself is a revelation of a condition that has existed now for two millennia also as a result of One Man's decision in another Garden.

Do we dare think that if this revelation gets out of every human heart where it resides into the collective consciousness of the human race that it could alter how we now understand ourselves, much less how we deal with and understand each other? I can't help but have that prospect enliven my soul.

I dare to think . . . And on Earth, peace.

Perhaps if the planet as a whole will embrace our peace with God, then we can certainly imagine the possibility that if the war between us and God is over, then the war that raged within each of us is over, too. Again, as Paul brilliantly wrote, war comes from within.

The implications are phenomenal.

Chapter 7

A Covenant of One

W e were at my Mom's aunt and great uncle's rural Tennessee home. Mom took me along for a visit there. I was four years old. I believe this was my first exposure to anything "spiritual."

It was the kind of house where the upstairs sat at ground level with the front porch facing the street, but because of the way the property was sloped there was a garage underneath the house on the back side. It was a small Tennessee home that was set along the side of a highway. After we sat visiting in the living room for a while, my mother's aunt said, "Oh, you have to see dad before you go!" So, we went outside, out the front door, down around the side of the house. When we got down there, they opened the garage door. There wasn't a regular door; there was just the garage door. Inside, there was a little apartment. It had a little living room and a little kitchen over in the corner, and there was a very elderly man there. My mom and I went in and they were telling the man, "Geneva's here and her son's with her."

They were all talking and pretty much ignoring the four year old that was just standing there. Suddenly when we got ready to leave, this elderly man turned all of the focus of his attention to me. He stopped and put his hand on my shoulder and said, "Young man, I want to give you something." He reached in his pocket and got out a brand new penny. He said, "I want to give you this, but I don't want you to spend it. I want you to keep it as a token to remind you to meet me at the Eastern Gate in heaven."

The power of that was overwhelming to me. I really cherished that coin for about 3 days, but when you can get a Super Bubble for one penny, it's hard to keep those tokens just to get into heaven when you're all of four years old. I kept that coin in my pocket for only three days but I thought about what the old man said, not just then but all these years later.

I had been awakened to the concept of heaven and spirituality.

I would always greatly regret giving away that penny and buying that piece of gum. I felt that I had no commitment to anything. The inner-insufficiency I experienced because of that one slip-up was immense.

The appeal from my great, great uncle left an indelible mark on my consciousness. His intentions were nothing but good. He wanted to help me when he gave me that penny. He thought he was giving me something to look forward to. He never would have imagined the guilt that heaped upon my four year old brain by giving me a penny and telling me to keep it *forever* as a token to remind me to meet an elderly gentleman at the Eastern Gate of heaven. He might as well have told me to not partake of the fruit on the tree in the Garden of Eden! This was an agreement—a covenant between me and my great, great uncle about something eternal—and

I couldn't even keep my end of the deal for a week! It was the first of many broken promises in my life where I couldn't keep my end of the bargain.

We make covenants in life all the time—verbal agreements, promises, handshake deals and signed contracts. One wonderful aspect of the gospel is the clarity that runs all the way through the Old and New Testament writings about the covenants of God. This clarity comes from the light of the scriptures being about Jesus and NOT about us. It's important to make sure that in our individual processes of understanding the gospel that we do not place ourselves into the equation. The moment that we see ourselves involved in this covenant with God is the point where you believe you have a reciprocal responsibility to be in covenant with God. Whatever you are taught or believe that reciprocation entails, your mind will tell you (and rightfully so) that you are absolutely not able to keep covenant with God. It's just the way we're built.

The problem with having to reciprocate with God is that reciprocation has to be absolute perfection—especially where the law is concerned. It is not just *a* law for *a* promise. It is *all* of the law or *none* of the promises. Even though there are single promises given for each and every law if you obey, it says at the very beginning of the law that you *must* keep *all* of the law to do it. There is no such thing as keeping *one* law, or keeping *any* degree of obedience and getting a specific *promise,* because the disobedience of another law removes your qualification of obedience to the one that you feel confident you have obeyed.

The law was designed to help (or even force us) to conclude and eliminate any perception that we would have any part in this.

Had we understood the law, had we accepted the law for what it said and for what it was designed to do, then we would have understood this reality accurately. It is designed, and does indeed bring us to the end of ourselves. The law condemns everyone. The law, as concluded by the prophets, proves that there is none righteous; no not one.

We are led in several ways to conclude that man is completely left out of this covenant. An important clue is when God dealt with sin in the Old Covenant.

God set up a selection process for the priesthood, the high priest, and for the sacrifice to be made for sin. There were very specific qualifications for all of them. All of the people were gathered together but there is no indication anywhere that God looked to the *people* for *any* qualification on their part for their sins to be covered. The emphasis was on whether the *high priest* was qualified and whether the animal sacrifices were qualified. The blood of bulls and goats could not *take away* sin, they could only *cover* sin. That's what this whole ritual was for, the *covering* of sin.

Christ does not cover sin. Christ obliterates sin!

Sin no longer exists. If the blood of Jesus is simply something that has to be re-applied over and over in confession to cover our sins, then the blood of Jesus is really no better than that of a bull or a goat—the ritual for the sin offering that was done once a year. Paul described it very eloquently in the New Testament book of Hebrews, chapters 9 and 10 in particular. He brings it out very clearly that as a foreshadowing the blood of bulls and goats was offered in the Holy of Holies by the high priest to cover the sins of Israel.

For us the Holy Spirit now made the way into the holiest of all.

It is amazing to think that the blood of a goat was sufficient for the covering of sin for an entire year. The children of Israel did not have to be reminded of their sins for an entire year. Yet, in Christianity whenever we "come to the Lord" and follow even the simplest method religion has prescribed for forgiveness of sin, the impact of the blood of Jesus is temporary at best. It doesn't even last for a moment because if there is another "sin" immediately following your last repentance, then you are going to be "in sin" again even with a thought according to what Jesus taught, as interpreted by the Christian religion. This is no different than the law. And I suppose it should be of no surprise, because Jesus was teaching the law in its fiercest application. The problem is Christianity has not been able to separate the old and new covenants. We see the "red letters" of Jesus' words and just assume it is applicable to the new covenant of grace because we have not understood Jesus' intent and purpose, as the prophet who was to come, as Moses prophesied about. However, even looking at how sin was dealt with in the old covenant, we can see it was better than what Christianity teaches now! Even the blood of a goat would take away the need for *confession* of sin, the need to *address* sin for an *entire year!*

Christianity's prescription for dealing with your sins implies the blood of Jesus doesn't take it away for a millisecond.

Paul said the system of priests and sacrifices was set up so that the Holy Spirit could teach us that it was obvious that the way *into* the Holy of Holies was not yet made manifest. He wrote that under the old covenant the holiest of all was *not yet made perfect* because sin had to be dealt with again once every year. Can you imagine how *imperfect* they are saying the blood of Jesus is? Christianity says Jesus' blood is sufficient only for the moment of confession! But the blood of a goat DID take away the need for confession of sin and of dealing with sin for an entire year! This old covenant system of sacrifices to cover sin is the means by which the Holy Spirit was to teach us that the way into the holiest of all was not yet made known.

Not only was there a sacrifice for sin that was required, it had to be offered by the high priest. There were all sorts of qualifications for the high priest to be ceremonially clean. This again is another way of showing that the way into the holiest of all was not yet made perfect because the high priest was only *ceremonially* cleansed to carry out this ritual. It was a very stringent cleansing process. Paul explained that it was "the cleansing of the flesh" that the high priests were going through to be able to take this sacrifice of the blood of a goat into the Holy of Holies as an offering for sin. It was not the people who went into the holiest of all. The high priest and the sacrifice were the only things that God was looking at to see whether or not the people qualified for their sins to be covered. It is important to note that the people were left completely out of this entire process. Their sin being covered in the Old Covenant was based on God's approval of the *high priest* and God's approval of the *sacrifice*. This is how God dealt with Israel's sin. He dealt with their sin through the high priest and through the sacrifice that was offered. Talk about a tremendous type and foreshadowing of what was to come!

The people of Israel were completely left out of the process even for the *covering* of sin, much less the *taking away* of sin. If the people in the type and foreshadowing were never a crucial factor in the covering of their own sin, why in the world would anyone conclude that in the taking away of our sin, we would be in any way involved in this incredible process?

In the children of Israel, God gave us the perfect picture of how He would eventually deal with the sin problem once and for all.

High Priest, Perfect? ☑ Check!
Sacrifice, Perfect? ☑ Check!
Sin Taken Away? ☑ Check!

Jesus himself was the high priest AND he was the sacrifice. The dual role that Jesus carried out is the only way that an absolutely perfect sacrifice and an absolutely perfect high priest could carry out this need for a perfect process. The reason Jesus was the perfect sacrifice was because he (and only he) was born of the Spirit. The reason Jesus was the perfect high priest was because he passed through death and lives forever and remains alive forevermore. The high priests under the Old Covenant all died. The blood of Jesus did not go into the Holy of Holies on *Earth,* as this was just a type and shadow as Paul explained of *the heavenly.* Instead Jesus became the Great High Priest when he rose from the dead. And when he rose from the dead he was fully qualified to be the Great High Priest. He took his own blood, not the blood of others, but his own blood, not into a Temple made with hands but into the very presence of God the Father himself.

No matter which way you look at it, if you stay with the proper comparisons you have to realize that God was not looking at the human race to see whether or not they qualified for forgiveness of sin. He was not looking at their confession. He was not looking at their sin. He wasn't looking at their ability or whether they deserved it. The whole process of the forgiveness of sin was only possible, even as just the covering of sin was only possible, if God left the people out of the equation. As God left the people completely out of the equation, an entire system was set up in the Old Testament so that the Holy Spirit could teach us!

In order for the blood of the animal's to be effective, it had to be accepted by God, *not* by the people of Israel. In the same way, the blood of Jesus had to be accepted by the Father, not by the human race. We did not, could not, and do not have to accept Jesus and his blood sacrifice. God DID accept it. And thank God for it!

Paul said that the reason they had to offer sacrifices every year was so that the Holy Spirit could teach us something. So, in becoming the Great High Priest, as Paul puts it so eloquently, Jesus took his own blood, not the blood of others, into the presence of God and offered that blood for the sin of the world; the *entire* world!

Catholicism forever desiring to close this gap between us and God came up with some pretty creative ways of doing this. And Luther's reformation did not reform their mistakes. The reformation challenged the authority of the Pope, but these pivotal issues were not really addressed even through Luther.

Is it time for another reformation?

Is it time for a reformation that would affect this planet in such a powerful way based on truth in a continuing progress and process of understanding the gospel? Some may ask, "But how can that be true? These things have been taught for centuries." To that we can reply, the things that were preached before Protestantism came along were preached for 1,500 years! 1,500 years before there was a change in the mindset, before there was a break from having to go through the Pope or a priest for remission of sin. 1,500 years! Now, we're only at 500 years since Luther! So, by comparison, we are talking about things moving forward quite rapidly really.

The Catholic view of confessing and dealing with sin has infected every aspect of Christianity whether you're Catholic *or* Protestant. The Catholics traditionally do it once a week; Protestants upped the ante and now we're supposed to do it all the time. Pentecostals piled on even more and now we're supposed to do it every moment with every breath all day long!

Thus, the mental illness grows. As you become more and more sin conscious, and less and less conscious of Christ and his perfect sacrifice, the insanity progresses.

Christianity creates the problems and then turns around and has the audacity to offer the answer for them. Sin consciousness is taught, which creates obsessions forbidden by the law, destroying relationships by requiring husbands to be perfect in their households and wives to submit to their tormented husbands—tormented by being coerced by Christianity to be examples of what God the Father is like to their children and spouses. Talk about a recipe for disaster!

The modern Christian religion is quite creative, but what the religion has spawned is not a good thing. It created the dilemma in order to provide the answer. Now that is crazy! And what a vicious cycle it is. Christianity misses the boat altogether. They are in a constant battle with *sin*. Yet, sin was destroyed 2,000 years ago!

Here's some good news for you and all people everywhere: not only is the battle over, so is the war!

The blood of Jesus not only *took away* sin, but it is also capable of *purging our conscience* from dead works. Humanity was completely left out of this entire process. The blood of Jesus took away sin *for* the people, not *with* the people. Once again, people were left out of this entire process. The moment people become part of the equation or process in anyway, that is the moment that doubt and unbelief begins to plague the human soul. Once we believe we are a part of the process and thereby have responsibility to initiate or maintain the quality of our relationship with God, our soul will be burdened.

When you believe you are part of the process of being "born again," you're traveling down a very dark trail that will never end in this life. For some people it does not end until their death. And what a shame that is. But I am very glad to be able to announce that the clarity of the gospel is becoming stronger and stronger in the Earth as more and more have the privilege of knowing that we are not a part of the glorious process that culminated two millennia ago. All of us being left *out* is the *only* way that we were all able to be included. This is the great mystery that Paul wrote about, this mystery of how everyone was *excluded* so that everybody could be *included* by the mercy of God, the grace of God. And thank God, this is not a mystery to us anymore!

Teachings and movies such as the *Left Behind* series have probably frightened more people than we will ever know that they might be left behind in the *Rapture* and would have to endure the so-called great tribulation and face a possible eternity in hell.

What an insult to the cross!

I have good news for all who have feared this tormenting view of the future. Nobody is going to be "left behind!" But thank God we ALL were "left out" of this incredible, God-ordained process.

What really happened is that "the catching away" (or what many Christians call "The Rapture"—another term that doesn't even appear anywhere in the Bible) already took place in the body of One Man, Jesus Christ. The entire human race was tucked securely into "the cleft of the rock" and under the "shadow of the Almighty." And it all took place 2,000 years ago as we rose out of darkness at the speed of light—his light—from the bondage of death and appeared in the presence of God *IN* Christ Jesus. Yes, even "The Rapture" already happened. Jesus delivered the whole lot of humanity wrapped in the righteousness of his blood to God the Father!

The only way that we are going to truly see the *love* of God is to see that all of the issues of sin have been resolved once and for ALL. If there is a Gospel of Peace, that the covenant that Isaiah proclaimed would never be removed off of the Earth, then there is no way that there could be anything called "sin" within the human race that God is still dealing with. Now we know that people have to cope with their actions and deeds, and their consequences within their families, communities, and respective societies. However, if we were completely freed in our minds from sin consciousness in relationship with God, I believe that it would bring an even greater sense of responsibility for our actions. When I do offend someone or hurt someone with my words, my actions, my deeds, then I can resolve that much more effectively and quickly because I am not trying to protect my righteousness. I no longer have to prove myself to be right in the sight of God, because I already am. I can say I was wrong and that I am truly sorry without bringing my relationship with God into question at all. What freedom!

Being wrong and owning it is a wonderful part of life. I remember when being wrong was the most tragic part of life, but once you understand the gospel, being wrong is just part and parcel of living the human experience—and an important part. Coming to grips with the wrongs that we have done can become something that is a part of everyday life. And it should be a good part of any given day. One of the most freeing things you'll ever say is "I was wrong."

Another of Paul's teachings pointing out the fact that we were completely left out of this entire issue of covenant with God was his discussion of marriage. He taught several things about marriage. He reminds us that, "I'm not talking about the marriage between a man and a woman," he said "I'm talking about it regarding Christ and the Church." So again, with Paul's help, we go back to a covenant—this time the covenant of marriage. This again was NOT about *people* but about *Christ and his Church*.

I once taught a series on the issue of scriptural marriage and scriptural divorce, concluding that nobody has a scriptural marriage and nobody's ever gotten a "scriptural" divorce. Marriage was established to bring us to a full understanding of the relationship between Christ and his Bride. Please understand the covenant left everyone in the human race out, so the covenant could *include* everyone in the human race. Like the brides of old, we had no choice, no role.

With ancient marriage, in its type and foreshadowing, it was the father of the groom who picked the bride. We still call them arranged marriages when they still happen today. Many times the groom didn't want to marry the bride, and the bride didn't want to marry the groom. Still, that was decided by a higher authority.

The bride had absolutely no say so. She was selected and that was it. So, if Paul was talking about Christ and the Church when he was talking about marriage we would be ill-advised to gloss-over this magnificent aspect of scriptural marriage—the part where the bride has no input whatsoever. We can't look at marriage in our western culture and say it is the same as what they experienced in the Bible for goodness sake. That would be the height of intellectual dishonesty. But that never seems to stop Christianity.

The Holy Spirit is the One that we really have to stop and acknowledge. He is our inner instructor and it is he that brings us into all understanding and the truth of this powerful and perfect mindset called the gospel. It is the gospel that Paul described as "the power of God." It is not a *source* of God's power. It's not a way to *get to* God's power. It is in and of itself the power of God! It doesn't plug you into God's power. It is not how you experience God's power. The gospel *IS* THE POWER OF GOD! And Paul said, it is the power of God "unto salvation." So, we know that its power is to affect us in a *saving* way. Saving what? The gospel is to the saving of our souls—our mind, will, intellect, and emotion. That is what needs saving—our brain.

Another way this could be said, is the gospel, the power of God (the power which created the Universe) is now here to do nothing less and nothing more than to rewire humanity's thinking. No small task, to be sure. But we're talking about the power of God here, folks!

The heart and the mind are designed to become congruent with absolute truth. Since the heart and the mind is the means of our thoughts, our feelings, and our emotions, it is obvious that by interfacing the heart and the mind with the absolute truth of *the power of God—the gospel*—this is the process that brings those areas of our life to their greatest fruitfulness and to their most effective place—not just for our lives but for the lives of everyone involved with us.

For me, the most beautiful part of this process we're in the midst of is to acknowledge how the gospel itself begins to integrate and interface that which is absolute truth—which is of the Spirit—with my heart and then my mind. This is indeed the renewing of the mind and the saving of the soul. It is the way the Holy Spirit reveals to us that which is absolute truth. Please don't let anyone tell you that there is no such thing as absolute truth because there absolutely is absolute truth. You might say "Well, how do we define absolute truth?"

This absolute truth is that which equally affects every living, breathing human being regardless of race, creed, color, age. It affects everybody absolutely the exact same way. The way gravity does for example. Gravity has the same effect on everyone regardless of where you are on the planet, regardless of your age, regardless of your height, your weight—gravity will have the same effect. We're all under the same gravitational pull at all times.

So like gravity is an absolute truth, the gospel is absolute truth. Why? Because the gospel is affecting us all equally the same way at the same time. Unfortunately, like some folks with gravity from time to time, people don't know what they are dealing with in the gospel. They aren't aware of the gospel or simply want to ignore it. However, when we begin to fragment the gospel, the truth of the gospel gets distorted and religion steps in with its own answers. You might ask, "Well, how do we fragment the gospel?" We fragment the gospel by inserting ourselves into the equation. This makes Christ, the Spirit living within you, of no effect. You only have to add ONE law for this to happen, as Paul taught in Galatians. Remember that you are not a part of the equation. You *are* a beneficiary of the equation, but the equation does not include us at all.

We can fragment the gospel when we try to place ourselves in an equation that we have no business being in or any justification trying to apply to ourselves or to our societies. Again, in the scriptural marriage covenant we see that the bride is not included at all. That should teach us something! You want a divorce, a scriptural divorce? Well, ladies, there is no scriptural divorce for women! Thank God there is *legal* divorce for women nowadays. But there is no such thing as a "scriptural divorce." The only divorce laws given were for the man, that he could "put away" his wife and only for a specific reason.

We must understand that Jesus is the Bridegroom and we, all humans, are the Bride. This marriage has been made by the selection of the Father, by *his* will, by *his* decision. We have entered into that marriage of the Spirit with God himself. Now that we have been betrothed as the bride, the only one who can possibly get out of it is the groom—the husband. The husband is the only one that has a right to a divorce scripturally. But guess what? We've already got the verdict on how committed this husband is to his bride. Husband Jesus made a commitment. He said in this marriage, "I will never leave you nor forsake you." That is a marriage term, people. Jesus the Bridegroom—the Husband of this Human Race—married all of us, joined together, united together—a marriage truly made in heaven.

And what God has joined together let no man put asunder!

I put every preacher, teacher, and minister on this planet on notice: STOP saying that man can put asunder that which God has joined together. God has joined together the entire human race. Jesus prayed to the Father before this all took place, before this marriage took place, "Father I pray that they'll be one with us even as we are ONE."

Paul teaches specifically on this covenant in Hebrews. He explains how this covenant has nothing to do with us. The covenant was *for* us but it wasn't *with* us. That is Paul's magnificent understanding. He explains the difference between the covenants that God made with man and this covenant. It is drastically different than all of the others before. He said in all the other covenants that God had made with man that man had broken them all. He showed how man was eliminated from being qualified to have covenant made with him because man could never keep his end of the bargain of any that was ever attempted. The conclusion was that God decided to remedy this *broken-covenant* issue. He did it by determining this covenant would be between two unmovable forces. Now this is interesting because we see the equation as being between *two*. But in reality the equation is *singular.* We find out by the entirety of Paul's statement that God is *both parts* of the *unmovable force* of this incredible covenant.

There is no way Paul spoke of two unmovable forces and meant we somehow figured into that. It is foolish to think that we are one of the unmovable parts of this great covenant. In fact, it is repeated over and over—whether it's through the marriage or whether it's even the way that God dealt with sin through the nation of Israel—it is concluded that man's involvement always ended in disaster.

The only way that God could ever perform anything to fruition was to do it *in, of,* and *by* himself—not *with* man but *for* man. Even "sin" was imputed to the entire race without their involvement, all because of the disobedience of one man, Adam. So, you see, because sin was established strictly by the disobedience of just one man, the eradication of sin and the establishment of righteousness throughout the Earth could only be by just One Man, too, "the Last Adam" Jesus Christ!

This covenant between these two immutable (or unchanging) forces had to be done by God himself because it is impossible for God to lie. These are the two unmovable forces—God the Father and God the Son. It is in this covenant, void of man's participation on any level, where it is impossible for a lie to exist. That's the reason this New Covenant is perfectly successful. It only pertains to perfection.

So, please, for the love of God, let's leave ourselves out.

God left us out. It is so foolish for us to insert ourselves into this covenant. In fact, the only way that we became the recipients of the covenant is by virtue of the fact that we were totally left out of the covenant.

It is with one voice to all humans that the gospel speaks. There is not a multiplicity of voices saying different things to different people. The gospel does not say "This one's righteous, this one's not," or "This one's making it, this one's not," or "This one's going to hell, this one's going to purgatory, this one's going to heaven." The gospel does not say, "This one has relationship with God; this one does not have relationship with God."

The gospel says in Christ we are all ONE!

So regardless of how many voices, and how many preachers you hear that say who is excluded, who doesn't qualify, who has now "fallen from the grace of God;" when you hear anything like that, do yourself a favor and please hit the mute button.

Don't let that fragmented, illogical message have place in your precious soul. It is not congruent with the truth. It is not the truth. It will never be the truth. It has never been the truth.

The truth will make you *free*. It will free your heart. It will free your soul. It will free your mind. You will not have to walk in that bondage of the fear of separation from God for the rest of your life like Israel did and like so many millions of modern day people do today. And when that fear is gone, the heart, the soul, the mind become a much healthier place. They become a place that can deal with what life serves up because it is infused with and exposed to the power of God. It is immersed (or baptized) with the truth. It is immersed with confidence that is produced from knowing our relationship with God is settled forever. You never, and I mean never, have to be concerned about you and God ever again. You can be absolutely confident about it.

When you share this glorious gospel then do as Isaiah did. Get up into the high mountain and say to the people, "Behold your God!"

Please don't tell them who their God could be. Let them know who their God *is*. The God who did not, and does not, need, want, or demand humanity's involvement to redeem them—any of them.

The power of this revelation is going to set this planet free in a manifested way. The struggle to be one with God, to please God, has ripped us apart at the seams for thousand of years.

The gospel alleviates ALL of that. The gospel revealed from our hearts to our minds restores our souls to the place where we can actually resolve our problems. With the power of the gospel, the power of God, we can cope, endure, recover, and overcome the issues that reside within our own selves first and then with each other.

This is the prescription for true healing for a hurting world from its Great Physician.

Chapter 8

The Faith of One

"I praise you 24/7 and this is how you do me? You expect me to learn from this? How?! I will never forget this . . . ever. Thanks though."

How many Christians could have sent that "tweet?"

This specific one, though, was sent in 2010 from an American football player. He was exasperated and blamed God for his dropping an easy pass which would have resulted in a crucial score for his team. The story and the tweet made national news.

This is a perfect little peek into the collective souls of those affected by cause-and-effect religion. It was just that in this case the athlete had a public persona and an immediate 21st century platform to express his frustration. This is the kind of turmoil that often ensues when one embraces the perspective that God is out there blessing you, helping you, intervening for you, taking over for you, getting you that touchdown, or avoiding that wreck for you. Just by a *hair*, you avoided that wreck! God must have sent an angel.

What an excellent illustration of how Christianity teaches the world to avoid taking responsibility. This crisis of faith is a glimpse into the mind of the average Evangelical Christian.

This kind of anger is always just under the surface right next to its cause—fear. It's akin to someone walking away from the Emperor who has the authority to have his head chopped-off. Reading between the lines, it's like he's really saying, "You know, I'm going to be brave enough to tell you I don't like this, but I'll thank you anyway. I've got to throw my thanks in there, because I know that you could also wipe me out. If you made me miss that pass, you could also send a bolt of lightning and strike me dead. So, here's my token 'thank you.'"

The football player's statement is an example of someone expressing a desperate need for salvation. He said he "praises 24/7" but he obviously does it for a reason. He does it for a reward. He does it for protection. He does it in the hope that God will intervene. It's like a religious "crossing of the fingers" for luck. The reasons why he praises are now obvious. When you publicly cite that you praise God 24/7 and that you're disappointed with the payback, your perspective is glaring.

A good dose of real salvation for this young man (who "praises" 24/7) would be just what the doctor ordered. And please *always* remember what needs to be saved, our souls, our minds. Our redemption is a fact and is as sure as Jesus himself. The salvation that our football player needs, and which we all need on an ongoing basis, is for our brains. It's for the cleansing and renewing of our intellect, emotions, will, and thoughts to the reality that we truly are one.

Many of us can easily relate to this story because we lived that life for so long. And *I* was really good at it. I did well while *doing* it.

But it did not do me well just as it is obviously not serving this pro athlete very well either. The conflict and the reality of what could only be described as a "multi-personality disorder" almost made me like the Ecclesiastes preacher in the Old Testament instead of the preacher of the gospel. I wanted to exclaim, "What's the use?" In the psalms, David says he will never see the righteous forsaken. Then the Ecclesiastes preacher says I've watched the good people beg and grovel and I've watched the wicked go scot free. I was preaching a message of salvation, I thought, but I was the one desperate for salvation.

There's that word again, *salvation.* What an important word, salvation! "Salvation" can be applicable to any subject.

Salvation is applicable to redemption. Redemption is a salvation. Reconciliation is a salvation. The renewing of the mind is a salvation. Where we made the gravest mistake was in taking the word salvation and narrowing its meaning rather than allowing it to be the very descriptively broad word that it is. Salvation can be as simple a term as if we were standing on the street corner and I started to step off the corner onto the path of an oncoming bus and you reached and grabbed my arm and pulled me back. That's a salvation. You *saved* me. If you sell all your stock in a particular company the day before it crashes, that's a salvation. It's a salvation I wish I'd had a few years ago!

However, when it comes to terms like "redemption" and "reconciliation" (that Christianity often equates to salvation or being saved), those terms are absolutes. They are fixed. It is that terribly simple. It is just that we have been trained to think that, "Johnny went to church on Sunday and got saved!" Well, that could be true if Johnny became aware at some point of his redemption in Christ. But it is so horribly misrepresented by Christianity. They say this is when Johnny's sins were forgiven. This was his salvation *experience.* But there's a huge difference between salvation *experiences* and salvation *facts*.

Redemption is a salvation fact. Redemption is not an experience that we have. To come to the knowledge of the saving fact of redemption and reconciliation is a salvation of the mind or the soul. The *saving of the soul*, Paul called it. Redemption literally means "to buy back." And that, again, is a *salvation*. So, when you're studying, especially the New Testament, and you see the term "saved" or "salvation" you must look at it (like every other topic) in the *context* to see what the *subject* of the salvation is.

In Ephesians Paul says, "For by grace are ye *saved* through faith; and that *not of yourselves*." It's interesting because Paul writes numerous times of the faith *of* Christ—the faith of the One Man.

As we consider the *faith* of one man it is congruent to include the *obedience* of one man because they are coupled together within the entire requirement for redemption. God was looking for faith and obedience. The reason he was looking for faith *and* obedience was because *that is what was lost* in the garden. That is what led to the condition of sin, which failed the relationship between God and man. It was disobedience and unbelief. It is not a stretch of the imagination to understand that the remedy for disobedience and unbelief would be *obedience* and *faith*. So, as we have learned throughout the gospel, this always turns out to be about just one man, and that One Man is always Jesus.

The first Adam's disobedience was brought on by *unbelief*. The obedience of the Last Adam led to the restoration *of* faith and *of* belief, and that faith and belief was and is of just the One Man. God put the human race through our paces and we had to go through the exercise of the requirement for obedience and faith. These are things that the human race just could not achieve or attain to God's standard which was always perfection. The prophets concluded "There is none righteous . . . no, not one."

As the prophet declared, "They've all gone astray. They have turned everyone to his own way." But the interesting thing even about that insight, in speaking about the coming Messiah and his work, the prophet spoke that "the Lord hath laid on him *the iniquity* of us all." It didn't say he laid on him all of our *iniquities*. It says he laid on him *the iniquity* of us all, and "the iniquity of us all" really was "unbelief," the original sin, the condition of iniquity—not the actions of iniquities.

Just as there are the "works" of the flesh, those "works" are not what Paul considered *the flesh* itself. This is another one of those concepts that if we just could get it right, all the pieces would fall together and everything would actually make sense. We would actually understand what is meant by such things as "the flesh" and "the iniquity."

The gospel has an incredibly powerful effect on the soul as we consistently contemplate and speak of *what Jesus died for*. There are so many areas of misconception in the Christian world that I hesitate to say that this is the most egregious. Still, it certainly is such a major theme throughout the Christian world, and even the *non-Christian* world, that they believe that Jesus died for man's disobedience to laws, rules, and regulations. However, this just is not true.

Jesus died for ONE sin.

To be the author of the one faith that redeemed all of us from unbelief, it was necessary for Jesus to take upon himself "the sin of the whole world." Or another way to put it is the afore-mentioned "God laid upon him the iniquity of us all."

God experienced the kind of separation that man had been living under since Adam, all this in order to re-establish our oneness. Such a deal! What a God!

The enormity of the reality of this sin-destroying, relationship-healing event may very well have been expressed when Jesus was on the cross and he cried out "My God! My God! Why hast thou forsaken me?"

There was a huge debate in The Word of Faith movement. It pretty much split the movement in two. They were arguing about whether or not Jesus died spiritually. They called it J.D.S. and J.D.D.S—Jesus Died Spiritually and Jesus Didn't Die Spiritually. Kenneth and Gloria Copeland, a well-known couple with an international television broadcast, were some of those proponents that said Jesus died spiritually because they believed he had to die spiritually to bring us back to life spiritually. I don't believe that is necessarily so. I doubt very seriously that Jesus died spiritually. In all likelihood when Jesus cried out "My God! My God! Why hast thou forsaken me?" I believe this was the full expression of the iniquity that was laid upon him; *the* sin of the whole world; *the* sin that was the problem. The immensity of that experience may have produced what came out of his mouth at that incredible moment.

As far as transgressions against the law, Paul made it very clear that Jesus did *not* die for the things *we did*.

One of the most profound forms of spiritual abuse to church-going children and teens is to be taught that Jesus died for their lying, their cheating, their stealing; their being bad boys and girls—that Jesus suffered on the cross for *what they did*. Hopefully, and thankfully, few young people take that completely to heart. The potential abuse of that statement runs deep. I know that it did with me because its potential was realized in my soul for sure.

Crucifying the Son of God afresh is a statement found in Hebrews. It does not mean when someone breaks a law, or does something wrong or any type of "sin" that you're causing Christ to suffer anew. In context, it is referring to believing that you have to go back and start all over again. This isn't even a possibility because when Christ died, his sacrifice was *once* and *for all*.

For those who think that there is some *re-application* of forgiveness whether it is through confession, contrition, whatever it be . . . anyone who believes that there is a need for a personal application of the blood of Jesus to take away specific sins—that, in effect, is crucifying Jesus afresh in one's own soul.

As always, PLEASE read these things in context. In that context, it means they are crucifying to "themselves" the Son of God afresh. They are literally in their own minds crucifying Jesus all over again. And that's why it's such a deadly doctrine. That is exactly what it turned into for me. I was taught that when I sinned within myself I was crucifying *to myself* the Son of God afresh, and I was counting the blood of the covenant wherewith I had been sanctified as *an unholy thing*.

To reduce the blood of Jesus to something that needs to be constantly re-applied to be valid is like cruising around a drive-thru at McDonalds over and over again. That's how absolutely degrading to the entire concept of the work of the cross it is.

Nobody was ever found to be in obedience. No one, NO ONE, was ever found to be in faith. The only way out for the entire world was the same way the world got into this mess. The world got "into this mess" based on the actions of one man—the First Adam. And the *only* way to come out of this was based on One Man—the Last Adam. In God's eyes this was always about one man. This isn't two different people to God. In God's economy, in God's way of reckoning and counting, this was always about just one man. It was by one man, and *is* by one man, as Paul's genius brings out.

So, what was "the faith" then? We know that Jesus was obedient even unto death. A lot can be said about that but we will take it at face value that Jesus was obedient *even unto death*. Please note that Jesus was not necessarily obedient *unto the law* unto death. He was obedient *unto God* unto death.

What would be counted as obedience for Jesus to the Father? It has nothing to do with the laws of Moses because Jesus was born *of the Spirit*. There was not a law that governed his relationship with God. They were and are always literally ONE. Whatever was meant by his obedience, the one thing we cannot do is equate it to any obedience to God's law as a prerequisite for him being the perfect sacrifice. Jesus was the perfect sacrifice by virtue of how he was conceived, by the Spirit, without the seed of man. It is not anything Jesus *did* that qualified him. His qualification was simply and profoundly because of who he *was*. We do know according to Paul, that Jesus' obedience was even unto death, even unto death on the cross.

The process Jesus went through to have righteousness imputed to the human race, and have it be credited to everyone (and the type of faith that was required) was to exactly reverse what had happened to and by the First Adam.

Jesus successfully defeated the temptation to fall into *the* same sin, or the same *unbelief*, that the First Adam committed. This was what his battle was right up until the cross. He was tempted by the devil and all three temptations were to challenge "*If* you are the Son of God." That was the same challenge to the First Adam, the challenge to him of who he really was, who he believed himself to be as had been articulated by God. This was the sin: Adam did *not* believe who God said Adam was. But the Last Adam believed unto death. And he resisted the ultimate temptation to be tripped-up by unbelief and totally defeated it. Now that is what you call a triumph!

Jesus never went into unbelief; *unbelief went into him*!

The Lord laid upon him the iniquity, *the* sin of us all. And it was the sin of us all because God had imputed sin to everyone through the deed of one man.

To keep the clarity of the gospel in its purest form we must keep focused on this. When you begin to add or multiply in any direction when it comes to the work of God, that's when you lose all perspective and clarity about the cross, the gospel, and the work of Christ; a work that did indeed redeem the entire planet.

If we were to examine the degree of each and every individual's faith as some kind of proof, the work of Christ fails. It doesn't just fail in *some* people's lives; it fails in *every* person's life when we begin to examine the individual instead of staying zeroed in on the faith *of* Christ.

Paul's confidence about this matter was very strong. Any time he shared his testimony—regardless of Christianity's attempt to remove it from the New Testament writings—the term "the faith *of* God" or "the faith *of* Christ" is the fact that Paul enunciated and always turned his reader's attention to. They can call it a *mistranslation*. However, Peter, James, and John didn't talk about the faith *of* God or the faith *of* Christ. This has been exclusively "mistranslated" in *Paul's* letters for some strange reason! It was only "mistranslated" in Paul's writings? Really? It has been labeled a mistranslation in Paul's writing because Peter, James, and John never talked about it! The fact is, it was only *in* Paul's writings because Paul was the only one of these gentlemen who carried this mystery and wrote about it. Paul's take on the gospel was so unique at the time that he was the only New Testament writer who referred to it as "my gospel." Wow!

This *one-man mystery* is so powerful that it brought freedom to every single human being who ever lived, is living, and ever will live. We are utterly and completely free! It's just that most of humanity does not know it, *yet.*

If there's any mistranslation at all regarding faith in the Bible, it's not mistranslated from "the faith *in* Christ" to "the faith *of* Christ." If there is a translation issue, it's the other way around. It is being misunderstood as "faith *IN* Christ" rather than "the faith *OF* Christ." Whenever he's talking about redemption, Paul's testimony and his comments about it constantly refers to "the faith *of* God" or "the faith *of* Christ." He attributed his redemption to "the faith *OF* Christ." The moment you get to the point that you attribute your righteousness, your holiness, your redemption, your relationship with God Almighty to *his* faith and not your own—when you place it all into the realm of the faith and the obedience of the One Man—that's when freedom begins its wonderful work inside your soul. To speak of the incredible impact of that work from one's heart to one's soul would take *lifetimes* to tell.

The teaching series I did entitled *Freed from Your Own Faith* sounds like an odd thing for a Bible teacher to present. As is usual with me, this was not the title that I started with as I prepared for the sessions. It is just what came *out,* out from the great teacher who resides in my heart, and yours, the Holy Spirit of God.

While Christianity is trying to teach people to *have* faith, and to "believe" God, and to put this massive effort into *our* faith, here I was up in front of a congregation of people teaching them the glory of being delivered from your own faith and being set free from *your own faith.*

There is not a law that was any crueler to the human soul than the requirement to believe. There is not a heinous demand like that in the entire 613 laws of Moses that was so cruel. To demand an individual person to have their own faith be a requirement for their own redemption is cruel and unusual punishment indeed.

That demand in and of itself actually creates a *lack* of faith.

Isn't it odd that faith is something that is strictly of the heart, yet we teach people that it needs to be applied as a rule? "You *must* do this." How could we ever wrap our brains around this issue of faith by making it a requirement? The moment it is *required* it becomes completely *illusive*. If faith is ever going to "come alive" in the heart of a human being, it will happen there because it grows. It will live there because it's nurtured. It will live there because of the nutrition and nourishment that comes from the wonderful good news that is the gospel and which saves the soul.

It will never live because concrete was poured in there. The concrete of a required human faith is far from nutrition. It is an unattainable requirement that was and is being demanded. It *was* demanded by the "pre-cross Jesus." The greatest teacher of the law who ever lived. And this same pre-cross Jesus, the Last Adam, should also have been the last teacher of the law. You don't ever need to teach about something that doesn't exist anymore. But, sadly, Christianity "resurrected" the law, in its own fragmented, twisted way. And at the top of their list of "dos and don'ts" is the requirement for a personal redemptive faith.

No matter how much you eventually feel that you *do* get to a place where you have some faith, please don't ever revert back to trusting in *your* faith in anything pertaining to relationship with God. I hope your faith grows. I hope your faith becomes spoken of throughout the world as Paul spoke of some of the people's he knew. But no matter how well spoken of your faith may become, whatever you do, do not fall to the deception and the misguided direction of trying to build a confident relationship with God by your own faith. It is NOT possible. Please, always rely on the faith *of* the Son of God even as Paul did. Allow the faith *of* the Son of God to free you from your own faith. You will never be disappointed.

We also need to be set free from our own obedience regarding our relationship with the Almighty.

To whatever degree that we think our own obedience is measuring up, to whatever degree we think our obedience is gaining favor or our disobedience is losing favor or bringing God's blessing onto the scene—that is the same degree to which we are enslaved to self righteousness. This is not something to play with. It won't affect your relationship with God one iota. But it is "deadly." Because when you revert back to the old thinking, you'll feel like it has negatively impacted your relationship in God. The mortal threat is not to your relationship with God or your eternal destiny with him as one. It is "life-threatening" to your thought process, your emotions, your ability to think right, to your soul.

If you've tried it, you know now how it is to feel like you were stepping onto solid ground. But you'll also remember how it felt when you thought "the solid ground" you thought you were on began to shake beneath your feet! Remember how it gave way when you tried to stand on your *own* faith and on your *own* obedience? And while you stood there quaking, trembling, shaking, falling, and stumbling, you had to smile and pretend you were strong in the faith.

Well, guess what? We don't have to pretend any more. We do not have to stand on shaky ground ever again. Hallelujah!

At this magnificent point of history in the development of spiritual understanding and the true nature of the gospel, my plea to you is this: I'm calling you to place your feet and to stand firmly on the faith *of* the Son of God!

Please place your reliance completely on the obedience *of* Christ and be *not* tempted with falling into the trap of relying on yourself or anybody else's faith.

Jesus endured this temptation and you can, too. You have the same Spirit that raised Christ from the dead resident and active inside of you! You can endure the temptation of SELF—righteousness! You can overcome the temptation of being hoodwinked into believing that reliance upon your own faith is a requirement from God.

This deception runs deep in Christianity and has for thousands of years. Still, it is a deception that is being exposed even as you read this. People are being set free all over the world by taking this one step out of self-righteous thinking. They are no longer relying on their *own* faith but instead finding their righteousness in the faith *OF* the Son of God, Jesus the Christ.

Chapter 9

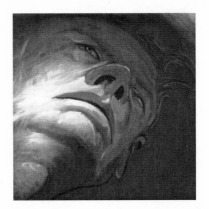

The Mystery of Temptation

My wife Hazel, our two young daughters Sarah and Geneva and I were living just east of Indianapolis. I'd left the comfort and the sense of security with the ministry I started out with. I was now an associate pastor of a "deliverance ministry." By virtue of its description you may have deduced that this church was focused on "casting out devils," addressing demons, and commanding them out. We had people coming for deliverance from everywhere—out of state and from far and wide they traveled desperate for relief.

I did not see eye to eye exactly with the church about their techniques or their persuasion about casting out devils. Methods and procedures could be overlooked, but the one thing we were very much in agreement with was the importance of and the need for casting out devils.

It had been about five years from my own "deliverance" from homosexuality.

Actually, I had never been freed or changed in the least from my sexuality. I was simply in denial. The desire to have some encounter with another male was simply overwhelming. I had made a trip into Indianapolis about an hour's drive west of where this deliverance ministry was located. While I was there on this particular trip I did meet someone with whom I had a sexual experience. If I were to tell people what that encounter actually entailed, some people would probably laugh at me for thinking this was such a serious offence. Still, for me it was a very serious offence because I "went back" into an area of sexuality from which I said I was completely delivered.

This event led to a trip to the mental hospital.

The Baptist church of my childhood told me that every time I sinned, I was crucifying Jesus all over again. The increasing amount of temptation that arose from that teaching was immense. I became even more conscious of the temptation when I found out that Jesus said if you even think about breaking one of those rules that you've actually done it. It was a huge challenge for me to think that I could not resist temptation. When my friends and I were kids, we used to talk about this stuff because it really meant a lot to me even as a very young child. I remember the son of the Baptist preacher would constantly remind me, "Well, you know it says it's just as bad to think it as do it, so . . . you might as well do it!" That was his resolve. That was a logical conclusion to the Baptist doctrine and one which multiple millions still practice quietly.

The whole issue of temptation truly is a mystery that has been perfectly revealed in the scriptures. This flies in the face of the very core of modern-day Christianity. The reason it does is because Christianity and most other religions define temptation as being something that is trying to get you to break God's laws and commandments. They imply that temptation, whatever the source, is constantly trying to lure you away from God by tempting you to break his commandments. I'm so aware of this dynamic because of my very personal experience with it and its consequences. You will see how and why I can say this as you read on.

The thing I have found is that I am actually perfectly capable of resisting all temptation because I learned it has nothing to do with keeping God's laws. It has nothing to do with my moral behavior, whether that morality is acceptable or unacceptable to society or not. This was a monumental challenge for me. However, I can now unequivocally say that I am capable of resisting all temptation. I have been resisting temptation for several years now.

What is this great mystery of temptation?

By seeing now how dramatically Evangelical Christianity missed the perfect simplicity of God's one man plan, it is now much easier to understand how they've mucked-up many other subjects. Temptation is one of them. Sin is another. Virtually *every* subject needs to be re-addressed after you comprehend God's equation of the One Man. You cannot allow former concepts to go unchallenged. You must take another look. I mean, if they missed it so badly about Jesus, what else did they miss? And as with all spiritual issues we must approach temptation through the prism of the scriptures.

It's now amazing to read the writings of Paul, and even James to some extent, about resisting temptation. I went back and actually studied those writings in context and realized that their teachings, for the most part, were all focused on or around resisting the temptation of going back under the law! It was shocking. It was wild to see that resisting the devil meant to resist going back under the law mentally and going back to a search for righteousness or validation through your performance. The emphasis was clearly not on behavior. This called for more questioning.

Why was Jesus the perfect sacrifice?

Was Jesus the perfect sacrifice because he never did anything wrong? Was he the perfect sacrifice because he was non-human? Was he the perfect sacrifice because he never had a sexual thought or that he ever had a sexual experience of any kind? As far as experiencing sexuality, or any issue of the heart is concerned, it wouldn't even have to involve doing it to be a violation of the law because Jesus himself taught that if you even think about it you've done it.

Many people dismiss the work of the cross because of the impossible thought that a real human being lived on this Earth and was without behavioral (or mental) sin based on God's commands.

I'm not saying that Jesus broke any commandments. I am saying that our focus should not be on whether Jesus broke any law or not. Instead, we should concentrate on the means by which he was made the perfect sacrifice.

Remember the controversy that was getting a lot of public attention a few years ago of whether or not Jesus actually had sex with Mary Magdalene? I do not believe that he did. Actually, the argument that he had sex with her is just an attempt to take away the validation of Jesus being a perfect sacrifice for sin. I once considered what it would have meant if he had had sex. I realized that even if Jesus had a sexual relationship with Mary Magdalene, or if he did have a child by Mary Magdalene, it would not affect him being the perfect sacrifice.

As we've already dealt with, Jesus was the perfect sacrifice because he was born of the Spirit.

Being born of the Spirit through Christ is the thing that makes us all perfect and acceptable in the eyes of God. Jesus was born of the Spirit and then he was born again from the dead, where he brought all of humanity in a second birth back to spiritual life. We are without sin because we are born of the Spirit. He was conceived by the Spirit without the disqualifier of the seed of man. He was indeed the seed of God himself.

When we look at "the fall of man" or "the original sin," we can conclude that if there were original *sin*, there had to be original *temptation*. The original sin is spoken of very clearly in the books of Galatians and Romans. God concluded *all* to be in unbelief, and unbelief is the sin that "doth so easily beset us" as Hebrews 12 relates to us. It was the sin, the transgression of unbelief that caused the entire world to have sin imputed to it by God.

What was the original temptation? What was Adam tempted with? Was he tempted with eating of the Tree of the Knowledge of Good and Evil? He succumbed to doing that because of temptation, but the temptation was "God knows that if you partake of this, that you will be like him." You will find very clearly in the book of Genesis that God had created man "in his own image." Then the temptation came. You have to realize that the temptation was to be like God. But they already were like God being made in his image. Realize who this temptation came from. It came from one who, according to the scriptural account, had attempted that very feat in heaven, Lucifer.

Looking at the issue of sin, look into heaven first, because sin did not originate on this planet. Sin actually originated in heaven. The story in the scriptures when Lucifer attempted to make himself like God is our first clue as to the real original sin. So, here we have this same being, creature, angel or whatever you want to call him having now been cast to Earth. Of all of God's creation, it is the man who was created in God's own image. That was an envious place for Lucifer—now Satan. He had failed at his attempt to become equal with God. And he certainly didn't want anybody else to experience the incredible position of being *like God*.

Presuming Satan influenced the serpent in the Garden of Eden—however that worked—Eve was tempted with the "forbidden fruit" and shared the temptation with her mate. And they succumbed. The serpent shed doubt on the reality of the state in which God had created man. He had created them in his own image. Eating the fruit was NOT *the* sin. Eating the fruit was just a vehicle to a destination; a means to an end. Eating the fruit of the Tree of the Knowledge of Good and Evil was simply accessing the system by which one must live, if one was going to live outside of truth. That system of living outside of truth was there if that was man's choice. Man had to deny his very existence of "being in the image of God" before he could partake of the forbidden fruit.

For a moment let's look at Adam as though he had not been influenced by Lucifer or been tempted with being like God. Let's suppose he could have gotten around the rule not to eat of the Tree of Knowledge. Adam in that scenario, if he had taken a bite from the fruit could almost be heard saying, "Wow, this is horrible! It just doesn't taste right! What in the world is wrong with this?!" Unfortunately, the thing that made it appetizing to them was that they had already gone into being a human *doing* and left their original God-given position as a human *being*.

There have been many motivational speakers that have picked up on that perspective I taught a couple of decades or more ago that God created us as "human beings" but we decided to be "human doings." Someone who worked for me back then brought it up in a weekend self-help group meeting, and the guy in charge picked up on it and made it part of their curriculum. That aside, we have a tremendous insight into this temptation and the evidence of us becoming "human doings" instead of who we were created as (or recreated as in Christ). The intriguing thing is where the temptation is actually originating from.

The temptation is not coming from the prostitutes on the street. The temptation is not coming from pornography. The temptation is coming from the pulpits of churches and all kinds of places of worship around the planet because religion is still appealing to people to strive to "become like God." One of the most devious instruments of this teaching is when they instruct us to become "Christ-like."

W.W.J.D.? What Would Jesus Do? Jesus would walk on water. Jesus would turn water into wine. Jesus would ransack the place of worship. Ultimately, Jesus would hang on a cross for the sin of the world. Is that what *we* should be doing? That would truly be "Christ-like," wouldn't it?

"Christ-like" comes from the term "Christian." There is no such thing as being like Christ in what Christ taught. The term "Christian" came from a group of people that were mocking those who were believers in Jesus or "People of the Way" as they were called at the time. Fast forward a couple of thousand of years and now we have this incredible, mammoth religious structure that is still rooted in the old Tree of the Knowledge of Good and Evil and appeals to people to be "Christ-like." Really?

Jesus did not die so that we could be like him. Jesus died on the cross so that I could be like me and you could be like you and together we could really make a great difference on the face of this Earth. We could never make a difference if we all acted the same. As an aside, how boring a world would that be to live in? Even think about the term, making a *difference*. We cannot make it *different*, whatever one is referring to, by being the *same*. The reality is we are NOT the same. We're equal but we are not and never have been the same except in one important way that we had no choice in becoming. Religion wants us to line-up in formation and surrender to its cookie cutter disciplining techniques because then we are easier to manipulate into supporting the system that supports its hierarchy.

However, because of the understanding the power of the gospel has brought to our souls, knowing the one place we are the *same*—in the realm of the Spirit—we can now rejoice in our diversity. I know diversity is a word that is tossed around a lot right now in our society, but it really is true. To celebrate diversity is truly a part of the plan that was completed at the cross 2,000 years ago. Every conceivable way in which humans can be seen to differ from each other, is the same number of ways in which God invites us to creatively celebrate those differences.

The cross is the foundation for the celebration of that diversity.

Adam was tempted and he failed at resisting that temptation back in the garden. Then God, in his authority, completely threw the entire human race into a condition called "sin," ALL because of Adam's sin and because of God's prerogative to impute the condition of sin to everyone.

As we look at the temptation of the Last Adam, please see it in the light of the issue of temptation using Paul's comparison of the First Adam to the Last Adam.

We conclude that the entire world was thrown into a condition of sin because of one man's disobedience—the First Adam. God concluded that sin to be "unbelief" because Adam failed to resist the temptation to try to become like God when the reality of it was he was *already* in the image of God. A Redeemer comes to the world, foretold in the law, the psalms, and the prophets—the scripture—as Jesus noted. And he came to bring reconciliation to the entire situation. Jesus, the Last Adam, was going to reconcile man back to God.

There are some incredibly strong analogies between the First Adam and the Last Adam. Paul believed that there were such strong ties between the two that he gave them the same name to make sure we understood the power of this comparison. So, if the First Adam suffered temptation and failed the temptation, we absolutely need to consider then that the Last Adam, Christ Jesus, suffered temptation but overcame the temptation! This is why it is so vital for us to look at what Jesus was actually tempted with.

Initially John the Baptist refused to baptize Jesus. But Jesus encouraged him to do it so they may "fulfill all righteousness." When John lifted Jesus back out of the water, the Spirit descended upon Jesus and there came a voice from heaven saying "This is my beloved son in whom I am well pleased." That same voice came another time at the mount of transfiguration where Moses and Elijah appeared and Peter wanted to build a tabernacle to honor all three of them. But God spoke up again and said, "This is my beloved son. Hear ye him." What a magnificent picture of the process that was underway. God was literally fulfilling the law (Moses) and the prophets (Elijah) into the body of One Man. We know Peter missed its meaning wanting to equate and recognize the equality of the law and the prophets with the one who they represented and foreshadowed. Yet, the Father would have none of it.

The validation and the acknowledgment that Jesus got were powerful. We don't know to what extent Jesus' vast knowledge of the scriptures gave him the understanding about who he was prior to what he experienced at his immersion by John. We can conclude that after this day he knew beyond the shadow of a doubt that he was totally approved of by God. "This *is* my beloved son in whom I am well pleased."

It is important to note that there is no record of Jesus performing any miracles before this unarguably public validation by God. He had certainly been on the scene prior. He had certainly been acknowledged by the doctors of the law at the age of 12 when he was found in the synagogue putting on quite an impressive performance. The gospels say he was both listening and asking them questions. He must have had some amazing things to say too because they all were astonished. The records in the New Testament "Gospels" do not document anything between that time and his baptism. He reappears in the Gospels right at the time of this baptism, which immediately precedes being driven into the desert to be tempted by the devil. Jesus' temptation, and his resistance of it, reveals the depth of his understanding of just who he was—that he was the one without sin. For him to be without sin, he would have to defeat the temptation that the First Adam fell to. He did resist, perfectly.

Jesus was born of the spirit, but so was Adam. Jesus got his absolute acknowledgment which was akin to Adam's when God said he had created Adam in his own image.

The Bible tells us that nobody else could understand what that voice had proclaimed at Christ's baptism. Some thought it had thundered, but Jesus heard the voice affirming that "This is my beloved son in whom I am well pleased."

After that, it's interesting that the writer says the *Spirit* drove him into the desert to be tempted by the devil immediately. As far as we can tell, the exact same player who showed up in the Garden of Eden with the First shows up again in the desert to tempt the Last. There's no mention that the Spirit wanted Adam to be tempted, but this time the Spirit apparently wanted Jesus to be tempted. What was the Spirit up to? Why did the Spirit want Jesus now to be tempted? The Spirit had just heard of course, exactly what Jesus heard: "This is my beloved son in whom I am well pleased."

Jesus heads into the desert directed by the Spirit to be tempted. I remember when I first read that. I so wanted to somehow read into it that it was the devil that took him there to be tempted. However, there is no way around it. It was the Spirit of God that drove Jesus into the desert. Then it says that Jesus fasted for 40 days. Imagine what Jesus must have looked like at that time. He had to be extremely weak. He had to have had a completely emaciated body. I saw what happened to the man who fasted for me 40 days. The transformation of his body was unbelievable. He was unrecognizable compared to what he looked like just 40 days before.

The Spirit had to know what the temptation would be and why it would occur. It was time to see what was what. It was time for THE test, because this was God's plan for the redemption of the entire world, according to the scriptures. This was the time that the Spirit was looking for. This incredible moment needed to be accomplished and fulfilled. He was inspired by the Spirit, joined by the Spirit, and now led by the Spirit to this remarkable place of temptation. It's known throughout the annals of the religious world as "The temptation of Christ."

So, what temptation was Christ actually tempted with?

It certainly was not sex, drugs, or rock 'n roll that the Lord was tempted with or with anything that Christianity presents as the great temptations we must stand fast against. The reality of this incredible temptation had absolutely nothing to do with anything that Christianity and other religions describe as temptation and warn us against.

How could the nature of the temptation of Christ have been overlooked for so long?

In the temptations of Christ that are listed in the Gospels, the devil starts out "IF you be the Son of God . . . IF you are the Son of God." What did he tempt Jesus to *do*? He was tempted to turn stones into bread. Then the devil took him to a high mountain and said "Look at all the kingdoms of the world." The devil showed Jesus all the kingdoms of the world, and said "If you will bow down and worship me, I will give all of this to you." Now, Jesus by that point said "Get thee behind me Satan; for it is written thou shalt worship the Lord thy God and him only shalt thou serve." He tempted him to cast himself to the ground from the pinnacle of the Temple, as the devil quoted scripture and said the angels "shall bear thee up, lest at any time thou dash thy foot against a stone."

The true temptation was not in the breaking of any of God's laws, except "Thou shalt worship the Lord God and him only shalt thou serve." But the other temptations had nothing to do with breaking God's law. What the devil wanted to do, was to entice Jesus to prove who he was *by his deeds*. That is absolutely clear. He wanted Jesus to prove who he was *by what he could do*. Remember at this point Jesus had performed no miracles. If he had, Jesus could have pulled his résumé out and said, "Oh I'm the Son of God. I've healed the sick, and cleansed the lepers, and raised the dead." But no résumé existed. He had no record of the miraculous to fall back on for his defense in proving that he indeed *was* the Son of God.

At the end of this time of temptation, the Gospels tell us that the devil left Jesus . . . for a time! If you think that your temptation with self-righteousness has ended, believe me, it will find its way back around to you again. It always has and always will so long as we are in this physical body. And your temptation with self-righteousness may be to try to keep God's laws so that you can be and feel righteous. In fact I guarantee that's exactly what form the temptation will be in. Either that or you will be tempted to be righteous by keeping God's laws or you'll be sold a bill of goods to make you believe you are unrighteous because you have broken God's law. We read of the temptation that Jesus went through and what happened afterward? This is beautiful. Jesus returned in the power of the Spirit! There was no record that he had broken his fast yet, but he felt good. He was in power, in control.

Jesus had been empowered.

The monumental defeat that Satan suffered at the hands of the Anointed One must have marked the demise of religion in the mind of the chief of religiosity himself, the devil. The frustration that he experienced must have been absolutely palpable. The resulting effect it had on Jesus was absolutely palpable, too, because he returned from the encounter in the power of the Spirit. The rest of the story goes on to tell how Jesus, after he had resisted the temptation, multiplied bread and turned water into wine. In fact, this was his first recorded miracle. He turned water into wine. He did it when his mother asked. He did not do what the devil had requested as proof of his status as Messiah. But he did do what Momma asked of him.

That might be a good topic for a sermon some day. Do what your momma says to do. Just don't do what the devil tempts you to do!

The motivations of each were two very different things. Mary wanted to make sure there was enough wine at a wedding they were attending that was apparently very important to her. The devil could have done the same thing, but you see his temptation would have been totally different. It's as if Jesus said, "Oh that's my Momma! I can do what she's telling me she wants me to do." He knew it couldn't have been the devil, because Satan would have said "*IF* you are the Son of God, turn this water into wine!" This time it was his momma. Mary already knew he could turn water into wine. That's what you call confidence in your boy. She did not challenge *who* he was; she didn't challenge his identity at all. She simply said, "We need more wine." The Gospel of John tells us that it was the beginning of the great miracles that Jesus performed.

There is no real record at all of Jesus ever breaking God's laws. There are places that people cite where Jesus may have broken the law, but whether he did or not is irrelevant in his capacity as the perfect sacrifice for the sin—*the* sin (singular) of the world. His qualification as the perfect sacrifice for sin was validated by defeating that temptation. What would have happened if Jesus had succumbed to that temptation? I shudder to think what it would have meant had Jesus given in to that temptation to prove his worthiness by *doing* something.

So, what for us does it mean to be tempted? How are we confronted by temptation within the context of the gospel?

Focus on the picture we get from the One Man equation. Again, this is and always was all about Jesus—not about you, me, or anyone else. The power of the cross is realized in an upside-down way due to the way Christianity has presented it. Christianity teaches that Jesus saved us from our sins (plural) that we commit by breaking God's law. Then they say he wiped our slate clean.

I was taught that when I went up to the front in a church altar call and accepted Jesus that I got born again, which of course was fictitious in and of itself. They said "the slate was wiped clean" for me. Now that was a glorious moment, as you can imagine. You want to feel like you're saved? Let somebody tell you that the slate is clean. I was so excited! I was enthralled! Then they began to explain to me afterwards that I now had to *keep* the slate clean. The "joy of the Lord" did not hang around for long. My mind got lost in a flurry of monitoring my actions and my deeds AND my thoughts. The responsibility for monitoring my righteous and unrighteous actions switched from God to me! Talk about upside down thinking. I tried to stop my mind from thinking about sex. I tried to stop my mind from thinking about anything because even if I got angry the Bible said and I was taught that I was equivalent to a *murderer.* This must have been the temptation they told me about. They told me "the devil's going to come and he's going to try to get you to do this and do that." They were right. The thing that made their predictions accurate was that *they* forbade those things to me. Legalism works every time.

It wasn't God who forbade me to do anything by threatening me with eternal hell; it was *them!* The "men of God" reinforced my inability to keep my mind focused. This caused my mind to literally become obsessed with things that should have just been no big deal, simple issues of life and living. Instead, as a young man I developed obsessions with certain things because they had been absolutely and totally forbidden by my Christian mentors.

What I didn't know was that I had already fallen to the great temptation, the temptation of self-righteousness.

The very same people who introduced me to the work of the cross then taught me a doctrine that stripped me and my soul from the power of the cross. This is why I had all the problems I had while growing up and while so many other Christian young men and women are so tormented. This is a massive injustice. The person who leads you to understanding that Jesus died for your sin should not be the same person who strips you completely of all the understanding of that.

This is simply diabolical.

I hadn't realized they had stripped my confidence in God away because their teaching put the focus back on me and my actions and thoughts and away from the actions and thoughts of Christ. We're supposed to look to Christ. We're supposed to be honoring him for what he did. But the whole thing gets turned back on us. Then those same people offered the solution to the very problems they created in our souls! Can you see the insanity in that?

Their doctrine and teaching had it all about Jesus for only a split second. I entreat you to take that split second of focus (and what that focus was and is all about) and expand it for the rest of the days of your life, every day. Enjoy your redemption, your righteousness, and experience your salvation—and everyone else's, too! The moment you saw what Jesus did for you was a very powerful moment; I have no doubt about that. But the thing that moment did for you did NOT redeem you. We all were already redeemed before we ever knew it or had an encounter with salvation or Jesus, or Yeshua. (Yeshua in Hebrew literally means salvation!) Before we ever had the emotional experience of the feeling that is the relief from sin and of guilt, we were righteous. Salvation is not the point at which you are freed from sin and guilt. Salvation is when you actually learn about it and then experience the resulting emotional and psychological lift from it. Redemption took place in Jerusalem at the Place of the Skull two millennia ago for me, for you, for all humanity.

Our whole focus has to change and remain on our new focus. Whether it does or not will NEVER affect God's view and opinion of us. This will save us from double mindedness, self-righteousness, and spiritual restlessness forever. That is as set as the Rock of Ages. It will have a dramatic and on-going impact on the way we see ourselves and be worth whatever effort and discipline one determines to put into it. We can and need to be getting *saved* on a consistent basis for the benefit of our respective souls and those we come in contact with on a daily basis.

So, what is temptation to us now? Remember earlier how I made the comment that I am perfectly capable of resisting temptation? Temptation has gotten weaker and weaker throughout my experience in the gospel. I know this now only in retrospect. I certainly did not know that this would be the case as I first walked my gospel road. But I know it now, and am happy to be able to confirm the stabilizing effect of this process on the soul for you. It does take some time. It takes the gospel renewing our minds and strengthening our souls first just to be able to identify temptation. After a few years of Evangelical Christianity and its twisted thinking, your biggest challenge is going to be identifying real temptation, much less being able to resist it.

The only real temptation that we have to contend with is the one that tries to tell us that "we need to do something to be something for God" or that our efforts and meditations will result in us "being closer to God."

People end up walking away from their understanding of Jesus and the cross because they know they can't keep the laws—that they simply cannot measure up—even to Christianity's watered down, fragmentation of the law. The fact is many people walk away from Christ because of the emphasis that is placed on resisting and defeating "temptations" that are frankly just part of life and what it means to be human. The smart ones have been the ones who have walked away entirely. Other victims of this heinous mindset have stayed around only to have been seduced, tempted and beguiled to deal with sin over and over again when it has, of course, been dealt with once and for ALL at the cross.

They either continue to confess sin or do penance or ask forgiveness from God over and over to try to get back to a place of right-standing with the Creator of the Universe and then try their level best to maintain that standing. The whole concept is an anathema to the very Christ they say they honor

How bizarre is it to think that God would go to the effort to send his Son into the world to bring absolute union between God and man (take thousands of years to foreshadow that coming involving multiple millions of lives) and then leave it up to man to be the one who has to work at maintaining that union—a union man had nothing to do with creating in the first place?!

God proved over a few thousand years of scriptural history that man could not create union with God, let alone maintain it. This is a union man had no choice in, no say in and no part in bringing about. How then can man, by doing or not doing something break this or maintain this union in any way? It is an absolute joke when you really think about it!

This is why an emphasis on temptation being the resistance of breaking one of God's laws is so erroneous, destructive, insidious, and damaging to life. It demands that *you* still "sin"—sin that has not existed since Christ's triumph. Jesus bore it all on the cross. He took THE sin of the world and that sin was unbelief.

When considering the mystery of temptation, it is vital to understand that Jesus did not shed his blood on the cross to wash away your sins of transgressing God's laws. Hebrews makes it quite clear that Jesus only had to eradicate the sins that were under the first covenant. There are NO sins under the second covenant! There was only *one* sin and that one was eradicated for eternity.

The power of the cross is real. The power of the cross is true. The power of the temptation—to be tempted to revert to self-righteousness and to fall back into unbelief about the nature of Christ and therefore your nature—is real and true, too. That temptation began in the Garden of Eden where Satan tempted Adam, who was already the image of God to try to *become* like God. When Adam gave in, that was the fall of humankind into unbelief. Jesus, having resisted the temptation to "un-believe" God's glorious declaration about his status as Christ.

Then he died on the cross for the First Adam's unbelief—for all of *our* unbelief. He took the sin of unbelief away completely and utterly!

There is no such thing as "the sin of unbelief" anymore.

We were *all* concluded to be in unbelief so that he might have mercy upon *all*. This is clearly presented in Paul's letters to the Romans and the Galatians. Christianity has turned the redemptive work of the cross upside down. This needs to be thoroughly and clearly understood. And once understood, it needs to be thoroughly and loudly denounced. Christianity emphasizes that Jesus died for your transgression of the law AND that he did not die for your unbelief! The core doctrine of Christianity is that you MUST believe. However, that completely diverts us from the very reason for the accomplishment of the cross. What Jesus died for was our unbelief and he *freed* us from the laws that caused us to be transgressors. Jesus did not die so that you would never break a law again. There is no law to break—not as far as God is concerned. Jesus' death pertaining to law had to do with taking the law *away* so that "where there is no law there is no transgression!" Was not Jesus the "word made flesh?" Was not Jesus the "lively oracles" embodied in human form? That's what it means in Ephesians when it talks of that very law, Jesus, being nailed to the tree, so it would be such an obvious, open show. The cross was such a momentous day, for it is the day Christ died, and all humanity was judged in his body. I don't think it is a stretch to imagine something earth-shattering happened on the day Jesus died.

Let your soul soak in this reality a while and then forever.

Allow this wonderful reality to be turned back right-side up so that your foundation is that you (and everyone else) are forgiven for unbelief. The law was removed in the dead body of Christ so that you could not transgress that law ever again. Jesus did not die to make you a good law-keeper! Jesus died to take the law off from us and to reverse what the First Adam did by not believing who he was and what God had done. Jesus did not die to make you a *good* person. Jesus died to make you a *whole* person.

In the end, the mystery of temptation is not a mystery at all. It's actually quite clear.

The great temptation is to be tempted to try to be what you already are.

Chapter 10

Identity

When I was around five years old I was in the grocery store with my mom.

While she was checking out, I reached up and got a piece of Super Bubble gum and put it in my pocket. When we got home my mom was putting away the groceries, and I reached into my pocket and while I was pulling the twisted ends of the wrapper, the bubble gum popped out. I stuck it in my mouth. My mom stopped dead in her tracks, turned around, looked at me and said, "Mikey, *where* did you get that?"

I *knew* I was in trouble! I knew I was in *big* trouble. So, I broke into tears immediately and told her I got it at the store. She didn't flinch. "Did you pay for it?" she asked. I said, "No," crying profusely. She said "I'm going to finish putting up the groceries. Then you and I have to go back to the store." Oh, I was so hoping for a beating, but instead she took me back to the grocery store. I cried all the way there. We went to the cashier. My mother asked for the manager of the store. When he came out, she said, "My son has something to tell you." I just broke into tears, screaming. I was gasping for air. I couldn't even breathe anymore. I cried so hard. But Mom was unflinching. She was unmoved by my tears. I stood there and gasped out, "I'm sorry I stole this gum and here's a penny to pay for it." The manager didn't want to be there. I didn't want to be there. I think the only one that wanted to be there was my mom. Nobody but my mom wanted any part of this.

While we were riding back in our blue and white 1956 station wagon, I was in the front seat and still gasping for air, and then Mom said, "Mikey, there's something that you have to know. You are a Williams, and *Williams' don't steal*." Now, my mom did not tell me that I would not *be* a Williams if I stole, or that I would be kicked out of the family. She never disciplined me for that, never once. She didn't spank me. She didn't give me a time-out. She didn't take away my privileges. She didn't ground me, none of that. She just explained that this is who I was and what I was, and that as a member in "good-standing" of this group, there are certain things that we do and don't do.

So, that was probably my first lesson about the gospel. Much later I would learn a great deal more through seeing it in the scriptures. It is the pivotal issue of identity that we operate out of who we are, not out of whom we want to be or to try to become.

Most of us have mistaken the issue of faith to be connected with circumstances when in fact it is rather an issue of identity, how one sees him or herself and everyone else. The entire issue of faith takes on a completely different understanding when we remove circumstances out of the equation. In reality, the reason that faith has been tied to circumstances, especially through the teachings of Jesus, was to demonstrate to the world that *our own faith* was simply not good enough (and would never be good enough) even and especially pertaining to circumstances. When faith becomes an issue of identity, then we have an entirely different subject on our hands: the trying of one's faith.

What's really happening when your faith is being *tried?* Does it mean that you are being tested to see whether or not you can alter your circumstances? Or is the trying of your faith to see if the circumstance has the ability to change *you?*

The most powerful thing in the human experience is NOT the ability to change circumstances but the ability to prevent circumstances from changing *us*.

During the course of our lives, human beings can begin relatively early-on to become bitter, jaded, disinterested, lose their zeal for life and find life increasingly dull—all because a person's circumstances begin to change them and alter the way they view themselves and life. We so desire for *our* faith to change our circumstances. However, the most important thing we can ever learn about faith is that it's there not to change our life's circumstances, but that along life's path, faith is what is in place to keep *circumstances from changing us*. Now that subject alone is a subject worthy of an entire book.

The world of faith is just that messed up.

When considering the original temptation, the whole issue in the Garden of Eden was not the circumstances Adam and Eve found themselves in; it was their misunderstanding of their identity.

God's reaction to Adam's disobedience at having partaken of the fruit of the Tree of the Knowledge of Good and Evil was certainly not one of being upset. He definitely did not approach them in an angry way after Adam had acted out of a misplaced sense of his identity. Perhaps that is why God gave them the first commandment that he did. He did want them to not to eat of that tree because he knew what would happen. He said, "in the day you eat thereof, you will surely die." And there was a death that took place. Adam and Eve's identity died. Adam, that one man within whom was the human race, really did die on *that* day. God did not say *some* day you'll die. So, he couldn't have been talking about his physical death, even though we know that certainly occurred eventually. But he said, "In the day that you do, you shall surely die." So, this has been the whole issue from the very beginning of time through today. It is not about circumstances. It is about identity or about how we see ourselves.

Now what about the requirement that was upon the human race to believe in Jesus? Is it to believe in him, to believe that he was the Son of God, to believe that he was all these things and more, to believe that he was sent of God, to believe that he was the Messiah, to believe that he lives? So, which one(s) do you have to believe?

The requirement for faith seems to be focused on the human race all the way through. But the fulfillment of faith, like every spiritual fulfillment, falls at the feet of Jesus himself because as it turns out, the rest of the human race just couldn't believe in Jesus. The one who still believed in Jesus at the cross was Jesus himself. He was the only one who believed what the Father said about him. The Bible even records that it was "For the joy that was set before him he was able to endure the cross." At its core, this is a statement of identity. The joy of that relationship, the joy of relationship being restored, and the absolute joy of watching an entire history of a planet completely reversed as far as its inhabitants' relationship with God is concerned was the source of that joy. That joy had such a powerful hold on his identity. He could endure anything.

Jesus was able to express his belief in the Father by believing what the Father said about him! Jesus had to believe in himself. Jesus was the only believer when he went to the cross. John Chapter 12 makes it very clear that he was the only believer. The prophets foretold there would be no believers because that wasn't God's plan. It was never God's plan to redeem man through the belief or faith of each individual.

John quotes two places in Isaiah where it's very clear that God stopped their ears and blinded their eyes because he said if I don't blind their eyes and stop their ears they might actually believe and I will have to heal them; "but," he says, that's not God's plan. So, God made sure man couldn't do what was required to have redemption, because the plan was that Jesus would be the only believer, and he would be the only one to believe in *him*.

In the story, Satan certainly knew this was not about circumstances, but that it was about identity; the very *survival* of Jesus' identity. That's why the devil's temptation was "*If* you are the Son of God," because he knew the circumstances were irrelevant. There were three things in play here: the circumstances (Jesus was hungry), Jesus' abilities (he could have set a miracle table for himself), and Jesus' identity. Satan went right past the circumstances and even Jesus' abilities and went straight for the jugular—Jesus' identity!

What the devil did do was to try to use the circumstances to destroy THE identity.

When Jesus went to the cross he fulfilled all the demands for faith *in him*. He fulfilled the law, too, as he took the law upon himself. He *was* the law. He *became* the law *itself*. What had to survive the cross was the challenge to his identity. Through ultimate humiliation, and even though it looked as though God his Father had abandoned him completely, what needed to live on during this horrendous test was for him to maintain the security of his identity in order to benefit everyone on the planet.

The good news is that Jesus never relinquished his identity, even though all the circumstances to that moment seemed to point to him not being who he knew he was.

Hebrews 6 lays down the things we are not supposed to be teaching anymore: "the foundational doctrines." Christianity actually still teaches them as the foundational doctrines to adhere to up to this very day. They will go back once a year and teach that these are the foundational doctrines just to make sure we do not get away from the foundational "truths." However, when read in context, it says that these are the things we should *not* be teaching ever again. We should *not* be teaching repentance from dead works. We don't have to start from there. You should not be teaching people that they have to start all over again. That's why the writer of Hebrews brings this up again. There is no need to go back and re-do this all over again and to resurrect the doctrine of repentance. We do not need repentance from sin because the entire issue of sin has been resolved. People shouldn't be teaching repentance anymore regarding how one gets to have relationship with God.

The last doctrine listed is eternal judgment.

We absolutely should not be teaching people about eternal judgment anymore. In addition, and as a fascinating point, the writer of Hebrews says we should also not be teaching anymore about "faith *toward* God." What a fantastic thing to read and understand! We should not be teaching faith *toward* God. Our faith is not an issue in any way anymore. *His* faith toward *us* was and remains the key factor in our relationship.

So how does this impact the human race? How do the gospel and the sacrifice of Jesus come into play here? The most powerful thing that can ever happen to a human being is to believe in himself or herself. This is true whether a person is an atheist or any kind of believer at all. One of the greatest influences in a person's life is to have the privilege of being raised by parents who are constantly telling you there is nothing you can't do; that you can accomplish anything that is in your heart to do. It instills in them an identity that says, "I can do anything."

On the contrary, one of the most horrendous things a child can experience is to be raised in a family where his or her identity for achievement is completely stripped away. They are left believing circumstances (many of which are completely out of one's control) are what's left to determine our own value and our worth. Discovering one's worth and value through our circumstances is a clear exercise in unbelief and a lack of faith! Why? Because to be obsessed with making sure our circumstances are correct in order to determine our happiness or sense of satisfaction is a sure sign that we have lost our true identity. Thank God that even when we lose our true identity (as I have myself many times) we can have that identity restored. However, if we think our identity is going to be restored because our circumstances have improved, we are in for a rude awakening, again and again, until we learn we cannot find ourselves in our circumstances.

We should not allow our inner-foundation to be built upon such flimsy things as circumstances. Whether it is finances, relationships, natural or personal disasters, or world events, we just cannot allow our soul to be established on such shifting sand. Circumstances always change, guaranteed. If our identity is built upon the circumstances of our lives, then we will have nothing but shifting sand under our feet. Here's some good news: we don't have to live that way. We do not have to live with circumstances influencing how we see ourselves. God has already determined who we are through Christ.

One of our greatest needs as humans is to be able to accept God's verdict about us, even as Jesus accepted God's verdict about him. Before Jesus did any mighty works, he heard this coming from the Father: "This is my beloved son in whom I am well pleased." In this we get to witness God beginning to nurture the soul of Jesus, not only through the scriptures in which Jesus was studying, but God himself directly began nurturing the soul of Jesus, preparing him to endure the impending temptation that would come immediately afterwards. The first time that he heard this voice of approval was at his baptism where John immersed him in the Jordan River. And immediately, *immediately,* after he heard these words of validation, approving of his identity, he was taken by the Spirit, not an evil spirit, but by the Spirit of God to be tempted. Because of the critical nature of the issue of identity, the Son of God had to go through and pass this test. And, so, he was *driven* into the desert.

Please note: Jesus was not tempted to do something wrong. The temptation was to do something meaningful, something powerful something God-like. "Turn these stones into bread." "It is written . . ." Satan even used the scriptures, "If you dash your foot against a stone it will not hurt you." But the temptation was based on the accusation: "If you are the Son of God . . ."

The importance of Jesus passing this test was paramount and critical in his ability and willingness to endure the cross. It was his knowing his identity that enabled him to complete his mission. He knew exactly who he was.

Through the preaching and meditation of the gospel, we gain the strength of that identity that is already inside each of us. It is a progressive process. The effect is nothing less than the renewing of our minds and the cleansing of our souls.

So, what does it mean to live a life of faith? If I say I'm living by "faith," am I saying I'm trusting God to take care of everything for me? What kind of reality is this? While I can't speak for anybody else, any time I have believed God's going to take care of everything for me I've been sorely disappointed! I could always go back and say, "Yeah, but in the long run, this turned out just fine."

In reality, it's just life. Life happens. It happens for atheists, believers and non-believers, alike. If you just don't give up, things will often turn out okay. You will meet new people. You will find another job. You will be in a different home. Circumstances do change. But, again, this is not about circumstances. It's not about losing or gaining a job. It's not about new or old relationships. It is about identity!

Here is your strongest belief to express about God. It is NOT what YOU believe about God but what GOD believes about YOU! This is the only true way to accurately explain, the only way I believe to articulate faith regarding Jesus: I don't know how to have faith in Jesus!

How would you have faith in Jesus?

People are constantly extolling the virtues of believing and having faith. Billions of dollars are given and spent trying to get people to believe. But how do you believe? How do you express your belief? Do you bow down so many times a day? Do you start speaking *Christianese?* Do you attend church? Do you join the choir?

The reason we've had so many addictions to these religious practices is because someone else, some religious leader of some form or another, has put a demand on us to believe and to have faith, and absolutely nobody can tell you how to do it all just right!

There is only one expression of true belief in Jesus Christ and that is to believe in y*ou!* To believe in his righteousness is to believe you are the way he made you. You are already exactly what he has been passing down through all the generations of the human race. You are created in God! You are God in the flesh! You are an extension of his holiness and perfection.

The religious people challenged Jesus about saying that he was the Son of God, and how did he respond? He challenged them from the psalms. He said, "In your own book of psalms, have you not read 'for you are gods?'" That's, of course, an entirely whole other subject. Still, Jesus brought the point up and it's a valid one for us to consider.

We must begin to realize who we really are!

At the risk of being too repetitive, you cannot come to grips with who you are if your circumstances are telling you who you are. *This* is the trying of our faith. The trying of our faith is more precious than that of silver or gold. Our faith will be tried, but what is being tried?

Recently a friend of mine watched his 16-year-old son go from a 190-pound strapping football player with a bright future to having his entire diseased colon and part of his intestines surgically removed. One day the young man started bleeding, and the next thing they knew they were looking at their precious boy having lost 40 pounds and with a colostomy bag. Sixteen years old! His dad expressed to me the temptation he experienced, the temptation to try to change the circumstance through prayer. Because of his past religious experience he was tempted to try to manipulate things through something he really had no means and the ability to do. He was a spectator in watching what others were doing, even the medical professionals who were involved. He had no control over helping his son whatsoever.

We had a brief discussion about this. The true trying of faith here was not in trying to overcome his and his son's physical, life-threatening circumstances. He determined that the circumstances were not going to dictate whether he had faith or not. Regardless of the outcome, the question of his faith would not come into question. In fact, he told well-meaning people "do not pray!" That is how confident he was/is in his identity as righteous regardless of outward appearance. His security in his identity through the entire episode shone brighter than the sun. It certainly was not the circumstantial results. While my friend's son survived and is on the mend today, this was no miracle. He is never getting his colon or intestines back no matter how many prayers or "healing services" he would attend. Those are the facts.

So, what is his family left with? They are left with the most powerful result one could ever have regardless of how things "work-out." They came through this crisis with their identity more than intact. It is now clearer and more secure in their collective hearts than ever.

I don't even try to express to people anymore where I am in the light of what I've gone through. Frankly, my circumstances have given me no reason to have peace in my heart. All of these negative experiences should have left me bitter. They should have left me jaded. They should have left me with little or no compassion. They should have left me with all kinds of battered emotions, hardened, less resilient, and less willing to open myself up to others. I do recognize that I felt my heart being pulled toward a results-driven identity. I'm relating this to you from the "observation-deck" of my life, on the other side, in the rearview mirror. I have been through such loss and trauma over the years, like so many of you. If somebody would have asked me about it all in the middle of all the loss and heartache, there's no way in the world I would have been able to communicate what I have now to you at the time it was taking place.

This is how the power of the gospel manifests itself. When the gospel is consistently focused on, it does its work silently, stealthily, and profoundly.

The soul of an individual is such a complicated aspect of our being that the constant influence of the gospel and its anchoring and stabilizing effect on our minds—on our identity—is the only remedy for the temptation of our souls. Having to do our Gospel Revolution radio webcast every week has transformed life for me because of the repetition of getting to rehearse, rehash and revisit the gospel over and over from every angle imaginable.

So, it gets boiled-down to this: Am I living a life of faith? Am I a believer? How do I express my belief? What do I do if I am a believer? How does it affect me if I am a believer? Those questions have been dangled out in front of us for eons. Now is the time for them to stop succeeding in their temptation of human souls, tempting us to judge faith through circumstances, conditions, and results.

If we are honest, we know we don't have the faith to change circumstances. So, what to do? Forget it! This is not about circumstances. Jesus proved nobody has faith to change circumstances. You don't have it and I don't have it! Jesus said if you have faith the size of a mustard seed you would be able to pluck-up mountains and throw them into the sea! Before you start telling me about your faith and your ability to change your circumstances, show me that mountain you or anyone has thrown into the sea. I guarantee you that my friend would have rather seen his son totally healed before he would have ever wanted to move any mountain. But alas, that is not what our lot is in this life.

The culmination of the wonderful gospel is not rooted in our ability to change circumstances through our faith. What it does do *is* supernatural—way more than what would occur naturally without the gospel. The amazing true miracle is for the human being to stand and keep his or her identity regardless of what their circumstances are. This is the power of God, the gospel. This is the gospel Paul said he was not ashamed of: "the power of God to the saving of the soul to everyone that *believeth.*" Believeth *what??* Believe what the gospel, the good news, says about *you* and about all other people.

You say, "Well, I believe the gospel." What does that even mean? What does it mean that you believe the gospel? What does it mean that you believe in Jesus? If they mean anything that needs external evidence to prove it, then they are all just platitudes. It's just so much religious gibberish.

There is no faith in Christ; there is no belief in the gospel unless you believe what the gospel says that Christ has done to secure our identity before God. Now that is something to believe in! That is something you *can* believe. That is a place where faith abides. Faith abides *not* in circumstances and whether they change or not. Faith abides in identity and the fact that circumstances do not have the ability to change your identity.

One of the most important things I get to share with people may be the *application* of the gospel to one's life. The importance of the paradigm shift from circumstances to identity for me is so clear now. Life just *cannot* be about circumstances. It *must* be about identity and identity alone.

I never will forget the very first time, as I began to come to grips with my own sexuality, I got a call from a young man. He was asking me to help him because he had heard my "ex-gay testimony." He asked me if he could come and talk to me. Now, I had not yet opened up to people to tell people that I accepted my sexuality. But I knew I could not impose this lack of openness on someone else. When he asked me if he could come and sit and talk with me and said he was going to have to travel a good distance to do so, I told him "I will talk to you, but you must understand before you get here I will not talk to you about how to change your sexuality. I will speak to you about how to deal with your sexuality, but I will not talk to you about how to change your sexuality." That's as much as I could tell him at the time.

So, as you now know, this issue of identity is absolutely vital. We've got to get away from circumstances informing our faith. We must come to the true reality of faith and belief that it's all about your identity, about how you view yourself.

The raging battle that you are engaged in is within yourself. It is not an external struggle between the devil and God or between the devil and you. From my vantage point, the knowledge and consistent meditation and focus on this incredible gospel is the only thing that will penetrate and deal with that confusion. This is the battlefield. This is where the sword has been beaten into the plowshare. This is where the lion and the lamb lie down. It's the only thing that will calm the storm of disturbed emotions and misplaced motivation. As these seemingly external, conflicting aspects of each human being are infused with the gospel, they rest in peace. They want to co-exist. They are made to co-exist. It's just that nobody ever told them they could.

My sexuality has learned to co-exist with my spirituality. My spirituality has fully embraced my sexuality. My humanity and godliness are one. I am a very *human* person! If you're around me for very long, you're going to get a full dose of that *humanness*. My God, am I human! I say that, of course, in full acceptance of everything that means: the good, the bad, and the ugly. And, now, I wouldn't have it any other way.

In my past religious life, I spent most of my waking hours trying to get rid of my flaws. But I can now tell you that the only way you'll ever deal with your flaws is to embrace them. It will never be by trying to eliminate them. You are who you are. You are what you are, and that *has* to be reconciled with who *God* says you are. And it *can* be done. You don't do it by starting to try to *become* what God says you are. You already *are* what God says you are.

Simply and directly put, here is what God says about you and the entirety of the human race: You are holy, righteous, perfect, sinless, blameless, and without fault. This is your identity in God's sight. Someone's strongly held and communicated opinion of you *will* form your identity. What is your identity in your mind? Has the strength and clarity of God's opinion of you and all others been accurately communicated to you?

For God's opinion of you was formed *in* Christ and in Christ alone.

You should just simply mentally embrace the truth about *what* and *who* you already are through Christ. As you mentally internalize the spiritual reality that lives in you, the process of the salvation of your soul ensues. This process of salvation is the most dynamic experience that will ever happen to you. There is nothing else that *causes* peaceful co-existence with our seeming contradictions. This is what I call the "psychology of the gospel," which definitely crosses into the bounds of sociology or how we relate to each other.

As people everywhere become more and more secure in their identity as a perfect humanity, the psychological and sociological effects of the gospel may manifest in a peace within ourselves and with each other that heretofore we could only dream about.

Chapter 11

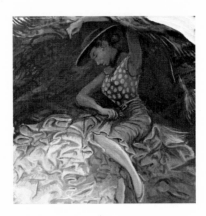

The New Creation

Miserable year upon miserable year came and went.

Then came my "deliverance" in the living room of a "Full Gospel Businessman" on the evening of August 15, 1974. The Full Gospel Business Men's Fellowship was an evangelistic outreach of the Charismatic movement. This new form of Christianity I was introduced to that night was certainly a vast departure from my Baptist roots.

Hazel and I had been married almost two years without having "consummated" our marriage. I kept subjecting myself to whatever these so called "spirit-filled" people deemed to be necessary for me to be free from my sexuality. They would pray and "lay hands" on me. A loud authoritative voice would yell, "Come OUT of him in

Jesus name" as the pressure from the ball of his hand pressed deeper and deeper into my stomach. "Come OUT I said! Obey me and come OUT!"

Regardless of my own story that came out of that evening, the fact a man had been on a water-only fast for 40 days for my deliverance was truly remarkable. I may be the only homosexual in history that had someone so concerned for my eternal destiny that he fasted for 40 days and 40 nights! It was all for naught. I was swept from my own normal environment to being surrounded by three other men whose job it was to keep me confessing I was free from homosexuality.

Eventually I did consummate my marriage, and we had three children. Still, I was as gay as I ever was.

I knew I needed to become a new creature, a new creation in Christ. However, the lack of true internal change in my life proved to me I was NOT a new creature. I was the same old Mike. The only difference now was I had the exterior and with it society's approval I so desperately wanted and needed even if it was based on a total fabrication.

At that time I had no clue that the 40 day fast, which was supposedly a necessary component for my freedom and would theoretically soon envelop me in a miraculous transformation from gay to straight, would make me a new creature. Little did I know then that transformation had already occurred 2,000 years before by the only true Deliverer, the only true Redeemer that ever was and ever will be, Jesus Christ.

Whenever Paul writes about the new creation he literally means the new creature. And when he talks about the new creature, it's akin to a new "creation." There's a lot to learn and understand about this, and the main point to know is just how totally different this new creation actually is.

Jesus' teaching out of Mark profoundly compares the stark contrast of new things versus old things. He said "No man sews a new cloth to an old garment." The reason why you wouldn't do that is because the new piece when it shrinks will actually tear away from the old and the tear is made worse. This is a very interesting concept. The other thing he said was "No man puts new wine into old wineskins." Now the problem with putting new wine into old wineskins is that the new wine will burst the old wineskins and the new wine gets spilled out and is lost. So, the new wine must be put in a new wineskin.

There is a scriptural understanding regarding the mingling of the new and the old, too. It is very clear what Jesus' understanding was that you never mingle new with old. If Christianity had taken only this one concept from the teaching of Jesus and let it be the standard by which we measure the doctrines they promote, most of what Christianity teaches never would have been taught in the first place. Without a doubt Christianity is a total mixture of the new and the old on every level. It is a mixture of law and grace, the old pertaining to the law and the new pertaining to the limitless grace of God. In fact, it is their main concept that somehow this is a very unique and very indefinable mixture of law and grace. Grace, yes—a gift from God. But also a certain amount of law—because at the very least faith without works is dead! Nobody can tell you exactly what proportion of grace there is in relation to the law, but they make sure you understand it is a mixture of the two that determines salvation, or if they were to word it correctly, what determines redemption. Now that is truly a mixture.

When I was growing up in the Baptist Church they told us that all of this was a completely free gift but, of course, applying my own belief would activate it. It wasn't until after I received this so-called "free gift" I had to believe for, that I began to be instructed about the rules and the laws. I was told I had to keep the rules and laws to be able to maintain this relationship with God.

Jesus' teaching is very clear about mixing new with old. By looking at the hazards a little bit closer, I think it will help us understand the new creation and its implications. The reasoning for not mixing old with new is very clear. Concerning the garment, Jesus said the one reason why you do not sew a new piece of cloth onto an old garment is because the new will shrink and take away from the old. What religionists do not understand is that by mixing grace (new) with law (old) they are taking away from the old. Not only are they taking away from the old but they are making the tear that much bigger. The problem is not solved. The hole is made even worse.

Christianity appears to have never taken these verses and applied them to their teachings about the new and the old, especially the new creature or the new creation. We're not talking about fixing an old life. When we talk about the new creation, we are not adjusting a life or a lifestyle. The new creation is something much greater than focusing on individual life choices.

In both the wineskin and garment examples Jesus makes it clear that the old has done its job. It's very interesting that he uses the phrase "it takes away" from the old garment. And it indeed does "take away."

I don't know of another Bible teacher who can tell you that they truly *love* and passionately protect the *whole* of God's law. This is mostly because they have yet to understand its ultimate purpose and believe that all of it is true without being selective about any one particular law. There is no law higher than another law. Still, it was the law that was done away with, and that is the only reason that anyone can respect God's law in its totality and see what it was used for. It's like the old garment. It was used until the new garment came along. We should not try to sew the new cloth onto the old garment. It will tear it asunder.

The problem with putting new wine into an old wineskin is that the old wineskin already accomplished its job. The old wineskin expanded with the wine. But once it is stretched out to accommodate the wine it's not going to stretch anymore. So, if you put the new wine in it and fill it to capacity, when the new wine begins to ferment and expand the wineskin, it's going to tear the old wineskin.

The only thing that totally preserves the authority, the righteousness and the purity of the law—or that which is old—is the gospel. Nothing holds the law as sacred as does the gospel. I believe the law is sacred. I believe the law is good. I believe it is pure. I believe that there is no fault in God's law whatsoever. I don't believe there's a single law that you need to go back and change. Christianity though, has done that throughout history. They voided certain laws to accommodate society. It is just as the prophet Malachi said about the priests of his day, using partiality in matters of the law, not bringing honor to it. But as Isaiah foretold, One would come and make God's law honorable. However, the law is not for today. It was for ancient Israel and for a purpose which was accomplished two millennia ago by "the One." We do well to leave the entirety of God's law completely intact and in its full glory.

We must go on to understand why the law condemned everything. It was so that everyone would know that through our own pursuit nothing could be made new. Nothing! The old wasn't there to be repaired. We don't need to repair the law. We need to honor God's law for what it was given for. The complete and utter separation of God's law and God's grace is the only thing that gives each their proper due and dignity.

The mixing of the gospel with the Old Covenant, the mixing of the blood of Jesus with the blood of animals, is just something you do not want to do! The gospel is the *only* message that does not denigrate the Old Covenant. We honor the Old Covenant. Now we turn to the Old Covenant to see its wisdom and to look at its wisdom for what its total picture shows us. The old brought us to the glorious revelation of righteousness in Christ and of us to a revelation of the new creation.

The law works death.

This is what Paul was explaining when he went into Romans Chapter 7 saying "when I want to do good, I can't do good. There's something within me when I try not to do evil I don't find the strength to do it. Woe is me. What's the problem?" So, I then identify because the law breaks me down. It leaves me to understand that the law is standing there pointing saying "There's the sin! There is the problem! Don't lose focus of the REAL problem!"

The sad and somewhat ironic thing is if you respect God's law for any other reason or purpose than for what it was given and for, you will lose the incredible revelation of the "*there's* the problem" as a focus. There's *that* problem. There's that *man*. That man was Adam. There's *his* problem. The problem was *his* unbelief. That problem was imputed to the entire human race by God's choice. The law not only stands and says "There's the problem," the law turns around and looks to the cross and says, "There's THE answer!" "There is the ONE answer! There's only ONE answer!" The Last Adam, he's THE answer!

There was never a multitude of offences. The one offence led to many offenders, and the many offenders led to one answer. Multitudes were not involved in this equation whatsoever. The equation is "one." The equation has always been "one." The equation will always be "one." The multitudes of people and laws between were simply there to give us a full revelation of the issue of "One."

Consider the power of this very simple concept a bit closer. At the same time, this is both the most profound and the most simple concept that this world has ever encountered.

If you can count to one, you can understand all things spiritual.

In fact, the problem is when you learn to count to two, and then when you learn to count to three, then four—look out! The things of the eternal *can* and *must* be understood through the number one.

However, with the purity of "One"—it cuts out all confusion. So, while the multitude was on the stage, the multitude of laws, the multitude of humanity, the multitude of the tribes of Israel, the multitude of people on Earth, we must conclude that all of these multitudes were put in place to help us understand the issue of "one"—the one man, the one sin, the one man Jesus, and the one righteousness. One.

As this ONE thought begins to dawn on humanity, we are in for some dynamic changes worldwide, the very same type of thing that occurred when Martin Luther took us through the portal of realizing that we didn't have to turn to the Pope for approval any longer. This led to an amazing revolution of thought, and a degree of freedom that is enjoyed to this very day. The question is, did Martin Luther get a full revelation? Did he do what he was supposed to do, and did he do all that was to be done? I believe Martin Luther did all that he could possibly do and all that was put before him. Do I believe he did all that needed to be done? No, I do not believe that. No more than I believe that Jonas Salk discovering the polio vaccine did all that needed to be done in medicine. What has been done in medicine since then has been remarkable.

So we do have an experience because what Martin Luther taught us wasn't something new; it was simply something we didn't know. We were never bound to have to go through another man to get to God. Did Martin Luther create that truth? No, Martin Luther just introduced the Christian world to a truth they had not heard. The things I'm sharing with you are not new things. These things were established 2,000 years ago. Please don't be fooled into thinking that just because now you're finding out something new that it means it's a new truth. It would be silly to think that. That's like saying that Isaac Newton was sitting under a tree and an apple fell on his head and that day gravity was invented or that's when gravity became real. That's not the day gravity became real. That was the day when someone got knocked in the head and realized what gravity was and that it was applicable to all human beings.

What we have here in the Gospel Revolution is an Isaac Newton moment! A gospel Isaac Newton moment! Maybe the proverbial apple from the first tree has hit our heads, and maybe when it hit our heads we suddenly realized that this great redemption did include all. Just like Isaac Newton realized that gravity in its application was applicable to all, so, too, we've had an Isaac Newton moment—the gospel, God's redemption and perfection is applicable to ALL!

This is more than just intriguing. It is life transforming and on a social level could culturally transform everything we see today to something totally new.

Please scour through what I've taught you in this book. See if there's anything really new in it. You'll find out that the information isn't a new doctrine. The information has in fact always been there. There's not one thing that has been developed in this book that is a doctrine that's been developed *after* the cross. All of it was developed *because* of the cross. It's all understandable because of the cross, and because of the results of what happened at the cross. I don't know of one shred of information that I've given you that tries to alter that magnificent moment in history. I simply present what the cross means in its entirety, in its fullness, and to all humanity.

We will always need the Old Covenant to show us the types, the shadows, the teachings and the validation of the successful mission of Christ. Where do we go to find out if the concepts we learn are true? How do we find out if what is written in the book you have before your eyes is true or not?

You go to the scriptures.

I'm not the one who says you have to go to the scriptures. Jesus said you have to go to the scriptures. As we've already noted, all of the Apostles agreed and understood what the scriptures were—the law, psalms, and the prophets—which is now what we call *old*. ALL scripture is now old! There is no such thing as a new scripture. Scripture is part of that which is old. Still, it is priceless in the revelation that it brings. Part of that revelation is the understanding of the new creation or the new creature.

Paul focuses on this in several places, one of which is in Corinthians. Paul teaches about leaven and says a little leaven leavens the whole lump in that it changes it into something else. Please do not change the Old Covenant into something else, something that it is not. It must remain and maintain its own rightful glory. That's the term Paul used—"glory." It is the glory of the first as opposed to the glory of the last. In the term "glory" he said that by virtue of the glory that now exists, the old has no glory whatsoever. It has lost its glory because of the new existing glory. You cannot do away with the old as far as its understanding is concerned or you will never understand the glory of the new.

In all of this newness, what is new?

The Christian community is waiting for the New Jerusalem. The Christian community is waiting for a new heaven, a new Earth. Christianity has Christians waiting for their lives to be transformed. They are waiting for all things to become new. But the good news about the gospel is that the new creation is already here. You were changed. It was not at the moment that you became a believer. You were changed 2,000 years ago when Jesus rose from the dead. And so was everybody else.

There's already a new heaven and a new Earth in which dwells righteousness. We're not waiting on a new heaven, new Earth or a New Jerusalem. All things have been fulfilled. All things have been made manifest. All things are ours. All things - A - L - L are complete. There's nothing left undone. There are no untied ends. There are no bluffs, cliffs, no dangers. There's nothing in this new creation to fall off from or a place to fall into error. There may be errors in your thoughts but there will never be an error in your relationship with God. That's so powerful to know, isn't it? You may not treat people or yourself perfectly. You may err in your conduct. You may have blown it in every area of your life. Please understand though, dear one, that on this side of the cross you can never have an error in your relationship with God because you have no responsibility (and therefore no credit or glory, no discredit or failure) in it. God himself took responsibility for it. He said *he's* the one that makes this perfect. He created it all new.

Now, that's the other thing about everything being made new. Who's making it new? "Behold *I* make all things new." It's not man who's making anything new. Spiritually speaking, we cannot make anything new. All components of things spiritual are God's department, God's will, God's manifestation of his will. We can only have it revealed. We have no participating role. We are not participants—we are beneficiaries! We can only enjoy our spirituality. We do not participate in it in any way, shape or form. If we could, would Jesus have to share his glory with the individuals that could do it right? Yes, he would!

Since Calvary, human will and capacity is now very open, powerful, and can accomplish many wonderful things. Our will can do many negative things, too. The only thing that is taken out of the equation is the element of being blessed by God because you do well or being punished because you do badly. Removing that element from the human/God equation, spells death to this horrific cause and effect religion. It actually begins to allow the real heart of humanity to be revealed; the truth that you and others are really better than you think. That is the power of the gospel and I'm sticking with it! The gospel is the power of God, after all!

We also have to remember to be careful because we are, in effect, reading another's mail. This was written to 1st century Corinthians, not 21st century Americans. Now, I do believe we can discover the intention of these letters, but we have to remember that it won't be as clear as it would be if there was an "epistle to the Americans." So, Paul compares the old to the new: this is the default setting. However, so many times when Paul is presenting the old in order to compare it to the new, people miss it because they never were taught that the old is OLD and has passed away. This is just one example of how we actually trick ourselves into mixing the law and grace.

So when Paul is saying that we're going to have to stand and be judged for the deeds done in our body whether good or evil, Christian doctrine ignores the fact that Paul has already taught that all judgment has already passed and been accomplished in the body of Jesus Christ.

Paul teaches this judgment in the very next verse and says therefore knowing the terror of the Lord we are trying to persuade men. Paul made it very clear regarding this judgment, that standing and being judged for your deeds whether they be good or evil is indeed a terrifying thing! The scriptures tell us that one of our benefits on this side of the cross is that we are far from terror. Now when the scriptures say we'd be far from terror, what terror would we be far from? It's not the terror from the devil that we'd be far from. We would be far from the terror of the Lord! We would never have to think that God was a terrorist any more, that we were going to be terrorized by a coming judgment. It is a terrorizing thing to stand and be judged for your deeds whether they be good or evil, especially when the sentence is death! The sentence was always death. If you failed the test to any degree, the sentence was death.

Paul said this is such a terrorizing thought and a way to live life that he was out there trying to persuade people of its fulfillment. The beautiful progression in 2 Corinthians Chapter 5 goes all the way to the point where he says "therefore if any man be in Christ he is a new creature."

Here again, please stop and examine this. I know that this is presented as "if any man, if *any* man, is in Christ." He's not saying "if you're fortunate enough to be one of those who are in Christ." He's already taught that all men are in Christ. He taught it in Philippians. He taught it in Ephesians. Paul is the one who preached this doctrine of *all* being in Christ. He is simply making the point, now if anybody is in Christ, now that I've taught you that *all* are there, if anybody's there, this is the reality. So, what Paul is saying is, "This is the reality for the entire human race." Again this *is* the ONE Man doctrine. That is why Paul was able to narrow it all down to just one person because he knew what was applicable to one was applicable to all.

This is the magnificent introduction to this thought that he's about to bring. It is such a shame that it is denigrated because of the lack of understanding within Christianity as to why it starts out this way and therefore it puts it into a questionable situation. They say, "Well, you may be in Christ or you may not." No! That is not what he's saying! He's saying if anybody's in there at all, this is a reality for EVERYBODY! This was simply Paul's teaching style, which is very evident and so crystal clear for me that it's hard to imagine anyone screwing it up this badly. He said if any man be in Christ he is a new creature. So, here is Paul trying to let us know that the entire human race was all in Christ, as he taught all went into Christ before the death of Jesus. Then when Jesus went to the cross, He drew all Jews and all Gentiles into his body in ONE man that He might make of the two, ONE NEW MAN.

Did Jesus do a complete work? Was he successful? Was it thorough? Was it scriptural? Is it restricted by our sense of justice or by our sense of righteousness? Here is where the revelation of the gospel escapes the bounds of man's imagination. The gospel is not restricted to man's definition of righteousness. The gospel is not restricted to man's definition of the scriptures, not what they actually are, nor their fulfillment. The gospel jumps outside our bounds and gives an incredible revelation of the fulfillment of all things. If it's One Man, it's all. And because of this One Man, he said if any man be in Christ he is a new creature.

Now that term "creature" in the Greek literally means "creation." Being in Christ means to be in a whole new creation. "If any man be in Christ he is a new creature. Old things are passed away, behold all things are become new." Please understand this in the context of Paul's teaching rather than in the context of Christianity's. Christian context bases their concept of righteousness on works, especially the "work" of belief. They tell you, as I was told as a young person, that if *you* are in Christ, *you* are a new creature and old things are passed away behold all things are become new. This is what convinced me I wasn't going to make it. Because they told me that everything about my former life would pass away and now that I'm a new creature that everything would become new.

This is so incredibly deadly.

Only the dishonest can survive in Christianity. An honest soul cannot survive in Christianity. The people who fall away from Christianity are not those who failed at it. The people that leave are those who are honest about the religion and themselves.

In Evangelical Christianity people give personal testimonies along these lines: "Old things passed away. I used to have dirty thoughts, I used to actually want sex, I used to be this person who used to have the propensity to lie occasionally. I used to be this person who got angry. But now I'm a new creature. All that old stuff has passed away. It's all gone." That's why I say only the dishonest can maintain the act (the façade) of Christianity. And that's just what it is: an act, a masquerade that has been perpetrated for thousands of years. It wasn't a role you signed up for. It was imposed on you and the planet. You can resign from this role. You can quit. You can put a full stop to the role and the act that you're playing because you know in your heart it is as fake and as phony as it felt from the start until the day when you decided to roll over and play dead until it's all over with. You don't have to roll over and play dead until life is over with.

You don't have to pretend that this is all working. It doesn't work and it's ok to admit it. In fact, it is the truth that it doesn't work. Know that truth! And you will see what happens when you recognize and contemplate the truth—it will make you FREE! Free from what? Free from a mentality and life of guilt and judgment, that's what!

How does it work? It works through one man becoming sin, one man taking judgment upon himself, one man, this man Jesus Christ, taking to the cross the entire creation. We have to understand that this is not a transition. This is a complete and utter death to the old and a brand-spanking new life. The man that God created in the garden is dead. The man created in the image of God no longer exists. We who were and are born on this side of the cross are not in the *image* of God. We are now all IN God!

Jesus prayed before he went to the cross, Father I pray they may be one with us, even as we are ONE. This is not a shadow of something Jesus was crossing his fingers for. This is something HE accomplished at Golgotha. That's why the law had to come as an image. The law had to come as a shadow. The law had to come as a type. All of these things had to be an image, a shadow, a type—because that was what man was, an image, and an image of God at that. God created images to relate to man. But to try to get the law to be applicable in current times after Christ's sacrifice, to be looking for prophecies yet to be fulfilled in the future, is akin to relating and looking to an image that doesn't exist anymore. It all departed the Earth in one man.

There are many brands of Christianity under the foolish notion that God's will was to "fix" man in this "new creation." Then we would be returned to living in the garden exactly the way Adam did before he sinned. That is fallacious at best. The truth is God, through the Last Adam, placed the garden in each and every one of *us*!

It is simply false to think that the work of the cross is to undo the problem and to fix the problem. The cross did not fix the problem. The cross destroyed the problem. The problem was man was made in the image of God. Adam was the problem. He was irreparable. There was only one way for God to have a creation at all. And it was to bring about the end of the world, the end of the ages, and the cataclysmic destruction of all things. He destroyed his own creation in its entirety. Christianity has missed it. The power of the revelation is that in one man all things have been destroyed and all things have been made new!

People might look at this as being way too deep, way too mysterious. However, it's really simple, as simple as the number 1. Please don't get outside the simple equation of "One." There is nothing outside of the One. At the cross is where all things were fulfilled and all things were made new. Paul said "therefore if any man be in Christ." I re-emphasize that because of the history of abuse of this verse. They put the "if" in a mode as if it were "optional." However, Paul said all were there. So, if any are there (and we know they are) this is what's true—he is a new creature; old things have passed away and all things have become new. Then he says, "And all things are of God who hath reconciled us to himself by Jesus Christ and have given unto us the ministry of reconciliation."

This verse has been twisted and distorted beyond all recognition for multiple millions of Christians throughout history and the whole world has suffered because of it.

Because of this he says, "To the wit God was in Christ reconciling the world to himself not imputing their trespasses unto them, and has committed unto us the word of reconciliation. Now then we are ambassadors for Christ as though God did beseech you by us. We pray you in Christ stead be ye reconciled to God. For he hath made him to be sin for us who knew no sin, that we might be made the righteousness of God in Christ."

Paul said "I know no man after the flesh even though we did know Christ after the flesh, but now we don't even know *him* after the flesh." And the awesome reality is Paul was talking about the Adam. When Paul called Jesus "Adam," that is the Adam he is referring to. He's saying this man no longer exists. This is where Adam died. This is where the entire human race of that day died. The entire image of God was destroyed in Christ.

Isn't it ironic and poignant that one of the commandments that God gave to the Israelites first was "thou shall have no images?" Destroy all images he told them. Don't ever have an image. Don't ever create an image. There are people in certain religions who won't even take photographs today and rightfully so. If we were trying to keep the law do you know you couldn't even have a photograph? You couldn't have a statue! You could not have an image replicating something, anything else. Built into the law is God's understanding—God's will. He knew that which was created in his image was going to have to be destroyed. There were kings who were made famous in Biblical times because they went throughout the country destroying all graven images. We have sects of Christianity today who will not allow a picture of them to be taken because they have tried to follow this one law.

It's amazing how most doctrines in Christianity are made because somebody finds a law—not because somebody finds *truth*—it's because they find a law. They preach Jesus, and then they add a law: "We can't have any pictures taken of us" for example. Then somebody else finds another law and says, "Now, everybody left *this* law out! So, we're going to focus on this law which they missed so we'll be *closer* to God and what he desires." The reality of the gospel makes you free from *all* law. You are not in the image of God. I know nobody's ever said that to you before. Christianity is trying to repair the man who was created in the image of God, trying to repair something that does not exist anymore.

Talk about "Mission Impossible!"

God destroyed that very image of himself. Why? Look at the corrupting and corroding effect that took place *in God*. God created an image of himself. What followed? God called himself jealous in the wake of that creation! Look at the problems it caused. Problems even or especially *for* God! And if God had "problems" because of it, what did that mean for his image? You've heard the saying, "if mama ain't happy, ain't nobody happy?" Well, in our example, "Daddy was not happy!" When something is in your image you feel a sense of ownership, but at the same time you have no control. Talk about frustration.

Parents taught child-rearing by Christianity are going to be especially disappointed. And it works the same way for the children. Christianity teaches that our kids are created in our image and it causes the same kind of mental instability and division for parents that we see in the scriptures.

There is only *one* resolution, answer or remedy. And the *one* resolution, answer or remedy is One. God took all things and put them all back on and in himself. He took responsibility for the whole mess. And now it's ALL hidden under the shadow of the Almighty, the cleft of the rock that we've been taken into. To the degree this understanding permeates this planet is the degree this orb is going to progressively become a better place to live.

The image was destroyed. The new creation is now not in the image of God, it's just God. Period. End of story. ALL things have been made new. We are already in the new heaven and the new Earth AND the New Jerusalem. And it's ALL in us where righteousness abides. There's the new heaven because there's no God with a reflective image on Earth any more. We are not a reflection of *anything* anymore! We are part and parcel of God himself. There's no way that a human's will and decision could have brought any of us to this point. Only the will of him who created all things could recreate all things, could have gotten the job done, complete, finished.

There have been two times when creation took place. And both took place in gardens. The first was in the Garden of Eden and the last was in the Garden of Gethsemane.

The new creation began in this garden before Jesus was crucified right near the very same location on the Mount of Olives. The new creation was about to spring forth. But for the NEW to spring forth, the OLD had to die. And die it did.

Christianity is trying to repair what they see as the damaged image of God. That might have been okay if that had been God's plan. However, God's plan was never to repair his damaged image. God's plan was to destroy the image and bring all things to ONE.

And one you are.

One we are.

One he is.

And ONE we shall forever be.

Chapter 12

Guilt Obliterated

Indianapolis.

The feelings of guilt and inner turmoil I had after the encounter with a man there were virtually indescribable. When I got back from my trip the next day, I went directly to the pastor of the church and told him I had to talk to him. I confessed that I had sinned and that the sin was of the homosexual kind.

I was removed from ministry at the church immediately.

When I went back home, I sat down and told Hazel what had happened. The guilt that surged through me was overpowering. A great deal of the anxiety, depression, and intense feelings of suicide began to come back into my soul and began to overwhelm me.

Five years after going through "deliverance" from being a homosexual, I found myself back in the mental institution again, this time for a very long stay. It was so bizarre to be back there again. Right back to the darkness—the depression was back.

Shortly thereafter I started learning and understanding the Gospel of Peace. That process would soon bring me to the Gospel of Grace as well because the two are inseparable.

I have taught on the grace of God extensively over the past few decades. Still God's grace is so vast and so endless that I haven't even scratched the surface.

There are three offences to the grace of God that are mentioned in the New Testament writings. The only person in the New Testament that teaches about offences to God's grace is Paul. John and Peter and James all taught about using the grace of God to go out and to justify committing lascivious acts. However, that was not Paul's concern. Paul *never* taught that people used God's grace to go out and do something wrong. In reality, Peter and the others were actually warning against Paul's teachings about grace. Paul did address what they were saying by responding, "That's what we are maliciously spoken of as saying."

Paul often battled the others' misunderstanding of the quotes from his own writings.

The preaching of the gospel does not demand change. Yet, the contemplation and meditation and preaching of the gospel can allow people to find the peace which resides inside each of us. Change that is attained through human effort is not change. Change that is *done to you* is perfect change. When I teach the gospel, there is no preaching that I do that encourages people to change. I encourage people to receive the gospel right where they are.

What do you have to change? Nothing. What do you have to believe? You don't have to believe anything. You just need to know what God's opinion is of you and all others. And that is the essence of the gospel. That is the power of God to the saving of the soul.

An amazing thing about having the gospel active in one's life is that we watch these incredible changes take place. Yet, there is zero emphasis of the gospel upon change for the human life. There is no requirement to change. You don't measure God's grace by measuring change in someone. We just allow God's grace to have its perfect work which it will.

We are the ones that must allow the grace of God to work its work in our hearts, impacting our souls and our lives. There's nothing you have to do to get grace to work. The gospel's power and simplicity is the extent of it. The power at work in the soul does two major things. The most important things that any human being could have developed from their heart are: 1 - the removal of all sense of guiltiness before God, and 2 - the removal of all judgment from the soul. If your morality affects your spirituality, this makes for a view of God that is very weak. Morality is variable; spirituality is absolute. We can't attach variable things to absolutes.

God's grace is not there to govern your moral behavior. Nor is your moral behavior or whatever you believe to be a morally acceptable measure of the degree of God's grace in your life. To think there is a moral standard to God's grace is a hideous thing. To believe that is to believe your or other's morality could somehow alter the grace of God.

I am well aware what people say about my teachings concerning grace. Paul reported that people of his day were saying it about him, too. So, at least I am in good company. We are accused of saying everybody ought to just go out and do whatever they want to do. I have never said that. And I will never say that connected in any way to the grace of God. The grace of God has nothing to do with morals—good ones or bad. Please remove morals from the equation. Morals are important. They just have nothing to do with the gospel. Morals are not a gospel issue. The gospel does not validate or invalidate morals. The gospel is not a way to change morals. They are two separate subjects altogether.

Of course, this rattles our religiously programmed brains. But please just stay with me.

Don't misunderstand; morality is a vital issue in society. We must discover morality. I've watched people who were raised in all kinds of families. I don't care how many children a family has; every one of the children is going to come up with his or her set of morals. However, when the grace of God does its work in the soul, no matter what your moral persuasions are, the things that you'll be relieved of more and more over time is hurting, using, and deceiving other people.

Looking back on my days of being dishonest, it was like my dishonesty had been imputed to me. It may seem like a copout, but the truth is that the religion I was in was fueled with "you've got to." You had to lie about your life if you're going to fit in the group. Morality is a very important issue and you need to establish what your morality is. But please don't think your morality is "the" standard because I guarantee you someone with higher morals is going to come along and make you look like a dirt-bag. You cannot measure up to what someone else believes to be moral. And no matter how high a person's moral standards are, a moral standard is by no means a measure of God's grace.

The measure of God's grace being active in our souls is only reflected by two things: the removal of guilt and the taking away of all judgment towards others. If I have anything in my thinking that judges somebody else's relationship with God based on their works or performance or their beliefs, then grace cannot have its perfect work. There are things that will cause the grace of God not to work in our hearts to bring about the glorious process of removing guilt from the soul. I can't even think of the term "removing guilt from the soul" without just seeing that process in my own soul. Guilt is like a cancer. Guilt eats away at the soul. It does not benefit you. This cannot be overemphasized. The only thing that will root out the "Cancer of Guilt" is the gospel of God's grace. Religion has given guilt such a place that our society honors guilt! We honor guilt being in our very souls! We respect guilt. We think that we are somehow good people because we feel guilty. What a destructive mindset! Nothing could be further from the truth, because the more guilty you feel, the more deceptive you will be. That's just a fact.

Guilt does not lead to a clean conscience. It never has. It never will. That's why the gospel of the grace of God does not resolve your guilt . . . it roots it out! It takes the whole mechanism of guilt and obliterates it! When guilt is in charge, everything that relates to the creature that no longer exists—that was done away with at the cross—is still in play. It's like trying to resolve something a dead man used to have. You are a brand new creature through Jesus Christ. Every human being is a brand new creature. They just don't know it yet. This new creature really has no place for guilt to reside. Guilt is foreign matter to the new creation—a contagion. It is a squatter. It has no legal status.

Paul aptly taught this in his letter to the Romans. The power of God's grace being in the heart roots out guiltiness from our thinking and emotions. It takes away guiltiness in total! So, how does it re-root? How does it get "downloaded" again and again? You're going to see how guiltiness stays living in the souls of those who have become Christians. If it's not a part of the new creation, then why is it in me? It is NOT a part of the new creation. It is NOT a part of what brings forth fruit. It is NOT a part of the gifts of the spirit. It is NOT a part of the fruit of the spirit. It is the total antithesis to everything that the gospel is about.

The heart is a beautiful place, but when guilt resides in the mind, the heart will never come up with a right conclusion because there is no logic to guilt. How can one feel guilt from God when no judgment from God exists any longer and hasn't in two millennia? It is not logical to emote something that does not exist! The taking away of guiltiness from our brains is the impact of the gospel. And the other measure of the evidence of the gospel's impact is the taking away of judgment for others. Guilt and judgment are the "Diabolical Duo" to the human soul.

There are always people who have been around warning about taking the grace of God too far. Incredibly, they sometimes refer to what I teach as "cheap grace." You don't need a warning about the totality and the freedom grace presents to you. There are no warnings warranted. When you hear people cautioning you about the grace of God . . . BEWARE . . . because somebody wants to control your life. Somebody wants to influence you in a way that is for their perverse benefit . . . not for yours. No telling what their motives are. There can be many motives for others trying to dilute the grace of God in your life. It could be out of their own fear that they want to manipulate you. You can find intimate relationships—husbands and wives, parents and children, etc. where an unwillingness to embrace the grace of God exists because they realize even subconsciously that their ability to control somebody else is about to leave.

It is in the absence of that control, the absence of the guilt that releases honesty from your heart to your soul. Guilt brings on control. The control brings on the lack of purity of the heart in the relationship. We become deceptive with one another. It's like you're both saying, "Just lie to me. That's all I want you to do. Just lie to me because I don't want the truth. I just want you to lie to me, because I would rather feel that I have some element of control here rather than to offer you your freedom. And that way I don't have to face myself honestly, either."

The wonderful thing you are going to find out about God's grace is that so many things just are not necessary anymore. All of the energy wasted on manipulation and control and deception are just not needed any longer. It truly is a life of freedom. So, if we are going to try to lay a foundation for this about not offending the grace of God, then the understanding of God's grace is our starting-line. God's grace is powerful. There is no end to it.

Paul's teaching about grace always compares grace to law. Grace is the *opposite* of law. Paul's teaching was profound. He said "for what the law could not do—grace has done." Anything to do with the gospel is going to come to your understanding by perceiving its opposite, its antithesis, its backdrop, or its contrast. You are never going to learn the Gospel of Grace and the Gospel of Peace without understanding the backdrop. I don't like black background, but sometimes it takes a black backdrop for what is really there to show up. That truly is the difference between law and grace. They are totally at odds with each other. For what the law could not do—grace has done.

One of the terms Paul uses in teaching about the offenses to God's grace is "Doing despite to the spirit of grace." Paul talks about this in Hebrews, but we have to set the stage that led up to that statement. Before Paul mentioned anything about "doing despite," he said "For the law having a shadow of good things to come—not the very *image* of the things—can never with those sacrifices they offered year by year continually make the comers thereunto perfect." Alright, we've got the facts and nothing but the facts. He's presenting God's law and all the things that God's law demands. And he has come up with a conclusion.

The law and all of its sacrifices were only a shadow of good things to come. The law was only a shadow. The law never had any substance to it. That's why in Hebrews it says "Now faith is the substance of things hoped for, the evidence of things not seen." We have even seen that taken out of context, because Christianity teaches people that if they have enough faith it will create substance. No, faith has already become the substance of things hoped for—the things that were a shadow of the real thing. Faith has presented us with the substance of things hoped for, the evidence of things not seen. But we see clearly now. Paul says this is no longer a mystery. They have come into focus. When Hebrews is talking about faith being the substance of things hoped for and the evidence of things not seen, he's not talking about *your* faith. He's not talking about your circumstances. He is talking about the substance of identity. He's talking about the substance of who we have become in Jesus—our substantive identity in Christ—our oneness brought to us by the "faith of Christ."

So, the law was only a shadow of good things, and not the very image of the things. Whenever you hear ANYTHING about the law, regardless of what it is, the very next thought you should learn to think should be . . ."and that can NEVER get me anything with God!"

The law never, even with its ancient animal sacrifices, ever caused the participant to be perfect.

Not being perfect in the eyes of God . . . you can call that hell. You and God are not *one* if you are not perfect. God's standard is, and always has been, perfection. Period. God cannot embrace anything that is not absolute perfection. This is what the law proved; that God could not embrace anything that smacked of imperfection. The demand was for perfection. God did not lower his demand for perfection by giving us Jesus—far from it. God fulfilled his standard of perfection in Christ and by Christ and by him *alone*.

In Matthew Chapter 5, Jesus made it very clear. You are going to have to be as perfect as, well, as perfect as your Father which is in heaven. Who do you think Jesus might have been talking about there? You and he know it wasn't about you or about us. The law and the scriptures demand perfection, but the only way we can have perfection is if our sacrifice is perfect and if our High Priest is perfect. That is the only way to perfection. It is not our process. It is solely God's process. And thank God for it. He chose Jesus to be our perfect sacrifice and our perfect High Priest.

We were never, and are never, part of the process or the equation.

Paul said "For then would they have not ceased to be offered?" What is the first sign that perfection has been achieved? Sacrifices have stopped!

If the sacrifice worked, then it would mean perfection was attained because the worshippers, once purged, should have had no more conscience of sin. What is the very first indication that you know you've been made perfect? No more consciousness of sin. Did Israel continue to contemplate sin? Yes, they did! Why? Because the blood of bulls and goats was a stop-gap measure meant as a foreshadowing. And it certainly is not a "blueprint" (as Christianity describes it) for life in the 21st century.

Are we really perfect now?

First of all, let us rehearse "What the law can't do . . . grace did." What the sacrifices can't do—if they can't make you perfect—the body of Jesus Christ did. The one thing the law could not do is free the conscience from sin. Under the law there is a consciousness of sins. Paul says, "For in those sacrifices there's a remembrance again made of sins every year." I would have rather been Jewish getting to offer a goat for my sins than to be a Christian. At least Jewish people in scriptural days could completely forget about their sins for a whole year! Christians are supposed to repent every single blooming time they "sin!"

The blood of the Old Testament sacrificial system cannot take away sins but the blood of Jesus has taken away sin forever!

Hallelujah!

The law—the blood of bulls and goats—cannot take away sins, but the blood of Jesus has taken away sin in its totality. Talk about a better covenant. For perfection to come, sin had to be obliterated. Sin had to be done away with. What does that mean for us humans? No more consciousness of sins. Under the Old Covenant there's sin consciousness. Under the New Covenant there's no consciousness of sin. Under the Old Covenant there's a remembrance of sin. Under the New Covenant there is no remembrance of sin. The First Covenant can't take away sin. The Second Covenant did!

This was and is all the will of God. We are now rightly dividing the word of truth. God's will was not completed in the Old Testament. His will was *completely* fulfilled under the Second Covenant in Jesus Christ.

Do you ever find yourself wondering what God's will is? You, and the rest of the world can stop wondering and trying to decipher what is God's will. God's will *is* Jesus Christ. It's a very good will. And it's very good news.

Under the First Covenant there is no sanctification. With the Second Covenant there is complete sanctification. Under the First, there is no perfection. With the Second, absolute perfection resides.

Whoa! I'm reeling. I don't know about you but I'm absolutely reeling. I feel like I'm having one of Paul's euphoric moments . . ."Oh, the goodness of the grace of God! His wisdom is unsearchable!"

So, when it comes to doing despite (insult) to the spirit of grace, Paul is speaking in these terms: Once a human being is completely cleansed of all sin through the work and faith *of* Christ, and then you believe by doing something you have to go back and re-implement the blood of Christ or the sacrifice of Christ, or repent for something that does not exist in the sight of God, then you are doing despite to or insulting the spirit of grace. You are counting the blood of the covenant by which we *were* sanctified as an unholy thing.

The grace of God again is not something that we find. It is something that has found us. This first offense is one the Christian world needs to stop and take notice of. They need to repent! They need to change their minds!

Catholicism and Protestantism definitely insult the spirit of grace. Any time when believing that you have done something wrong, that you confess or re-apply the blood over again, thinking that that is going to re-justify you again or bring you back into relationship with God—you are insulting, doing despite to, the spirit of grace. It is this process of guilt and contrition that brings on more self-righteousness and more guilt and more control. What a vicious cycle! To think that grace is something that causes you to have the availability to apply the blood of Christ at your own whim, that is an offence to the spirit of grace. The grace of God is what has caused the blood of Christ to be shed for us, to do away with all sin forever. The "confession of sin," to hope to be forgiven all over again, is offensive and rude to the spirit of grace.

I stopped confessing sin a long time ago. Why? Because it's an affront to the grace of God, that is why. Confession is like saying that the blood of Jesus was less powerful than the blood of a goat! I can't do it anymore. Being taught all the things that I was taught about un-confessed sin, it certainly was not a light matter for me. Like so many of you, confession of sin was like drinking and eating. It was part of daily life. It was like taking in air and exhaling. To stop the habit of confession was like forcing me to stop breathing because I thought it was my life-support system. What I did not know was that in reality it was a death-support system! It was death to my soul to rob it of the pure revelation of the power of the work of the cross.

It was not a quick process to come to the point where I did away with the confession of sin when I realized it was offensive to God's grace. I didn't understand these teachings in the concise way you are reading about them now. It took time. However, over time it really did become very clear to me that my confession of sin was something very unhealthy spiritually speaking. It was a death sentence for my soul. I was perpetually living on a spiritual and emotional death row. It was a sign of unbelief, for goodness sake! It was my not believing the efficacy and all sufficiency of the work of Christ and his cross. You're not going to hear that in too many places. The confession of sin is a sign of unbelief? That is exactly what it is! It is a sign of unbelief and an act of unbelief and self-righteousness. It is like filthy rags to God who demanded and fulfilled perfection. It is an out and out act of unbelief to have to confess sin or resolve sin in any manner between you and God since the cross.

One of the major thrusts of my teaching and the Gospel Revolution is to see an end to insulting the spirit of grace. Stop thinking there is any application *we* can make of the blood of Christ. A human being *cannot* apply the blood. It is *God* who has applied the blood. Please stop making Adam's mistake over again by trying to be *like* God. *God* has applied the blood to our lives. *We* do not apply the blood to our own lives. It is God himself who has given his own Son and has redeemed us through the power of his blood from the condition of sin and from the transgression of the law.

All humanity has been completely redeemed! Glory to *his* name!

I call upon the entire Christian world to repent and stop insulting the spirit of grace. It is my dream. It is my dream to stop the persecution of lies imposed by the religious world upon people that lead them to guilt themselves into all kinds of self-deprecating acts. All kinds of visions come to my mind. I see young people and old people in confession booths. I see people at "altars" in churches. I see people crying and weeping and asking God once again to forgive them of their sins over and over and over again. Paul is "rolling in his grave" seeing these images, too, as all of Christendom is "doing despite to the spirit of grace."

Once the mind grasps this, the offense becomes so obvious and so heinous because the heart has been freed by the work of grace. Paul drove the point home, as he always did, through comparison. He said, "He that despises Moses law died without mercy under two or three witnesses." It was not I who said that. Paul said this is the law and that this is the conclusion of the First Covenant and the first sacrifices that sin was under. It is Paul who said this is the Mosaic law and this is the first sacrifice. He did not say that this is what happens under the blood of Jesus. He said this is what happens with the blood of bulls and goats. He said, "How dare you bring that faulty understanding into the last sacrifice, the Son of God, who has perfected us once and for all, and dragged that damnable heresy of sin into the consciousness of the minds of people who have clean escaped away from all of this stuff?" He is now talking about the New Covenant. "How much sorer punishment suppose ye should he be thought worthy"? He's told us how harsh this was under the Old Covenant of the law. Basically, Paul is saying, if you don't leave that mindset behind, you are in effect saying that things are *worse* under Jesus! If we "suppose" with such a mindset, the only conclusion a law-based and law-controlled worshipper can logically come to is that Jesus is going to punish us *even worse*!

Paul has given an opinion in his letter to these Hebrews. He's basically saying that, in his opinion, somebody who does this to the grace of God ought to have the crap beat out of them even worse than they did under the law! To take the grace of God and reduce it to the blood of animals, and to laws and rules and regulations; how much sorer punishment should he be thought worthy? Not to worry, though, there is NO sin under this covenant! Paul is only supposing, according to the mindsets of these Hebrew believers in Jesus. He says "Of how much sorer punishment suppose ye, should he be thought worthy who hath trodden underfoot the Son of God, and hath counted the blood of the covenant wherewith he WAS sanctified, an

UNHOLY thing." Do you understand the finality and the past tense that Paul uses?

How do you count the blood of the covenant wherewith you were sanctified as an unholy thing and do despite to the spirit of grace? Let me tell you the number one way: continue to confess your sins! You will continue to insult the spirit of God's grace. Think that you have to re-up, re-ante over and over again, re-apply the blood, re-do the blood, ask forgiveness over and over, make confession over and over and you will be insulting the spirit of grace. Now in that kind of insane atmosphere of obsessing over something that does not exist, do you think that grace can have its perfect work in your soul? It cannot! Can grace take out of a man's soul his guilt, when that man is persuaded of such irrational thinking? No. His progress is brought to a standstill.

To do despite to the spirit of grace is literally saying that I have to do the same with the blood of Jesus that they did with the blood of animals—only more so! God forbid! Don't mix the blood of Jesus with the blood of goats.

You may ask, "Well Mike, are you sure about the separation of law and grace?" I'm as sure of law and grace being as separate as the blood of goats and the blood of Jesus! Do you think we need just a *drop* of the blood of a goat to mingle with the blood of Jesus? Do you think we need just a little law to go along with grace, for morality's sake? How sickening is that?! I am revolted by the thought of taking a drop of the blood of a goat and adding it to the blood of Jesus. To somehow give credence and validity to the blood of a goat, are you kidding me? Thank God for the blood of the goat and thank God for the law. They did their work and they are dead and gone.

Why does Christianity keep resurrecting an old system when the world has a resurrected Savior? Why? If they stop, they know they lose all power, all credibility, all ability to control people's wealth and lives. They know their jig would be up.

There are times I feel inadequate to communicate this message in order to be clearly evident to open minds. We must rely on the Holy

Spirit as the Great Teacher as he resides within us all to bring these concepts forward because these are not concepts created by man. These are concepts of God. God himself needs to bring the clarity. As he does, it becomes oh so clear.

The blood of the goat needing *repetition* is what gives us the clarity about the blood of Jesus *never needing repetition*. It is truly finished.

Another way that the spirit of grace is insulted is by not accepting God's perfection.

God's will is perfection. The sacrifice of Jesus is all-sufficient. When Paul says, and he's quoting the scripture of Psalm 40: "Sacrifices and offerings, burnt offerings for sin thou wouldst not, neither hast thou pleasure in them which were OFFERED BY THE LAW," he is saying the law never produced anything. Why then would we now, under the blood of Jesus, be looking to the law to give us something? After all, it never gave anybody anything when it was in force! These sacrifices were by the law, but Paul says, "Then saith he, Lo I come to do thy will O God. He taketh away the first that he may establish the second."

How many times have I heard, "Mike Williams, how dare you have the audacity to say that the will of God is complete?"

I didn't say it. Paul did! Paul said that God took away the first and established the second—that *that* is the will of God! It's done. It's a brick wall!

You cannot carry the issue of the will of God past the cross. It's too big. It's too exhausting. AND it's already complete! If you continue to wonder what the will of God is for your respective life, it is going to befuddle your life. At best, you're going to be someone who's indecisive. At worst, you will be completely paralyzed.

So, you ask, how do I do this? How do I change my mind about the will of God being something to be strived for in my life to the understanding that the will of God was, is, and will forever be Jesus Christ? Just simply move forward. If I did it, you can for sure! I stepped out and I'm calling you to step out, too. I'm calling you to come into a life of freedom away from the absolute lunacy Christianity is force-feeding you.

The gospel and Christianity are opposing forces.

During the first years in ministry, I preached "Christianity." I did not preach "the gospel."

Christianity presents an intricate, detailed, explanation of why Jesus really never succeeded. It is still so muddled with law and grace that the statement Jesus made to those Jews in his day is applicable now: "You have a fine way of setting aside the commands of God and getting around the truth." Christianity is the perfect demonstration of the absolute ignorance of the will of God and the gospel. It is a mixing and continuation of the Old Covenant. There is no greater abomination on the face of the Earth detailing an absolute ignorance of the gospel than the religion of Christianity.

Now one might say, it's got to be Islam or Hinduism or Buddhism or one of the other "isms" that is the most offensive to Christ and his cross. No they are not. And here's why—the only religion that attempts to embrace Christ as Savior is Christianity. And then it systematically and categorically undoes the power of the cross, the power of God's grace, and the power of God—the gospel. That's right. You read it correctly. The power of God *can* be undone. Where can it be undone? It occurs in the same place where the power of God, the gospel, is *done*—in our brains, in our thinking, in our emotions, in our souls.

No other religion does that. All the other religions Christianity accuses of leading people to hell are not guilty of committing this grievous manipulation against the grace of God and people's ability to experience the freedom of their souls. They don't get to experience the freedom from the guilt of thinking they are somehow separated from their Father.

This is how powerful the grace of God Paul was presenting truly is—that even the people in religion who do despite to the Spirit of grace will never suffer for doing so.

Chapter 13

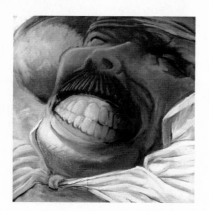

The Root of Bitterness

I returned from the mental institution to Hazel and our girls in the throes of severe depression. Let me explain.

One thing we always should remember about the word "gospel" is that it means "good news." In my own journey of struggling to come to terms with the contradictions in my life, I had to deal with the things I myself was disapproving of, let alone what I thought God and society disapproved of. It's one thing to believe God and society looks down on you but add that to self-hatred and you've got a recipe for some serious strong mental and emotional despair, to say the least. Good news is needed. A sense of God's approval had yet remained elusive to me, even though I had sought it so intensely.

Despair was an understatement about my condition when I got back home from the hospital. I even started smoking again. Unsure of everything, especially of myself, feeling so desperate, so lonely, so isolated, in such a state of mental and emotional turmoil; suicide was a serious consideration for me once again. Medicated for the depression, I once again was experiencing the cotton mouth, the inability to sleep, and the huge appetite that it created.

I was sitting there in the living room of our home. I was always up very late during those first few weeks back. All of the lights in the house were off. There was no sound, no music, no television, nothing. It was just me sitting in a chair with only the glow of my cigarette cutting through the darkness. As I sat there, the experience of my so-called "deliverance," my love for God, and my efforts not to be gay swirled around my head. My marriage, my daughters, and my "moral" failure in Indiana and the disappointment I had brought to everyone around me weighed heavily on me. I sat there all by myself. Every draw of the cigarette brought the only temporary light in the room. My mind drifted toward talking again to God. After repenting from that "sin" those few short months before, I had not even made an attempt to talk to God again. I realized I had emotions I just couldn't express.

What I had been taught to do was to surrender absolute control of my life over to God, and to the Holy Spirit, and to Jesus—which I had done or at least thought I had done. I did it anew every morning of my life. I gave the Holy Spirit control over my life. When this happened it was difficult for me to even take full responsibility for what I had done because I had honestly and earnestly given full control to God. I had trusted him to guide me, to direct my path. "Lord, light my path"!

I felt betrayed. I felt very much betrayed by Jesus himself.

As I sat there I actually began to mutter a prayer. I tried to explain to Jesus why I felt the way I felt, why I was about to say what I was going to say, and apologizing to him for what I was about to say. I halted and I kept trying to approach the moment when I would actually know the next thing to say. I opened my mouth and it just wouldn't come out. I knew, though, that it needed to.

Finally, I opened my mouth and these words came out: "Jesus, I do not trust you anymore."

I felt absolute death inside. I now know this feeling of death did not come from either God or the devil. I had been conditioned by my religious upbringing and by my Christianity. However, one thing not imposed on me nor instructed to me was to be honest with Jesus and to tell him how I actually felt. I thought, "I don't know what's going to happen when I tell Jesus I don't trust him." I knew what was supposed to happen when I told him I loved him. I knew what was supposed to happen when I told him I had faith in him. But now I was about to tell him "I don't trust you anymore." Nobody had taught a class on that. Nobody had said, "This is what happens when you tell Jesus you don't trust him. This is what happens when you're honest with yourself and with God."

So the words finally came out.

Every expectation I had about uttering them was a negative one. I don't know what it was I was expecting to happen once I said, "Jesus, I don't trust you anymore," but it surely didn't have a positive connotation to it in any way. Once those words came out of my mouth "Jesus, I do not trust you anymore" a sense of peace began to come over me and an awareness of God's love and his acceptance hit me. My mind almost went "tilt" because I was doing just the opposite of what I was taught I had to do to have "the presence of God,"—his love and peace to be experienced in a manifested way. I was not expressing how much I loved and trusted and had committed myself to him. I was telling God how disappointed I was in him, that he had failed me. But out of me expressing I did not trust him anymore, this incredible sense of peace and awareness that I was loved and that God cared for me began to flood my soul.

I sat there for quite some time astonished by what was going on. I put my cigarette out. I never had another smoke. I simply sat there with everything that I needed emotionally and mentally. All this came to me not after praying or worshipping or studying my Bible. This incredible sense of God came to my soul after expressing I did not trust Jesus.

It was from that point I learned the most important thing about spirituality and the most important thing about "a spiritual walk."

You accept where you are because where you are is where God is.

As long as you are in denial of where you are in reality, you cannot experience the sense of knowing you and God are one. It really doesn't matter where you are, because that is where God is. It's important that you come to that point of truth with yourself. King David said it this way, "Even if I make my bed in hell he is there."

I began to understand how I could experience this sense of peace but experience it outside of the Christian formula. It's a very powerful concept and one of the greatest teachings we can receive.

God is with us at all times. No matter what we're thinking or not thinking, no matter what we're doing or not doing, God is always inside all of us. We might not "be" with ourselves, especially if we don't or can't acknowledge where and what we actually are—holy, perfect, and righteous through the grace of God. It's at this point where it becomes harder and harder to know God and we are one. This is really what being "lost" is about. When you don't know who you are or where you are in truth.

The Apostle Paul had a concern that anyone should "fail of" the grace of God. He wrote about this in his letter to the Hebrews which is where we found him writing about doing despite to the spirit of grace in Chapter 10. In Chapter 12, Paul spoke about how they could *fail of* the grace of God. Paul brought it right down to its most elementary terms. He warned that if we still believe that there is something happening personally, individually, or any place on the face of Earth where God is punishing people after everything done at the cross, that *we should walk away from this*.

What Paul was making reference to was the root of bitterness. In religious circles the root of bitterness has been addressed regarding one's relationship with your mom or your dad or your son or daughter.

Or perhaps you've got a root of bitterness against a pastor. However, none of these things are applicable to Paul's teaching. Paul was speaking about a mindset which believes something happening to you or someone else was a chastening or scourging coming from God. He warned to be careful about thinking that way because in reality the root of bitterness is not against *someone else*. The root of bitterness is against *God* himself. And when that root takes hold, bitterness can spring up, defiling many. Now, it certainly has done that! I'm not theorizing about something that *could* happen. This is something that has already manifestly happened! A root of bitterness *has* sprung up. A root of bitterness *has* defiled many, and thereby *many have failed* of the grace of God.

This doesn't mean the grace of God has failed *them* or anyone. Paul's concern was with thinking something went down in your life as a result of a chastening or scourging or punishment from God. He said it would cause bitterness to come up in your heart against God himself and therefore would cause you to fail of the grace of God. You can fail of the grace that was perfectly provided for you by the finished work of the cross. And what a shame that is.

Isaiah said, "And the work of righteousness shall be peace. And the effect of righteousness shall be quietness and assurance forever." The entire Gospel of Peace is in this verse! The work of righteousness is the cross. That was when God made righteousness an imputed and imposed fact for the entire world. God did this. This is not what man has done or chose to believe, but rather what God has done as an accomplished fact. "And the work of righteousness shall be peace." The result of that work of righteousness was the declaration of peace. God made everyone righteous. God did not and could not declare peace with an unrighteous group of people. God did not say, "I give up on you. I'm just going to declare peace with you, anyways. You're all hopeless!" No. The reason God declared peace and could declare it is because he found us all righteous in his Son Jesus Christ. There was nothing and nobody to be angry with anymore. God had completely destroyed and removed sin off the Earth and established righteousness forever here on this planet. Therefore, the result of righteousness would be peace. Isaiah prophesied it. And Isaiah was a true prophet.

Righteousness was imputed by God to the entire human race after the cross, just as he had previously imputed sin to the whole of humanity after the Garden of Eden debacle. We were righteous even before we ever accepted our God-given status. Our belief did not put the righteousness there. Our belief had nothing at all to do with it. The righteousness is already present. Our awareness of it—*this* is what makes us believers. Our belief does not make us a part of this covenant. It's simply ridiculous to include man in the process of getting righteousness from heaven to Earth when God sent his own Son to accomplish that. And, of course, God is the One who did it all! It is fallacious to include ourselves in the wonderful equation of "One." It is and always has been about One Man. God declared peace because righteousness was imputed. The refusal to acknowledge the forever-established peace *is* an offense to grace. The writer of Hebrews says that is to fail of the grace of God. He said, "Looking diligently lest any man fail of the grace of God, lest any root of bitterness springing up trouble you, and thereby many be defiled."

Defiled in what? They're defiled in their own thinking, certainly not in God's view and opinion of them.

The term "to fail of the grace of God" simply means "to be deficient." You see, you should not be deficient of the grace of God. The other term in the definition means "to be inferior." You should never find yourself or anyone else in a position or an attitude of inferiority in any situation. We stand firmly in the gospel and the righteousness bestowed upon us by an act of God through the work of Jesus Christ. That glorious accomplishment is bereft of human belief, obedience, and involvement. The only thing we have to do with this is having it revealed to us. That reality is what can make a real believer out of me and anyone else. However, the process of believing does not constitute righteousness. Righteousness constitutes belief. The Christian doctrine of having to believe is so full of holes and leaves Jesus as such a pathetic creature it boggles the mind.

So if there is a deficiency in your own understanding about God's grace, if there's something there that brings God's grace to an inferior point in your thinking, we can see exactly what Paul means regarding this "deficiency," this "inferiority," this "failing of the grace of God."

Many Christian speakers teach on "the root of bitterness." They teach it regarding your relationship with other humans. They condemn people about it regarding their relationships with their boss or co-workers. They teach it about every possible relationship except the one actually being addressed here! This is not talking about a relationship with your dog, or your cat, or your mom, or your dad, or your brother, or your sister, or any human being or any other thing! This is talking about your relationship with God. It is directly referencing the grace of God and its implications with you and every person.

I can take you back through the entire scriptures and show you time after time where punishing God's children only made things worse. In fact, in the prophecies of Isaiah God spoke to Israel and said, "Why should I beat you up again? Why should I punish you again? Every time I punish you, you just get worse and worse." In fact, not only did they get worse, once the judgment was over, these people were ticked off at God. Sure they did their obligatory bow down and worship and asked forgiveness, etc. But after each judgment a root of bitterness sprung up. They were bitter against God. They were defiant against the one who they perceived was punishing them.

Chastisement does not correct anybody in their relationship to God. Man cannot live under the fear and the dread of a chastising, punishing, correcting God. We must understand that ALL of this took place at the cross—the chastening, the scourging. You may say, "How can you include chastisement in the equation?" Isaiah says, that "the chastisement of our peace was upon him." Why we drag chastisement into the New Covenant is just beyond me and certainly was beyond Paul. It may simply be because Hebrews Chapter 12 is regularly taught out of context by Christian leaders. The writer says, "Follow peace with all men and holiness, without which no man shall see the Lord." We can however do this when we realize what Paul was saying about chastisement, "whereof ALL are partakers," in Christ Jesus at the cross. No one is a "bastard." Paul is stepping into the mindset of a Hebrew and attempting to uproot the thought that one could somehow be left outside the work of the cross. Again, without holiness no one will see the Lord, and thank God for Jesus Christ, who was chastised and made us to be partakers so we can share in his holiness!

I totally agree! Christianity disagrees. They teach we get to holiness through our faith or belief and our works and our consecration, which they say should correspond with that "change of heart." Christian doctrine says holiness comes by what you do. I'll side with the prophets—holiness came through the blood of Jesus Christ.

We are not holy through our own works. We are holy through the power of the work of Jesus. Our belief does not get this holiness in us. The work of the cross got his holiness in us. How hard is this? We become believers because of the reality of our already=finished, imputed holiness. Paul says, "Looking diligently lest any man should fail of the grace of God, lest any root of bitterness springing up trouble you and thereby defile many."

How would "many" be defiled? We're defiled by living in a world that believes in any coming judgment, that's how. Looking at Hebrews 12, we can see Paul's warning when he said to "consider him who endured such contradiction from sinners, lest we grow weary and faint in our minds." We are walking around in a world full of people who sense separation between God and man. This is such an intense contradiction to the gospel, that we can easily grow weary in our minds, doubting the finished work of the cross and failing of the grace of God. Consider Jesus, who, as we dealt with earlier, maintained his identity as a son who was well-pleasing to the Father. And remember, in case you feel like you are bordering on blasphemy, that Jesus is NOT ASHAMED to call us brethren. When we consider him, we are realizing that we have been placed in the exact position as Jesus, as well-pleasing sons of God, as a pure gift. No judgment or chastisement needs to happen to make this so . . . because it already happened in its fullness!

Do you know that people look to you whether you realize it or like it or not. Everyone around you thinks they are less than what they actually are. People often think you are the one that's got it all together. Yet, I know you often think they are the ones who've got it all together, but that's what self-righteousness does. Self-righteousness causes us to constantly act like we're making up for a deficit while we all believe that the other people are better than we are, which never creates anything good relationally. Thereby, many are defiled. When my life becomes oppressed with anger toward God, then there's something about the gospel I don't understand yet.

Hebrews also says, "lest there be any fornicator or profane person as Esau who for one morsel of meat sold his birthright." Oh, you've got to understand what you've got or you'll give it away real easy! He goes on to say, "For you know that after that he would have inherited a blessing he was rejected because he found no place of repentance though he sought it carefully with tears." This isn't saying that this is what's going to happen to you; that you are going to find no place of repentance. He's showing you the power of being persuaded by something that's incorrect and how easily you will give up what you've got if you don't know what you have. Esau travelled down that road and we can all relate.

Esau did not know what he had. Please don't think the story of Esau is something it's not. It's not a story that you read and think, "well, if I'm like Esau then I will not get an inheritance into the Kingdom of God." These types and shadows are good for our instruction in righteousness. And we know who's righteousness we are talking about; it can only be God's. Therefore, as we receive the instruction about his righteousness from the sign/symbol of Esau, we are no longer in danger of "old garment" thinking. The reference to Esau being "profane" is trying to instruct us to *know* we are sacred, that we are not "godless." Along with so much of Paul's writing, it is teaching us not to abandon our incredible birthright for the mere "morsel of meat" that is Christianity or any religion or hollow philosophy, all things which are destined to "perish with use." It becomes so clear to us: we don't have to seek what we already have. Can we not see how this and countless other passages and verses in the Bible, as understood by Christianity, have tried to sew an old garment onto the new fabric, or new creation, that we already are? Both have been ruined for too long.

Moving on in that same Chapter 12 of Hebrews, "for you are not come unto the mount that might be touched and that burned with fire, nor unto blackness, and darkness, and tempest and the sound of a trumpet." The sound of a trumpet he is speaking of is that one long loud blast which signified judgment was coming. But Paul is saying you have not come unto that mountain. You have not come to the sound of the trumpet of judgment. All of Christianity is still teaching there's a trumpet sound we are waiting for. The fulfillment of the trumpets as prophesied in the scriptures happened 2,000 years ago! As we now know, the Son of God fulfilled the feast of trumpets like he said he would, like all scripture. You can read it for yourself and see! Go ahead, search the scriptures! You will find them just as Jesus said you would, speaking about HIM!

What else is said about what we are "not come unto?" Paul is referring to how Moses described this dreadful place: "You have not come to the sound of the trumpet and the voice of words, which they that heard, entreated that the words should not be spoken to them anymore for they could not endure that which was commanded. And if so much as a beast touched the mountain it should be stoned or thrust through with a dart, and so terrible was the sight" said Moses, "that I exceedingly fear and quake."

You have not come to *this* mountain where judgment lives. You've not come to this mountain where they waited for the sound of the trumpet of judgment. Can you imagine the dreaded sound of that trumpet sounding for judgment? You've not come to that mountain and you cannot. That mountain was cast into the sea of God's forgetfulness forever by the faith *of* Christ! You've not come to commandments and rules nobody can endure. Why is he going into great detail like this after saying "look diligently lest any man fail of the grace of God lest a root of bitterness springing up trouble you and thereby many be defiled." Why is he going into such detail? This is where the root of bitterness comes from, that's why!

If you do not understand, "this is *not* what you've come to," just drop back a moment. If you fear any judgment whatsoever, you're at the wrong mountain in your mind. People who believe there's a judgment still coming are dealing with an external kingdom, an external mountain, a physical mountain, and these are not the things that we are approaching any more. Those things happened in the scriptures. And the scriptures have been utterly and completely fulfilled in Christ. Again, that mountain was cast into the sea, into God's sea of forgetfulness through the One who had THE faith of a grain of a mustard seed in order to do it!!! How cool is that?! So, don't fear, but rejoice, when you see in the book of Revelation a big mountain all aflame being tossed into the sea!

We have a great hope. Are you hoping the writer of Hebrews is going to tell us what we have come to? Well, you're in luck—he does. He says, "But you are come unto Mt Zion, the city of the living God, the heavenly Jerusalem." These are all untouchable things, spiritual constructs. He goes on: "and to an innumerable company of angels, and to the general assembly and church of the firstborn which are written in heaven, and to God the judge of all, and to the spirits of just men made perfect."

Perfection needs no judgment. Perfection needs no chastisement. Perfection is, well, perfect. He goes on to say, "and to Jesus Christ the mediator of the new covenant, and to the blood of sprinkling, that speaketh better things than that of Abel." Whatever your background, whatever you've been taught, don't allow the Christian religion and its twisted interpretations and self-serving doctrines to steal the gospel from your mind and therefore your life and reality. When they begin to preach judgment and say there's a judgment coming to your life, your country or to the Earth as a whole, that there's some judgment unfulfilled, or that "chastisement isn't judgment, chastisement is the way of correction" . . . ask yourself, "what are they talking about?" The book of Hebrews speaks of "chastening and scourging." These people go into Hebrews and try to surgically remove the term "chastisement" out of these writings and make the claim that "chastisement isn't a judgment! Chastisement is just a correction." Let's deal with "scourging" then. It says "chastening" and "scourging." God chastens and scourges. The term scourge means to beat to pieces, to rip to shreds. Facts are stubborn things. To be consistent, if you believe that God is chastising you, you've got to believe he's scourging you, too.

How many sons did he receive? He only received ONE. You say "But what about us?" We are ALL in HIM! We all were partakers of this chastening in Christ. "For if you endure chastening, God dealeth with you as sons, for what son is he that the father chasteneth not. But if ye be without chastisement whereof all are partakers, then are ye bastards and not sons." For you to try to be a son on your own in your own works or faith is akin to being a bastard. The only way you can be a son and not a bastard is not because you have gone through your own chastisement but because of the fact that Jesus was chastised and scourged for us. As Paul says, "No chastening for the present seems to be joyous but grievous; nevertheless afterward it yields the peaceable fruit of righteousness." And, righteousness his chastening did yield!

In light of this statement of Paul's, how wonderfully consistent it is that the Bible reports Jesus endured the cross, despising the shame, for the joy that was set before him? There was no joy when he took *our* chastisement and scourging. Oh, but the joy that was set before him after the fact!

There is no chastening and scourging that results in righteousness other than the one Jesus endured and was victorious over. Please do not insult the blood of Jesus Christ by saying that God's chastening of you makes you righteous or more pure in his sight. That's like saying that God's punishment of you for sin brings more righteousness your way. To say one is being punished for sins is an insult to God's grace. The punishment for our sin was ALL and COMPLETELY on Jesus. So, too, was the chastisement for our falling short of the glory of God. It was ALL through him and by him.

To remove the term "chastisement" from its unity with the term "scourging" creates a doctrine keeping people subservient to pastors, elders, bishops, priests, and deacons, when in fact we are equal to all of them and subject to none. To tell people when things go wrong, "Oh that's God chastising you or correcting you" is the height of ignorance, hypocrisy, and manipulation. We need to grow up in the Lord in our own selves and not rely on anybody else to be your supplier of anything else other than what Jesus Christ provided for all. I'm not supplying you with anything. I'm telling you what you've been supplied with! I'm not the supplier. He is the supplier.

You've been fully supplied, fully equipped. You've been supplied so fully and completely that God says, "You're perfect." You have come to perfection! Or perhaps even better said, perfection has come to you! Please let that sink in, and let yourself soak in that transforming thought. That's what you've come to: "to the spirits of just men made perfect." Perfect. It bears repeating yet again. YOU are perfect because Jesus became the Perfect High Priest and became the Perfect Sacrifice, resulting in a perfected people.

What can you, I, or anyone else do to add or detract from that perfection?

The perfection of this magnificent work being trampled in the mud of Christianity while people build organizations to provide themselves with lavish livings is an outrage, keeping you in a guilty conscience and thinking sin is still an issue between you and God, and confused about coming judgment and chastisement and correction from God, is despicable. It is an unparalleled human disaster. So much human misery and tragedy has sprung from it. And it is high time for it to cease on this planet forever.

Correction comes from your own heart because that's exactly where God resides. That's where the Kingdom of God exists. That's the heavenly Jerusalem. You can't touch it. You can't feel it. You can't see it. But as sure as you have breath, you have it. You can know you've got it. And you can know the Kingdom of God and the New Jerusalem and the New Heaven and the New Earth is not something to come. It's something already living in you and ALL people.

No half-hearted work has been done in resolving sin. We are not left having to confess sins that don't exist in the mind of the Almighty. There is no half-finished work of judgment leaving us waiting until we get chastised again, waiting for another judgment on the Earth. It would be tantamount to waiting for another cross!

No! We will no longer sit idly by and allow the finished work of Christ and his magnificent accomplishment to be disrespected and misrepresented by a corrupt clergy and the centuries-old institutions comprised to continue to prop them up.

I so desire for your heart to be released and your soul to be healed from any persuasion, of any preacher, in any form of Christianity, which has taught you God was chastening or scourging you or teaching you a lesson through tragic circumstances. They do not have the audacity to add "scourge" to "chastisement" in the way God might punish you. However, they do have the audacity to separate "scourge" from "chastisement" and concoct a diabolical doctrine to keep you under their ignorant thumbs.

"Lift up the hands that hang down"!

You don't have to have a root of bitterness towards God. Lift up the hands that are hanging down; help strengthen the feeble knees.

How can one fail of the grace of God? Simply just by giving up—that's how. You see, you cannot embrace a chastening and scourging and judgment of God while simultaneously soaking mentally and emotionally in the grace of God. These concepts are directly opposed to each other. Trying to embrace one will cause you to *fail of* the other.

I teach the grace of God so that people will fail of the *judgment* and *chastisement* of God. When you fail of the chastening of the Lord, what are you left with? The grace of God in all its loving fullness!

How great is it to fail at something that no longer is here? And then only to be reminded of the only thing which remains: God's unconditional love, acceptance, and favor—his grace—for all humanity?

Merciful God, it is so great!

Chapter 14

Stand Fast

My transition from the Christian sect I was immersed in, the Word of Faith movement, to my coming into an understanding of the gospel, was quite the process to say the least. It was a slow trek, day by day, week by week, month by month, and year by year. While it was slow, it was also sure.

The gospel in my heart began being embraced by my soul. I was making my best effort to let go of the false doctrines and the other misplaced, misused and misinterpreted Bible verses which had messed with my head for so long.

As I began sharing these things I was learning and beginning to understand, pastors started getting upset at me. Really upset. They reported back to my mentor Norvel Hayes about me and what I was saying. A wedge began to form between Norvel and me. This was tough for me because I relied on my relationship with Norvel a great deal. My desire to make sure that I did what he wanted me to do was very real.

Norvel was seemingly always pleased with what I did and how I was doing it. He constantly was comparing me to everybody else on the ministry team. "If they could only do it as well as Mike did," he'd say, "then everything would be fine." So, I was always being compared to others. By virtue of that, I was not liked a whole lot because I was the "favorite son." I was presented by Norvel to his audiences frequently.

When the challenge about me by some pastors first arose, Norvel's daughter Zona stood by me. She knew how vital Norvel's and my relationship was to the effort as she had watched the ministry literally skyrocket after I became involved with Norvel. She knew the importance of that. So, she wanted to attempt to smooth things over.

Norvel never told me what was wrong, why the schism developed. There was just silence. It was amazing to me that he did not confront me. He just started shunning me because of things some pastors had said concerning what I had taught about. But I had taught some of the very same things in front of Norvel and he was absolutely elated with them! However, when he heard complaints from pastors, he wasn't so elated any more. Norvel was a businessman. He knew that the business was wrapped up in pastors and their congregations. And if you displease the pastors, you are jeopardizing your client base. So, Zona, in an attempt to get me teaching in front of Norvel again as if to remind him that I was actually okay, arranged for me to be one of the guest speakers with Norvel and Dwight Thompson at a big seminar held in Gatlinburg, Tennessee.

Dwight Thompson is not a very big-named speaker anymore. However, he was at that time. He's pretty much fallen off the radar now for whatever reason. So, we were in Gatlinburg, Tennessee. I stayed on the 11th floor of the hotel, which was the top floor. It was built in a circle. When you'd walk out into the hallways, they would proceed around in a circle, and all of the hallways became balconies that looked across the hotel to the floor on the other side. You could look down all the way to the lobby on the main floor from the balconies. Norvel was particularly fond of that hotel for some reason and booked it every year.

During the meetings, I was sitting on the platform with these two men and Dwight Thompson was sharing his "great revelation" about how there won't be any thieves in heaven. Then he quoted Malachi, about "Will a man rob God? You have robbed me in tithes and offerings." So, he came up with the great revelation that if you are not current on your tithes when you die, you will not go to heaven. It was amazing how these people would preach on the saving blood of Jesus and then you could lose it all just because you weren't current on your bills to God! The contradiction of that hit me tremendously.

My understanding of grace versus law was really coming into focus at that time. I had not only learned about the Gospel of Peace but by then I had learned the difference between grace and law and between the righteousness of God and self-righteousness.

Jim Richards, another Bible teacher who travelled with me for awhile, taught me the things I first embraced about the righteousness of God. I taught Jim about the grace of God and he taught me about the righteousness of God. However, when I started teaching the tithe was fulfilled, Jim cut off all ties with me. I have to give Jim the credit though; he's the one who introduced me to the concept of righteousness through faith. I will always be thankful to Jim for that. He doesn't embrace anything I teach now and does not embrace me personally at all. But I did learn that very wonderful part of my journey from Jim Richards.

Also teaching that week at Gatlinburg was Norvel. He, too, had his own "great revelation." He said "I don't know if you know it or not, but Mutual of Omaha's *Wild Kingdom* (a popular old American TV show about wild animals) is the most demon-possessed show on TV." And everybody just sat there waiting for this great revelation and he said, "Any animal that would eat the flesh of another animal is totally demon possessed!" And everybody just sat there like "Yeah.

Praise the Lord!" I was sitting there thinking to myself, "Norvel, I sat with you at dinner yesterday. You ate *a steak!*" All these contradictions that were so galling to me were not an issue in any way with the rest of the speakers! The thing that blew me away was that these contradictions were so incredibly glaring to me, but they were not issues at all for these other men! It was an amazing, amazing experience for me.

Meanwhile, Norvel was terrified that I was going to say some of the things that some of those pastors had complained to him about. I was teaching on grace and law, but Norvel asked me to give my testimony. So, I did. Compared to what I had done before, it was *so* watered down. Norvel was *so* disappointed. He said, "Mike you didn't say *this*, you didn't say *that*"—all the things that I had been instructed to say from the inception of "my testimony," shared under Norvel's tutelage on *how* to share it, and *what* to share, and things that actually grew out of things *he* said, things that just were not true at all! But if Norvel said them, it had to be true! For the first time in my life he was very disappointed with the presentation of my testimony. It was, in all candor, half-hearted at best. I was almost sick to my stomach having to do it again.

That was the last time I ever "shared my testimony."

Then Norvel, trying to control the situation, said, "Now tomorrow Mike, tomorrow, in your session tomorrow, I want you to teach the people on *deliverance* Mike! Teach them on *deliverance.* There are a lot of pastors here. You'll get a lot of invitations. I want you to teach on *deliverance.*" (That's how Norvel talks.) He was very emphatic about it and I could tell he was trying very hard to steer what I was going to say because of those pastors' prior complaints.

That night was a torturous night for me.

I already knew from my heart I wanted to share on grace and law. But Norvel told me I was supposed to teach on deliverance. I had never disobeyed Norvel. Norvel will tell you I had never disobeyed him. I always did what he said and did a bit more.

So, I was awake much of that night before. I walked out to that balcony thinking, "I just need to throw myself from the pinnacle of this 'temple!' I cannot do this, I just cannot!" I was so torn. I came back inside and I remember I did a little Bible-roulette thing. I don't know if it was intentional or if I just opened my Bible randomly, but it just fell open and landed on Romans where it says "For Christ has *delivered* us *from the law."* I saw the term "delivered," and I about went through the roof of that hotel. I thought, "Oh my God! Christ has *delivered us* . . . it IS *deliverance!* Deliverance from the law! I felt like I'm supposed to speak on grace and law. Norvel says I'm supposed to teach on deliverance. I can obey Jesus *and* Norvel! So, I get to teach on deliverance! I'm teaching on deliverance tomorrow!"

I never will forget that next day. I made it very clear when I got up to speak. This was back when we used to make everyone repeat everything you say all the way through. So, I got up and said, "I want you to repeat after me, *This morning (This morning), brother Mike (brother Mike), is going to teach on deliverance! (is going to teach on deliverance!) Yay!! Say it again with me! This morning (This morning), brother Mike (brother Mike), is going to teach on deliverance! (is going to teach on deliverance!)"* So, everybody was excited.

I did get to teach on deliverance. And I watched "deliverance" happen that morning to the people who had sat there in bondage to legalism. Five of them collapsed into the arms of the person sitting next to them. The bondage was so deep and so hard and so cold, and then to hear Christ had delivered us from the law, they collapsed from the relief. I spoke directly against everything that had been taught that week. I made sure they knew: "If anybody was trying to tell you that you had to perform to receive from God, it was false doctrine."

Finally, I knew I was really sharing on *deliverance.*

When I first began my search concerning the grace of God, this was one of those thunderbolt moments for me. I had heard what "falling from grace" was all of my life. The Baptists taught me well. The Catholics taught it well. Everyone taught what "falling from grace" was. Without exception they taught that falling from grace was: doing something bad enough, or doing something not so bad often enough, that you would "fall from God's grace" and/or lose your salvation—you would no longer be in God's good graces.

When everything hit the fan in the media about Jim and Tammy-Faye Bakker's ministry (a huge ministry "empire" back in the '80s), the scandal began to unfurl. It was like a made-for-TV movie. There was sex and money and religion. Then they of course were put out of their ministry with a "hostile" takeover from Jerry Falwell (a conservative Christian minister and activist). Jerry rode down the slide at Jim and Tammy's amusement park and took the place over. During that time, Jim and Tammy were spoken of as having "fallen from grace." In fact, Hollywood even made the movie! And they had no problems speaking of Jim and Tammy-Faye Bakker in this context of "fallen from grace." In fact, they called the movie *Fall From Grace*. Now, when Hollywood begins to understand something like this, we need to sit up and take notice. However, Hollywood was only parroting what Christianity had taught them. Thank God in many other areas, the art world actually picks up on the *real* grace of God, the gospel it produced, and proclaims it in a very powerful way through their art.

When I began to open my mind to what grace was and what to compare it to, I realized the clearest way to understand anything you must know what to compare it to. All of Paul's teachings about the law compared it to grace. Comparative-teaching is oh so powerful! All of Paul's writings about grace compared it to the law. It is the comparison of these two subjects which give us full understanding of both. If you don't have a full understanding of the law, and its complete and ultimate purpose, then you're going to simply pick your way through what law you want to keep and which ones you want to discard. You begin to apply those that are applicable to other people's lives and you begin to excuse yourself for the ones that are applicable to you and yours. Or you feel inferior by a law that others have imposed on you. What a bunch of malarkey! But it is done every day and has been done for thousands of years.

For years "falling from grace," just the thought of it, was horrific for me. I considered falling from grace right up there with the blasphemy of the Holy Spirit (also called the "unpardonable sin" by many), or just *blasphemy* itself. What a frightening thing to think that you have blasphemed. What a terrifying thought to think you had fallen from grace.

As I read through the passage about falling from grace, I saw it all in the context of Paul's complete thought. I was truly blown away. I wasn't sure if I even read this to people, that they would believe what I was reading, because *I* had never read this in context. Somebody had *told* me what falling from grace supposedly was. Therefore when reading it, I was blinded to the reality of what falling from grace actually was because I had already had that long-held pre-conceived notion.

Even before I became a serious Christian, I knew about falling from grace. This is a universal statement that is made around the world with the same common understanding. Everybody knows what falling from grace is. You don't have to go to church to learn what it means to fall from grace. It doesn't even have to be pertaining to God. Falling from grace is just when you have done something bad that disqualifies you from being able to stay in the position you were in. You have "fallen from grace."

Paul spoke about falling from grace in Galatians Chapter 5. He starts out by saying "stand fast!" He says, "Stand fast therefore in the liberty/freedom, wherewith Christ has made/set us free." This particular phrase, "wherewith Christ has set us free," in the original Greek means to be freed from moral, mortal, and ceremonial law. Do you realize that means *all* law? All moral, mortal and ceremonial law is the entirety of God's law. All of God's law fits into these three categories—moral, mortal, and ceremonial. Christians try to teach you, if they believe in any kind of grace at all, that you are free from the ceremonial law. Some might even teach that you are free from some of the moral law, but none of the mortal law. They break sins down into these different categories—the aforementioned fragmenting of the law. What they allow you to be free from and what they won't allow you to be free from is up to their discretion. I'm telling you it's *not* up to their discretion to tell you what law you are free from!

Stand fast in your freedom!!!

Paul made it very clear in his teaching that everyone has been freed from everything written in stone and ink according to 1 Corinthians Chapter 3. Paul's magnificent teaching about this incredible freedom makes a very direct stand that the law has been done away with. You will hear many people say, "There's no place in the Bible that says God's law has been done away with!" Well, I'm sorry, but it was repeated several times that all of God's law, specifically that which is written in stone and specifically that which is written in ink, has been done away with.

"Stand fast." Just the instruction here says that you will have to put some effort into this. It's an interesting juxtaposition of words, isn't it? Stand. Fast. Now many folks want to accuse me and say you shouldn't have to put any effort into anything. That's just not true. In fact, it's a lie! You have to put effort into remaining in the gospel because of all the voices out there that have and continue to desire to pollute and dilute the message. Now, I'm not telling you not to listen to the other voices. There is a major difference between when you hear me teach the gospel and when you hear other people teach legalism. They will warn you not to listen to me, but I warn you that you *should* listen to them! Listen closely. Take in every word they say, because it is in what they say that disqualifies them from teaching a single word of what they say. You see, if I tell you not to listen, I am telling you that what the gospel is saying is so weak that you can't go out and listen to something else. Take in these guys. Turn them on and listen to them. I do. Listen to what they have to say. What you're going to hear is self-righteousness, pure and simple. You're going to hear three offenses to God's grace in every sermon almost without exception: falling from grace, doing despite to the spirit of grace, and failing of the grace God. I realize they might leave one of them out in some of their sermons. Listen to them long enough, though, and it isn't going to take too long before you hear all three offenses to God's grace. Stand fast. You're going to have to stand because these voices are all around. They are everywhere. You're going to have to hear them out and realize what you believe about the gospel and what you do not believe the gospel is about.

Paul's teaching on "falling from grace" in the book of Galatians is so very clear. Falling from grace would be described in the Christian world as either doing something that was *really wrong*, or doing something *wrong* too many times, and finally you just come to the point where you have "fallen from grace"—especially after you get caught. That's how Christianity would describe a fall from grace, and the "secular" community even subscribes to Christianity's definition of it! They will talk about a politician who was caught in a sex scandal and gets put out of office, or whatever scandalous act, and they will call it "a fall from grace."

When I first started understanding God's grace, I went to the Christian bookstore in our town. It was a large bookstore. I went in looking for books on grace because I was just beginning to see it and wanted more information. I realized the number of times grace is mentioned in the New Testament writings almost as many as the number of times faith is mentioned and I thought, "I need to know something about grace." So, I went into the bookstore and I could not find ANY books on the grace of God. Now, a lot has changed since then. Yes, the message of grace has permeated the Earth. A lot of people are increasing in their knowledge and understanding of grace. There is a lot of people who've moved dramatically towards grace. Many people are teaching now the same thing that I was teaching back in the '90s.

The reason people don't increase in the understanding of grace is because they are doing "despite" to the spirit of grace. They are failing of the grace of God, and they are falling from grace—all three. They started understanding and teaching on grace. They started teaching the difference between grace and law and giving people a little bit of freedom. That's what gives me hope. However, a little bit of freedom is never enough. If you taste freedom at all, you're going to want it all, and that is exactly where the gospel always goes. One of many of my previous colleagues called it "the slippery slope of grace." Let me tell you something; it's not just slippery. It is a freefall! When you get freed from the law you're not falling from grace, you're falling right straight into it!

Unfortunately, they are trying to teach you that grace gets you free from sin, but they are talking about *your* own sin, as if you had any. They don't understand that *your* sin, everyone's sin, *that imputed sin,* has already been dealt with.

The law was given by God to reveal ONE sin in ONE man, imputed to all!

What was imputed to all? Unbelief! If unbelief is the sin, can belief cure unbelief? NO, the law reveals that only death could bring relief to sin! You see, the only real difference is that we have identified the sin. We know that Jesus died for THE sin of the world. The question has always been "WHAT sin?" Obedience to the law could not cure the transgression to the law. The cure for transgression of law is not obedience. The cure for transgression of the law was the removal of the law through death. The cure for the sin of unbelief was revealed by the law. The only cure for the sin of unbelief was death!

What grace is there to free you from is the law because the law is the only thing that holds sin against *you*. You've got to get rid of the root.

You've got to get to the point to where you understand that we are delivered from the very essence of this issue of sin. In this "new economy of God," sin is not a commodity we deal in. In this "new world," "The New Heaven and the New Earth," THERE IS NO SIN! As Paul said, "where there is no law, there is no transgression." It is actually impossible for God to hold anything against you! The law, which "was against us," was nailed to the cross, in the form of a body, Jesus, the very Word made flesh. Let this good news permeate every part of you until your mind is totally renewed . . . and then STAND FAST!

You've got to stand fast!

Paul's definition however is quite different from how "fallen from grace" is used in the everyday vernacular. Paul wrote, "Christ has become of no effect unto you; whosoever of you is justified by the law you are fallen from grace." Paul's definition of this was drastically contrary to those pre-conceived notions about God's grace. Paul's teaching about it said "You who are justified by the law—you have fallen from grace." I couldn't even believe it when I read it! I had heard about falling from grace all of my Christian life! But, now it was clear, I had heard wrong!

What does it mean to have Christ to be of no effect to you? If it is that Christ is having no effect, then are we saying that righteousness is not having an effect? Christ is the one who brought us righteousness! That's what Christ was for. Christ was to usher in everlasting righteousness. Do you see how, by allowing those who acquiesce and succumb to the brow-beating of a preacher to believe, is doing despite to the spirit of grace to make the grace of God irrelevant? This is simply not what it's all about.

Let's go right back to Isaiah Chapter 32 to demonstrate what you lose if Christ has become of no effect: "And the work of righteousness shall be peace, and the effect of righteousness quietness and assurance forever." There's a liberty here because we know Christ is our righteousness. Jesus is your righteousness. We can read that this way for our understanding sake: "And the work of Christ shall be peace, and the effect of Christ quietness and assurance forever." So, when Christ becomes of no effect, what's happened? Does it mean that you've lost the quietness and assurance that you're not going to hell? Yes! It means that and so much more.

I must agree with Paul when he says that the *effect* of Christ and the *effect* of God's grace are indeed interrupted when we do despite to the spirit of grace. When we fail of the grace of God, and fall from grace, the effect of Christ and his righteousness begins to wane from our soul. However, it NEVER wanes pertaining to eternal truth, redemption and our destination. It does not affect eternal reality. This is the redemption of the world we're talking about—pure and simple. But now for those of us who are redeemed, which is everyone on the face of planet Earth, there is an effect this righteousness and this Christ should have in freeing us from God's law psychologically and emotionally and mentally. And what is that? It is quietness and assurance forever.

Quietness and assurance about what, you ask? Is it about your finances? Is it about your level of health? No. That's not what we're talking about. Quietness and assurance forever is about your relationship with God, your oneness, the fact that you and God are as close as you ever will be, and ever could be.

The quietness in your heart about your relationship with God is NEVER based upon anything you do or don't do. It is not based on any alteration of morality or ceremony on your part whatsoever. If you miss the ceremony of reading your Bible every day, do you feel guilty? If you miss the ceremony of going to church, or if you miss your hour of prayer, or your five minutes of prayer, do you still have quietness and assurance? If a failure to do something externally spiritual takes away your quietness and assurance, those things have become law to you. They've become your righteousness. You've become self-righteous and are doing despite to the spirit of grace.

There are going to be days when you have no quietness and no assurance about what's going to happen. You're going to face death, you're going to face sickness, the death of loved ones, you are going to face financial difficulty, and you are going to face relationship challenges. There may be no quietness and no assurance about those relationships or about your finances, etc. But you know what? You can have quietness and assurance forever pertaining to your relationship with God, even and especially during the trying times. That peace you should and can always have. These other things we can grow in. Can we grow in the understanding of grace and come to a better place where finances are not so desperately ruling your soul? Yes we can! It has been my experience personally and through the observation of others that it can be true. Can we come to a place where relationships and issues of life and death don't have the impact they used to have? I know so. But that's not the issue. The issue is this incredible quietness and assurance that reigns in our hearts regarding us and God. This is what you have to let have its full effect. And as it does, as the power of God has a greater and greater place in your thinking, the other issues facing you begin to pale in comparison.

A fall from grace does not mean you have fallen from God's favor any more than failing of God's grace means that God's grace has failed you. The fall from grace, according to the book of Galatians, is when you have some type of a thought or a persuasion that something you are *doing* is causing your relationship with God to be affected—or even if it causes you to believe that you *have* a relationship with God—either way. Maybe your persuasion is by doctrine because you've done something, and therefore *you have* grace with the Lord. Remember, we are no longer of those who are trying to *find* grace; we are of those *grace has found*. Thinking we have done something that could cause God's mercy to be upon us is a fall from grace. This is simply just something taking place in our *own* minds—never in the mind of God. It does not change the application of the power of grace that has come to our lives.

You can't try to make grace work. It sounds silly, but it bears repeating Paul's obvious statement in Romans: "otherwise grace is no longer grace." Making grace work means you are going back under the law again. Grace is grace and law is law. There is no mixing of the two. It's the old wineskin and the new wineskin, the old garment and the new garment. We all remember the parable teaching us not to mix the two, right? Jesus told us we would ruin BOTH! And that's exactly what has happened. We don't know the law and we don't know grace.

It is so powerful to understand when Paul started speaking about his own life it was because he had lived these things. The reason Paul understood these offences is because he had gone through them and been so guilty of them himself. The reason Paul taught them was because he had gotten rid of them. Paul's testimony is one of the highest recommendations for getting rid of all offence to God's grace.

Paul encapsulated this beautifully in his testimony. He said to embrace the righteousness of God imputed unto him, "I have to let go of my own righteousness." Now that's not a testimony you're going to hear in church. That's not a testimony you're going to hear in Christianity. You're going to hear "I just accepted Christ and I'm trying to give up cigarettes, I'm trying to give up booze, I'm trying to give up women, I'm trying to give up sex, I'm trying to give up eating too much. I'm trying. I'm trying or I DID!" That is not what Paul was trying to do. Paul didn't even try to give up the murder which he had been involved with prior to his conversion. Giving up murdering people: that would have been a good place to start, don't you think? "I want God's righteousness so I'm going to give up murder." Paul knew he didn't have to give up murder to have the righteousness of God. Paul knew he'd been given the righteousness of God while he was a murderer. That's what caused him to love the gospel so much.

You see, Paul was alive prior to the cross, when sin was still alive and an issue. Paul was alive when the law was still in effect. Paul was alive when there was nothing but self-righteousness and separation from God, nothing but sin. Paul was alive as Saul and preached when sin *was* the *condition* mankind was in. He *knew* what he was talking about.

And Paul was alive when sin was done away with once and for ALL!

Paul was alive when judgment was done away with. Paul was alive when all scripture was fulfilled.

Why does that make Paul's testimony even more valid and powerful? It's obvious. Here is a man who experienced both sides of this, both economies of God, if you will. It's like the people who have lived under both an oppressive Communist dictatorship and freedom. You KNOW the difference.

Born of the First Adam and dead and resurrected in the Last Adam, Paul knew what it was to be resurrected a new creation. He was one of the few human beings who ever lived who knew in reality both sides of the fence—talk about an "Iron Curtain!" He experienced that in his breathing, living years. And what was Paul's conversion about? What was his testimony concerning? Was it his conversion from being a murderer? No, not even close.

Here was Paul's testimony to the Philippians: Wow, this righteousness is so incredible! I must shed my own righteousness so I might know Christ and the Power of his Resurrection.

We should repent from only this one thing. We should repent from our own righteousness. Take your own righteousness and throw it away because it is all filthy rags in the eyes of God anyway.

In other words, stand fast!

God sees you as perfect IN Christ, in Christ's sinless nature, in his work and dedication and study and prayer and holiness and actions. Shouldn't we all see ourselves that way? It's not impossible. In fact, if you'll allow your soul to agree with what already exists in your heart, it's inevitable.

Please know what it's like to stand before God as righteous, holy, and perfect without blemish and without fault. These are the spiritual gifts that Paul taught on.

Stand fast!

Stand before God knowing even as I do and thousands upon thousands around this planet know, that whether you're straight or gay, whether you cheated on your taxes, whether you do it all right or whether you do it all wrong—you and the Father are as ONE as Jesus is.

So many of our lives were consumed with trying to do things right, so we could be right with God. We gave it up. We changed our minds. We repented. And we have found quietness and assurance forever with God because it is the *very* work of righteousness. This is the effect of Christ in the souls of those who have chosen to lay aside their own righteousness and trust in nothing but the blood of Jesus Christ and his righteousness. Nothing but the blood of Jesus . . . .

Chapter 15

The Manifold Grace of God

One thing that I have found to be an encouragement to me along my way, perhaps the only encouragement I got early on, was when I discovered the book entitled *The Legalist* written by Jack Stewart. It was a refreshing indication someone was on a path I was on.

I was still living in Southern Illinois. I told lots of people about this book. I recommended it all the time, and a few who I was close to read it. I'm not a real big reader. I was not taught very well in my formative years to enjoy reading. So, reading was never something I did for pleasure. On a side-note, I am so pleased all three of our daughters are avid readers. They definitely got that from Hazel.

There are very few books I can say I have read from cover to cover. But this one I absolutely did. I was so taken-aback by this book that I could not absorb everything in it.

One of the chapters was entitled *A Day in the Life of a Legalist*. There was a comment in it that said on any given day in the life of a legalist, they are either mean or miserable. They're mean when they think they're right. They're miserable when they find out they're wrong. He had all these comparisons about the mental illness of it all, the almost bi-polar mentality of legalism, the swings of emotions, and the shifts of disposition, all based on the legalism they embrace.

I had known about the book for some time before I realized that the author lived in Indianapolis. One day I decided to call directory assistance and asked them for a Jack Stewart in Indianapolis. And they *did* have a Jack Stewart! I didn't' call immediately, but when I did call Mrs. Stewart answered. She was very inquisitive as to why I was calling. I told her, "It's about Jack's book." Then she began to explain to me that Jack was not in good health. I explained to her the encouragement I had gotten from the book. I asked her if there was any way I could possibly meet Jack. She finally agreed that I could come by. I also asked her if they had any more books. I told her I would buy all the books they had left because the book was no longer in print.

So one evening I drove the couple of hours over to Indianapolis and found their home. It was a very modest home on a nice street. I went to the door and I was greeted by Jack's wife. Some other people were there as well. I can't really say who, but I think his daughter was one of them. When they took me in, they led me to the room where Jack was. He was in a recliner and was obviously in a state of great misery. I tried to talk to him about the book and was trying to tell him what it had meant to me. In a strained attempt to respond to me he told me that he should never have written the book. He said he was misguided and a lot of it had to do with the suffering he was going through at the time.

I knew he was in a great deal of pain. I don't know what the physical condition was, but I did learn later that he had recovered.

While I was there with him, his wife asked me to pray for him, which I did. Meanwhile, I had such respect for this man, so I was shocked at the response I got from him, the fact he felt he was misguided when he wrote the book and that he should never have written it.

I distinctly remember laying hands on him praying for him thinking, "There's no need in doing this, this is not going to help. There's nothing that's going to help this man." It wasn't the first time that thought had crossed my mind when praying for someone. But this was the first time I fully embraced that God would not answer this prayer. There was nothing I could do to help this man who had made such an impact on my life through the book that he had written.

I laid hands on Jack. I prayed for him and there was no change. I was so torn inside. Honestly, I could not wait until I walked out of the house because everything in me was colliding. There was such inner turmoil in me from this visit on every level. I was very disturbed because of Jack's condition. His mental and emotional state that night when I talked to him about his writing the book, and also about God, was unnerving. It was an amazing time for me. I walked out of that house with everything inside of me coming apart.

Driving away, I was literally trying to hold this outburst back because it was something of a magnitude I was not familiar with. Before I could get very far, probably just a few feet, everything within me began to fracture emotionally. I began to weep openly and then it got to the point of screaming and crying. I pounded my fist on the steering wheel and stomped my feet on the floor. I knew I had to get the van pulled over to the side and park it. My entire body was convulsing with screams of rage.

Broken-hearted for Jack, I was devastated at the reality that my laying hands on Jack or anybody else is not going to help. This man who had been such an influence on me and had helped me so much by his book was in a devastated situation physically, mentally, and emotionally. Why did he wish he had never written the book in the first place? How could I have been so helped and the man whose work had touched me so much was distraught for ever having written it?

I was confused and devastated.

A storm of confusion was raging inside of me—the many areas of my life that had been held together with the glue of superficial spiritual persuasions and religious edicts and doctrines—were colliding with this new vista of understanding the grace of God.

Everything was completely flying apart.

As all of this was taking place inside of me—it felt like the whole world was involved in this horrible swirl of devastating pain and anguish, anger and grief all at the same time. I was so angry at God. I was livid. I was broken. I screamed. I cried. I did not utter a formal prayer. I couldn't. It was a horrible gut-wrenching and mind-twisting experience. In the midst of all this, my body was literally flailing back and forth in the driver's seat of the van. I tried to hold onto the steering wheel to protect myself from the violence of what I was going through. If anyone from the religious sect I was in had seen me, they would definitely have, without a doubt, started casting the devil out of me. But right in the middle of the rage and anger and emotional cyclone, deep in my heart I heard something. (I've only had this happen on a handful of occasions. The only thing I know to do about these types of situations is to share them. I hope everyone will share their experiences whatever they are. How those experiences are defined is another thing. I just don't want to over-spiritualize them.)

In the middle of this emotionally violent situation I heard within my own heart:

> *You have learned enough grace to accept the fact that I do not judge you based on what you do or what you do not do. When will you receive the grace to be able to accept me not based on what I do or what I do not do?*

It would have taken a Hollywood production to demonstrate the instantaneous conversion in my soul from a convulsive violence, grief and anger to a peace that washed over me. It was as if someone had thrown a light switch. I couldn't tell you to this day whether they were turning a light on or turning a light off. All I know is there was profound quietness that had replaced this inner war. Suddenly there was an absolute peace inside of me.

When you look through the scriptures, the vast majority of the times when speaking about the characters in the Old Testament, it talks about them *finding* grace in the sight of the Lord or "looking for grace" or "trying to find grace." So, we understand that grace is not a new subject for the human race. However, the difference is that today nobody has to try to find grace in the eyes of the Lord. There were people such as Noah who found grace in the eyes of the Lord. Nobody has to look for grace anymore. Nobody has to pursue grace anymore. Now grace has pursued and found us. And this all because of the magnificent work that was done at the cross. We're told that it is by the grace of God through faith and by grace that we have been redeemed. So, the act of grace truly is the implementation of the redemption of the world.

When reading verses about grace, I attribute all of the work of God to the grace of God. However, there was one thing that I had to slow down to read because somebody had subdivided this verse and this understanding in my brain. I had to go back and let it stand for itself rather than let somebody separate it for me. It was in Paul's letter to the Ephesians, "For by grace are you saved through faith and that not of yourselves, it is the gift of God not of works lest anyone should boast." The powerful thing about it is that it's not just the *grace* of God, but it's also the *faith* of God by which we are saved. "For by grace are you saved through faith and that not of yourselves." So, neither the grace nor the faith is of our selves. The separation of those two subjects has been highlighted by Evangelical Christians who are willing to believe in "grace" as long as the "faith" is not attributed to God but made a requirement for the human race to handle.

Everybody in Christianity pretty well knows what grace is. The problem is just *where* they believe it is *appropriated*. You won't find a Catholic that doesn't believe in grace. You will not find any Protestant that does not believe in grace. However, it is the *degree* to which it is appropriated and *how* it is appropriated that comes into question. Again, in the Old Testament and throughout the scriptures, they *found* grace. Still, I am glad to report to you that we don't have to try to find grace in the eyes of the Lord. Grace has found *us* in the eyes of the Lord!

There probably is no way any human being will ever be able to teach fully on the grace of God. I hope others do more study and research into it because there are so many little statements about grace that can reveal huge new understandings. For example, Peter called God's grace *the manifold grace of God,* which just about stupefied me. What an incredible thing that one of the writers of the New Testament would write about the manifold grace of God. The word "manifold" means many-sided and is indicative of something reflective. The term "manifold" also means the many faceted, many faces of the grace of God. When I hear about something being multifaceted, I think immediately of a diamond and all of the different ways that the reflection can come off of it. All we can do is get these beautiful reflections of God's grace. It's way too great. It's way too marvelous! It is many-sided like a diamond or cut crystal. You can look at the very same one and move your head just slightly, and now you see red, now you see green, now you see blue, and you don't even have to walk all the way around the thing to see the different reflections that are there.

Grace is not only applied for our redemption, but there is a *multi-facet-ness* to the grace of God. I think it really has more to do not so much with the application of grace but how grace reflects off certain situations in our lives. Grace is multi-faceted. It doesn't mean that grace is a *multiple thing.* Multi-faceted is simply the many ways it is reflected in the life of any human being. A multitude of stories could lead you to understand and to see the *multi-facet-ness* of the grace of God. I don't believe there is a multi-faceted *application* of God's grace. I believe there is a multi-faceted *reflection* of God's grace. God's grace is that powerful thing that has found us righteous and holy through the blood of Jesus Christ.

Grace! The manifold grace of God shows up everywhere.

As I watched the movie *Invictis* about Nelson Mandela, oh the grace! The numerous themes of the nature of grace throughout that film! When you look at the lives of Martin Luther King, Jr., and many others, you can see the *multi-facet-ness* of God's grace and forgiveness and the way it reflects out of certain people's lives. There is a multitude of ways it does! These are just people we know of in the forefront of our societies, but God's grace can be reflected through anyone. It is the manifold grace of God. Many times we get a reflection of God's grace out of someone who doesn't even claim to be a part of the family of God, but it doesn't matter what a human being claims. The awesome thing is that God's grace *has* found *us*. We are not finding God's grace. In many cases, people who have no concept about the grace of God can actually give off a beautiful reflection of the grace of God and its *multi-facet-ness*.

Christianity fell into thinking like many of the Disciples when they claimed the teachings of Paul were "using" the grace of God for some dubious purpose. Some of the Disciples thought, and some people think today, that Paul was teaching that in the book of Galatians as well. But that is simply not true. That's not what Paul was talking about whatsoever in Galatians. Now we see clearly what a powerful statement it was when Paul actually said "Not only have you fallen from grace, but he said Christ, *Christ* has become of no effect unto you." What an incredible statement! The *no effect* is not if you have *broken* the law; it is if you've *kept* the law! Christ becomes of no effect unto you if you've kept the law and you believe that law has gained you something in the eyes of God!

Once you understand Paul's teaching on the three offences to God's grace, it makes understanding what grace is much easier, especially in its comparison to law. The teachings of Paul in his comparison of law to grace are very strong indeed. It is born out of his constant determination to get people to understand that righteousness came by the grace of God and not by any performance of the law, period.

God's law and grace do not walk hand in hand, far from it. The law delivered us *into* God's grace. It was at that point the psalmist claimed "Righteousness and peace have kissed each other." What a powerful statement! Man, I love those verses. I love that description of righteousness and peace kissing one another. The cross made this possible, as the penalty and judgment of God's law could happen simultaneously with the outpouring of God's grace, with humanity being unwitting partakers of all that took place. Seeing the "handing off" if you will, of the law delivering us into grace is just beautiful. It's the very same thing when we see the law brought us to faith. The law brought us to peace, too! The law brought us to all of these things to deliver us into the grace of God and to deliver us into a righteousness the law itself could never, ever, ever bring us to. But the law has *delivered* us to the state we find ourselves in now: God's peaceful perfection, grace!

One of the most definitive statements about God's law that I can say is that I truly do love God's law. However, we do not have the latitude or the scriptural privilege to love God's law outside of why God's law was given.

As I've said many times before, David loved God's law, but he loved it for the reason that God gave it. David got a magnificent revelation of God's righteousness. So, he knew what the law of God was given for. He knew it was given for that very revelation that he carried around in his heart which was: "Blessed is the man that God makes righteous who has not done anything right, and blessed is the man to whom God will not count sin against him anymore." That's a powerful revelation AND was the basis for David's love for God's law. He loved it for what it was given for. But how could you love that which condemns you? David certainly stepped outside the bounds and stayed outside the bounds. David was never inside the bounds of God's law at any moment in his life. And he knew it! This law was given for a magnificent revelation of God's grace. The absoluteness of the law which would condemn all would eventually be compared with the absoluteness of God's grace, which would redeem all and bring all into righteousness that the law could not do. "For what the law could not do, grace has done." The law could not bring the righteousness which it demanded, but grace has delivered us into the righteousness that the law demanded.

Now that is good news!

Please understand God's law and respect God's law. Any time you teach on grace, and somebody thinks you are somehow insulting the law of God—let it be far from it in reality. In fact, those who *embrace* the law for *righteousness* are those who *offend* God's law. You could really do the same thing to God's law to offend God's law. To offend God's law is to add any *grace* to it! You might want to read that again. You cannot add grace to law, because law doesn't want any grace applied. Law wants to introduce you to God's grace. It does not want to have grace imply that there is some way around the law. The law was our school master to bring us *to* God's grace and *to* God's faith. To mix these either way: to add grace to law or to add law to grace, dilutes both to no effect. They are mutually exclusive, not in that they are opposing one another, but because the law is what Paul credits to have brought us to the faith and grace of God.

This dividing line is so powerful and critical.

Under the law there is nothing but wrath. Under the law there *is* reapplication of the blood. Under the law, if you break one law, you've broken them all. People have offended God's law and reduced it to a pharisaical view. That's why Jesus' teaching ministry was so poignant and misunderstood. He taught the law the way it was intended to be taught! He didn't add any grace to law. Jesus should have been the last teacher and preacher of the law. In fact, Isaiah said he came "to make his law honorable." He let the law *be* "the law." He let you know "It's not only if you *do it*, it's if you even *think about it!*" There's no grace offered in that at all, is there?! There's no leniency given to any law. In fact, if you broke *any* law, you have broken *every* law.

The law is profoundly rigid, conclusive and completely unforgiving.

If you're under the law, you're under wrath. If you were under the law there had to be reapplication of blood just for the "covering up" of sin and that never even brought *forgiveness* of sin. Now that the law has brought us to grace, to mix these two together is not only an insult to the work of Christ, but also blinds our understanding to the real good news of the gospel.

The law is *the* beautiful backdrop to God's grace.

We understand God's grace by *comparison* to, by *reflection* from, by *contrast* to the law. God's grace is something so profound, and the greatest feature to make grace come into its clearest focus is indeed the law. The law makes grace relevant. The law actually gives credence to the grace of God and to the faith of God. We see the conclusion of the law was "there is none righteous, no not one," and that "the righteous will live by faith." So, whose faith are we talking about here? If it were you or I that could live by our own faith, we would be righteous. But the law demands perfection or death. So, there came One whose faith was perfect, who never went through an identity crisis, maintaining by his faith that he was well-pleasing to God. God's law gives us this understanding because under the law there is punishment. Under the law, there is need to go back and re-do sacrifice for sin over and over and over again, and under the law when you break one law you've broken them all.

You needn't "make nice" with the law of God because, outside of its intended role of bringing us to grace, God's law is a non-issue. They are mutually exclusive yet they have no real meaning without each other. I know some people find that a hard concept to grasp. Really, it's very, very easy. It's just like a canvass on an easel. You have to paint the background first. And that's what makes the picture stand out—the background. Without the background, there wouldn't be the clarity of the total picture. There would be no depth. There would be no understanding of the picture being painted. So, I think one of the most important things that I learned in my life is not to mix any grace with God's law, not to mix any law with God's grace, and how deadly it is to do so. God's law is so very powerful and revealing. However, it cannot be revealing unless it's applied without compromise. When it is applied in full you will realize under the law there is nothing but wrath. Under grace, there's nothing but peace. Wrath is over. Peace is forever. The Gospel of Peace has been established and we should not be failing of the grace of God. Under the law there was a requirement every year that the blood of animals be reapplied for sin. The good news is that now under grace there is no more reapplication of blood needed because this is the blood of Jesus.

These comparisons are consistent throughout every offence: not to fail of the grace of God, not falling from grace, and not doing despite to grace. So, let's do away with these offences.

Thank God there is no punishment for offending God's grace. As Paul pointed out in Hebrews, if we mix the law of the Old Covenant with the grace of the New Covenant, it just doesn't work. Paul was brilliant at entering into a person's framework of understanding and bringing that framework to its logical conclusion for them. There is no need to go start all over again because you have offended God's grace or because you were self-righteous. It's time to change our minds!

A life absent from offending the grace of God looks likes a person who is free. This is so beautiful to me. What would it mean to clear *your* life of any offence to God's grace?

Number 1 - You'd leave behind forever any thought of a need to reapply the blood for sin, to once more confess your sin. Any thought that you would have to start all over again would be null and void. When we put that away, we don't revisit the issue of sin and put away for good any offence to God's grace.

Number 2 - When we no longer believe the things happening in life are the chastisement, or scourging, punishment or judgment coming from God, then we are putting away offences to God's grace.

Number 3 - When we cease to think that our obedience to any law could add to God's favor in our lives, we are putting away the offence to God's grace.

I could teach on grace itself for hours on end every day. You never lose anything with God. You only lose it in your *perception* of your relationship with God. When you fail of the grace of God, you've not caused the grace of God to leave your life. You've not lost relationship with God. Far from it. Rather, this most important relationship has been distorted. You've caused a schism in your thinking about your oneness that does not exist. You cannot believe in a potentially angry God and have a heartfelt and a peaceful relationship thriving in your heart as you and God are ONE!

You *must know* that the blood applied is the blood satisfied. It did not *cover* sin as the blood of a bull or a goat did. The blood of Jesus *TOOK SIN AWAY!* Please get this! The blood of Jesus did not *cover* sin; the blood of Jesus *took sin away!* Sin is gone! So, to re-visit sin with the blood of Jesus again, is an offence to God's grace. To believe there's some form of punishment still coming from God—whether to you or to the world—is an offence to God's grace. To think we could add a law and *enhance* our relationship with God and gain favor because of our performance, despite what Deuteronomy says, and *try* to be *obedient* and think the favor we seem to be experiencing comes from our obedience, it is a fall from grace.

Let's allow grace do its perfect work. Let's be gracious to grace!

Paul spoke of the grace of God doing its own work in our hearts and lives. Many times people want to know "Well *how* do I grow in grace? How do I let the grace of God abound? How do I?" There is no *how to.* I wish there was! You simply must take the brakes off of God's grace. And the above outlined areas are where to take your foot off the brake. I promise you if you take the limits off of God's grace in these three areas, the grace of God will do its work, guaranteed! Please remember that as long as you're thinking that there's some re-application that needs to be done, the grace of God cannot have its rightful place in your soul. If you believe there's an angry God, the grace of God is seemingly impotent. If you believe your obedience is going to enhance your relationship with God, you are in dangerous territory, not *with* God but within your own mind, intellect, will, and emotions.

You might ask, "Well, Michael, what's that going to be like when the grace of God has its full work?" I have no earthly clue! The grace of God has not had its full work in *my* life, yet. I don't expect I will ever be able to say that until I take my last breath. This is true for everyone on the planet. What we want is for the grace of God to be effective, to grow, and to manifest in its multi-faceted way in us more and more and more. I don't even know what *more* is! I don't even know the depth of that, but you see, that's the power of grace.

When I was initially trying to understand the grace of God, I prayed. I asked if there was a way that I could conceptualize the grace of God.

I no sooner made that request that I saw myself in my mind's eye. I was placed over the oceans of the world. I can see it as clearly today as I did that day many years ago. A huge hand had me by the nape of the neck. It's almost like how a momma dog carries her pup. I saw this hand up over me and had me by the scruff of the neck. Under me I saw the oceans of the world. This hand was lowering me very slowly. When I got down to where that I was just inches above the oceans of the world, this hand very quickly submerged me and pulled me right back out. It was a split second. I wasn't under the water more than a split second. I, of course, was totally wet. There wasn't a part of me that wasn't wet. There wasn't a portion of my body that was not completely soaked. I was saturated completely. In my mind I was still wondering, "What does this all mean?" Then these words came from my heart:

> *The amount of water that it took to get you wet is the amount of grace that you have experienced. The amount of grace that is available to you is like the amount of water that is left in the oceans of the world.*

I never will forget when that was over. I was—forgive the pun—*awash* with being stupefied. It was like "I appreciate you showing me that, but I still don't get it! This is way too big!" That is when I realized the grace of God is beyond man's ability to conceptualize. And I accept that. I accept I will never know the fullness of God's grace on this side of the grave. I will never know it all. But this I know; it will always be sufficient. You and I will always be wet. That is as sure as the blood of Christ is sure.

Always remember what the law could not do—grace has done. Everything that the law leaves unfinished is finished in grace. To borrow a phrase: "It is FINISHED!" Grace is not something you are waiting for.

God's grace is here in its totality and now we get to swim in it, forever. The oceans of God's grace are without horizons, without a shoreline.

The subject of God's grace is one of the most beautiful subjects that anyone can ever understand. But remember, it is through these comparisons with the law that grace becomes real, relevant and effective in our souls. It is the effectiveness of God's grace to the heart that we are concerned with. The grace of God supports the heart. The grace of God can build the heart up and causes clarity to come to the mind even and especially in the time of crisis and trouble.

Humans are biased to always believe we've got to re-do something somehow having displeased God we are in God's "doghouse" and that God is no longer happy with us. We also tend to think there is something we can *do* or perhaps *add* to enhance the grace of God. However, you must remember that God was angry. These are like our human "default" positions, and religion capitalizes on these tendencies. This is why we must continue to hear the gospel. Now God is never angry. Now, because of Christ, God is always at peace with this new creation.

Please simply *allow* the grace of God to be what it is, the gospel—the power of God. I cannot make the grace of God *more* than what it is by teaching on it. The only thing I can do is begin to encourage you even as I encourage myself—always in the grace of God—even though we have not come to a full understanding of God's grace. I have never seen the fullness of God's grace. One could only hope to see the fullness of God's grace in one's lifetime.

Chapter 16

The Observer

I am so proud of the gospel.

It may sound a little peculiar, but the gospel has truly done a number on me. In the last several years I have had the experience of observing myself become a witness to how this wonderful, stealthy, healthy gospel makes its way from the chambers of my heart to my soul, my mind. It's like being under a doctor's scalpel. You are anesthetized and have nothing to do with what the doctor is doing. Whatever the doctor does, you must trust. Notice I said this "surgery" is happening from my heart to my soul and mind—not to my behavior or life circumstances.

My ultimate goal in life is to point people toward realizing for themselves the magnificent honor of coming to know the full work of the cross and becoming the observer in the supernatural work of the gospel in their lives—all without involving Christianity and its polluting effect on the gospel. Again, this is a Christianity-free gospel. It's religion-free.

It's simply and profoundly, the gospel.

My journey out of the Word of Faith movement and Evangelical Christianity has been nothing short of a complete transformation. In the span of just 3 months in 2010, I was faced with a series of life-threatening events that, in retrospect, evidenced I was no longer the "I" that I once was.

In the summer of 2010, I was told I had cancer. Now, I cannot tell you what happened to me but it had no negative emotional impact on me. There was a growth on the side of my head. The dermatologist looked at it. I went in for surgery. They dug all the way to my skull to get that thing out. The dermatologist said "Mr. Williams, you need to prepare for the worst." So, I did! It was very "un-Word-of-Faith-like," but I prepared for the worst. In Word of Faith we would have cursed the growth, stood on the word, declared the growth a lie, refused to believe it and bind the devil. Instead, I just prepared for the worst.

I waited five days for a pathology report to come back and they called me in and told me, "You have a benign cist; there are zero cancer cells." You could have knocked me over with a feather! I was ready for cancer! Then it hit me, "Wait a minute . . . I was ready for cancer?!"

The reason I even went to my doctor in the first place was because I was a relatively new patient in her office. My old doctor used to periodically test my liver and kidneys because I had my gall bladder removed over a decade ago. Without a gall bladder it puts a little extra stress on those two organs. My new doctor had not done any tests to see how the liver and kidneys were functioning. So, she said we'd run those tests. It was during that visit she also saw the growth on my head.

Three days later I got a phone call from my doctor, not from the nurse but from the doctor. She said, "Michael, you have got to get back in here as soon as possible." And she started making statements like, "Michael, dialysis isn't fun." Dialysis?! What in the world is she talking about? I went back in and she showed me the report. I had it right in front of my face. I saw the numbers, and I was in the third stage of kidney failure. My kidneys were rapidly failing. I was either headed for a kidney transplant or death. So, here we go again. I was dying, *again*! I went back several weeks later to take the same test again and it was worse! Then she said, "There's another test we've got to run because it's *the* test of tests of tests!" So, I took the test of tests of tests, and I went back after that, and she said, "Michael, I'm in shock." I thought, "Oh well. This is it." She said, "There's nothing wrong with your kidneys."

I could have gone and given a testimony of the miraculous happenings in my life, that we prayed and God intervened. And at one time in my life I would have. It's a real crowd pleaser in the Word of Faith movement. The leaders of the movement really milk it financially. All I would have to do is leave out one little thread of information and I could say I was healed of cancer. "They *told* me I had *cancer* and *praise God* I went back in and the cancer was *gone!!*" That's how things are presented all the time in Word of Faith circles.

I've got two documents that show I was in the third stage of kidney failure rapidly going into stage four. The problem was the test she gave me is for a little guy with little muscle-mass. I am 6 feet, 5 inches tall and work out 5 days a week at the gym. The test didn't give me an accurate reading of the health of my kidneys. So, the whole test was wrong, but I could bring you those papers. I wouldn't have to tell you those tests they ran were completely the wrong tests for a guy my size. I could publish them in our weekly publication and show you I was in the bottom of the third stage of kidney failure and only 15 points away on a scale of 100 down to 15; I was 15 points away from total kidney failure!

Then on October 1ˢᵗ, I drove just across the street from the entrance to my neighborhood because I just had to have white vanilla icing. (I said I worked out a lot. My diet on the other hand, well . . .) I just had a hankering for white vanilla icing. Leaving the grocery store, I was pulling out of the parking lot going to turn left, and as I got across my lanes, the next thing I saw was a white *something* coming at me. I was broadsided in the middle of that highway. I was trapped in the car.

One of the funniest things in the process of this was the very first person on the scene of the accident was an off-duty emergency medical technician. My door was crushed in. So, he got in the back seat from the passenger side and was stabilizing my head as he explained to me what he was doing. Then I heard the accident being called in over his radio. The voice said, "All emergency responders to a major accident on Jones Road." The first thing that went through my mind was, "Oh no! I hope nobody was hurt!" My brain would not accept that *I* was the accident. I was 58 years old and had never been in an accident in my life.

They got me out of the car on a backboard. Talk about fun to watch. This should have been on *America's Funniest Home Videos*. They got me out of that car and I was in pain. They took me to the hospital. They x-rayed me. They gave me shots of morphine, shots of everything, and finally got the pain to stop. The emergency room doctor stood right there with me lying on my back immobilized. "Mr. Williams, you have a broken back. Now, it's not broken like when you take a bone and break it. Your vertebrate is crushed down like a box. "He said it was going to require surgery. I thought, "Ooookay . . . Here we go again!"

Two days later, the radiologist who read my report, not the emergency room doctor, reported to me "There's nothing wrong with your back at all."

Now at this point of me telling the story, people always say "Mike, I think I'd get a different doctor." But remember, these were three different doctors!

The old Mike Williams would have spiritualized these things and said God was doing something, teaching something, healing something. The fact is the emergency room doctor was not qualified to read the x-ray. But I've got the paper on which the emergency room doctor wrote down "broken back." I could have gotten up on stage behind a pulpit and said, "three days later, no broken back!" All I would have to do is leave out a *little* bit of the truth, just a little bit. I have zero interest in doing that. People ask, "Well, did you pray?" I have to admit, I didn't. I was just at peace through the whole thing. I wasn't trying to get God to do something for me and I didn't need a miracle.

This all happened in a period of three months.

Through these incredible 90 days I realized I was different inside. Something had changed in me. Each time they told me something was potentially life-changing or perhaps life-ending the only kind of thoughts that went through my head was "Wow! This is going to be a new experience. This is a new journey. I have never done this before." Previously, anytime in my life, my default position for ANY health related issues was that of a hypochondriac. For whatever reason, that was my natural bias; my default position. But the natural bias . . . the default position of this new Mike Williams was that of a simple observer watching as a story played out. All of those negative emotions that fed off all those worst case scenarios were completely absent.

When I went through these things and saw something had happened to me internally, mentally and emotionally, I realized the gospel really *is* the power of God and what its purpose is. This gospel did not keep me from being in the accident or from getting those bad medical reports; nor did the gospel heal me. What the gospel did do was give me a whole different mindset for approaching these things. I was able to think to myself, "Here we go. We're going to take this and we're going to do it. Whatever we need to do, we'll do it." I was broke and didn't have health care coverage. I was faced with the obvious question, "How's this going to be paid for?" My take was "It really doesn't make any difference how it's going to be paid for."

The big mind-shift for me is my perspectives on faith, the issue of prayer, the reason or "purpose" these things happen. All of these have nothing to do with my circumstances anymore (never really did in reality). It has to do with my identity. A constant state of prayer has to do with your identity. It's the state of thankfulness, perpetual thankfulness. During this time, there were people who said, "Michael I'll be praying for you," and I said thank you because I don't have a need to pull people away from where they are. When we are dealing with the respective souls of people, it means no two are in the same place on this journey. Knowing we can embrace each other where we are. But one thing I won't do is compromise the message and the reality of the gospel.

At no time have I ever worked hard in any way to attain a "higher" level. These are simply and profoundly things that *happened* from my heart to my soul and that's all. I don't ever want to share a story like that and put it in a context of "This is what we are striving for or what can be gained by following steps, a, b, and c." The only thing we are doing is listening and learning and discussing and reading and meditating the truth that is the gospel. And then the gospel does its powerful work. I guarantee you the gospel is already in your heart guiding your mind to think and feel and act and react differently to life than you have ever acted or reacted to life before.

I am so proud of the gospel. It has brought me mentally and emotionally to a place to where I don't have to go through the typical psychology of embracing trauma or death or loss. There was never a time during these potentially traumatic situations that I experienced any sensation of depression or anger. I was never in denial. I was able to absorb these things immediately. There was no going through the classic "stages of grieving." I simply received the information presented and thought, what's next?" I had no reason not to believe the information. I had no reason to think it wasn't true. While I never got emotional about anything on the outside, I felt enormous pride about the gospel inside and the way it stabilized my mind throughout.

I am overwhelmed with the "stealth" of the gospel. I love that word! I think I love it so because it signifies that you don't have to operate the gospel nor can you manipulate it. The gospel does its own surgery, it does its own work, it renews, it stabilizes, it does all of these things all by itself. It has been a slow process over these many years. However, with the focus of our Gospel Revolution weekly radio webcast, and all the thought, meditation, and discussion about the gospel that goes into it each week, this process has been highly accelerated over the last seven years. I am so proud of the gospel having lifted my soul, mind, and emotions into this position of peace, a position that has always been in my heart and has always been in yours. I have not pursued peace. Peace pursued me. Literally, it feels as though peace tracked me down and found me in the middle of my situations.

And all that I did was consistently, persistently, and repetitively expose my brain to what Paul called the "power of God," the gospel.

Christianity assigns people to positions and gives them specific roles and identities apart from Christ. Initially, Christianity relegates you first as a "sinner, a lost soul," and then promotes you to the position of a "saved person, a Christian." But what I have discovered about our position and role as human beings is the gospel totally eliminates all of that garbage. You are not "the guilty," you are not "the bound," you're not "the shamed," you are not "the abomination" and you are not "the judged." Whatever Christianity or other religions ascribe to you, the gospel eliminates that position. That role has been filled, and all of those other spots have been taken. Christianity absolutely refuses to believe that Jesus filled the role of "the shamed, the guilty, and the judged." All of the roles that could possibly be taken in relationship with God, the gospel totally liberates you from all of those positions and declares you as a righteous inheritor.

After the series of "crises" I went through with the various issues of my health coming one right after another, I got to thinking about the way I dealt with them. I observed that none of my reactions to these things as they were playing out were what I would consider a normal reaction for me. Others around me observed that also. In hindsight, they were *pseudo*-crises, but at the time they certainly seemed real. What I realized was I was not standing in the position of "the guilty" trying to work out what I had done wrong. I was not standing in the position of "the judged." I wasn't in the position of "the shamed"—none of them. I was not evaluating my situation from these perspectives.

When I had that near-fatal car accident and the doctor in the emergency room told me I had broken my back, one thing that made the potential outcome of this accident to be so frustrating was the motivation for the trip. I craved white icing! I could count the years since I had tasted white icing. I knew it was rush-hour traffic I was going out in. So, here is the doctor saying, "You have a broken back" and I'm thinking "I have a broken back because of white icing!" I didn't even consider any of the other things like I could have driven more defensively and all the what-ifs. Still, none of them caused any angst in me, not even the white icing thing. I just never took on that kind of position from which to view the accident or my injury. I didn't beat myself up because of anything. I can't tell you why, except to attribute the fact the gospel just would not let me settle into one of those positions. The stealthy work of the gospel had already placed me where I found myself by taking me out of all other positions. The reason I didn't go into the "white icing position" was because I had already been placed in a different position or vantage point. And that position was that I had simply become an observer of my own life.

Bible verses started clicking in my head.

I got a letter recently from a pastor who has a church in Oklahoma who I spoke to when he was associate pastor up in Minnesota some fifteen years ago. At the time, I was teaching on the subject of grace. Over the years, about every 5-8 years, I'd hear from him and now he's listening to the gospel again. In his letter he said "I have proceeded so far into the gospel now I feel like one more step and 'I' will disappear; 'I' will vanish." I knew then this guy was on track with the gospel and it was doing its stealthy work from his heart because when you hang in there with the gospel you will "disappear" out from that position. The "I" does disappear in respect to how you view things. You don't view them anymore from that position of "I," but rather you take on another position which is simply as an observer. You are now a spectator.

Here is a hypothesis I have about this. In a lot of crisis situations what is the most common thing you hear from people who went through it? When they go into crisis, when a "crash" begins, when the near-death experience commences, they often say "It was like I was outside of my body watching it." I have talked to so many people who in crisis get this overwhelming feeling they are literally standing outside of the situation *watching* it instead of *experiencing* it. They say, "The crash wasn't that bad, the experience wasn't that bad, because it was like I was watching it, not like I was experiencing it."

The truth of the gospel is already in *every* human being. It is quite possible that every human being has the opportunity of experiencing the gospel in some point of their respective lives. I don't want to say *ultimately* because I don't know where the gospel will take me from here, or anybody else from wherever they may be and at what point. This is not a goal to attain. This is just an experience to be had. Could it be this experience is the reality of the gospel kicking in, doing its stealthy work, and the reality of the gospel putting you in the only position giving you the ability to deal with life? Especially a crisis where it allows you to view it and your *whole* life more than experience it? So many who describe this crisis experience tell of the calm in which they watched the accident taking place. They often mention the absolute peace they sensed. They talk about it "being in slow motion."

I cannot tell you how much I have experienced this in previous years, but in these last four years—as my thoughts are consistently in the gospel—it has been in very much a state of viewing my life versus experiencing it.

Sometimes I miss speaking at so many meetings not just because of less opportunities to communicate the gospel; but because I am not listening to it as much. I need to listen to the gospel as much as I teach it and as much as anybody else needs to hear it. Teaching the gospel doesn't exempt me from *needing* the gospel and its influence in my soul. I would say this whole past year has been a communicative process in the gospel for me. I've never gone out of that peaceful I'm-watching-this-take-place position. It has been a continuously amazing experience for me. It certainly was not always my norm, I guarantee you that. But the observer is definitely the most powerful position for any circumstance in life one may face. The observer of any circumstance in life has the greatest power both mentally and emotionally to deal with any situation. The observer will always have the most impartial view, the most inclusive view and the most accurate view of what is occurring—even more than the most observant actor would have. The observer is going to have the most rational, vital, mental disposition about it. As the observer, he or she is going to see situations and circumstances in a different way than others do. Now, because one sees it differently, one experiences it differently.

So this position of the observer, as far as the impact the of gospel on my life is concerned, has been the most powerful thing that has ever happened to me. I am in the sixth decade of my life and can tell you it is the most important thing that has happened to me. I have been equipped to deal with life's circumstances. I can't tell you how I'm going to react to tomorrow's crises because I don't know. I can tell you that the position I view them from has changed. I can tell you that is the very same sensation people of all faiths, all denominations, atheists included, can describe they have in an immediate crisis. It's a mode where they feel like they have stepped out of their body and are observing this situation with a great sense of peace. The sense of peace is there because they temporarily entered the position of the observer. There's no need to do anything, to be anything else, but to just be at peace. And you experience that how? You can experience that on-going peace by simply being the observer, a witness of your own life.

This is one of the "stealthy" effects of meditating on and staying focused on the gospel.

The most powerful position we can ever have is that of the witness. In a court of law, it is the witness who has a much more powerful role than the others in the trial. Even the verdict of the judge is guided heavily by the witness. That is what they listen to, that is how a judge makes a decision, and even more so—a jury. If there's not a witness, often times they can't even go to trial. So, when you are dealing with the trials of your life, it would be a much better decision for you not to be the jury, not to be the judge, not be the prosecuting or defense attorney, or to be the criminal on trial, the accused. The most powerful position you will ever find yourself in is *as the witness, or the observer* of your life.

Just imagine this situation. You've got the defendant and he's anxious. The one who's bringing the charges is angry. There are all kinds of emotions going on here. The judge is going to have to make a ruling. The jury has to listen so that they can make a decision. Almost everyone is fully immersed in the event. The only one who's totally free and at peace is the witness. As long as he or she tells the truth, they are liable for nothing. They're not in a winning situation. They are not in a losing situation. Here's the irony: The knowledge of the gospel and knowing you are free from liability actually produces more of an inclination to be truthful. As you are witnessing your own life, observing your own life, the most important person to tell the truth to is yourself! One attribute that's been so powerful in my life has been coming to the point of self-honesty. I'm still coming to it. I can't tell you I am 100% honest with myself, but I certainly see the value of it. I'm not pursuing it because it is a *holy* pursuit. I am pursing honesty because I see its value to the saving of my soul. I have just got to accept me as I am. I have to admit I can be jealous, not *can be*, I *am*. I've got to admit, "Michael you can be a *jerk!*" You need to be able to tell yourself what you are observing about yourself is *true*. The observer has to witness *everything*. And, most powerfully during the process, when you realize God honestly knows you and is never judging you guilty because of the work of Christ.

In recent years it has become so much easier for me not only to look at and accept my contradictions but to even laugh about them. They are ironic; some of my contradictions are *so* ironic! I just watched Thomas Jefferson's biography by Ken Burns. It's a great documentary. Here was the man who penned "all men are created equal," yet he was the second largest slave owner in Virginia years after that. To be able to embrace your contradictions is a very powerful thing because that is true honesty. Whether or not I'm going to tell the truth on my taxes, or whatever the case which arises, the thing we are talking about here is the honesty that you don't need to lie to defend your character, or *who* you are, or *what* you are. As the witness of your own life, you must witness who you are to your core. You are a righteous, and holy, and perfect person. The witness needs to take this strongly into consideration. You see, once the witness takes that into consideration then it's easy; especially if it's the witness' own life. This has great precedence because I think we can look through the life of Jesus and if there's anything Jesus did, he was a witness to his whole life.

Jesus was an observer of his life. This is clearly demonstrated through the power of going through with the cross. It even says "for the joy that was set before him, despite the cross, enduring the shame." I believe Jesus went through all of this as an observer, and it is from this position you are able to deal with yourself in honesty. Jesus observed humanity, including his own, and did not entrust himself to that way of thinking. Therefore, it put him at greater peace around other people. This goes for us, too. Our interaction with others is much more fluid because we are not defending ourselves. We are not defending what we are. We know what our faults are, and if we don't know them we are more than willing to find out what they are and embrace them. We know our qualities, our faults, or our contradictions do not define us in the sight of God. Therefore, they should not define us in our own sight as an observer. All the pressure to either live down to certain aspects of our personality, or to live up to certain expectations of ourselves and others are diminished and we can manifest the person we actually are.

What would be the scriptural evidence that influence of the gospel is to produce this sole role of a witness, or an observer of our own life as opposed to living our lives toiling, struggling, and stressing? It would be that we can literally sit back in the Sabbath rest that is the Lord himself, Christ within you, and then observe and make life decisions and take responsibility for them based on that role of the observer. It is interesting to use the example of the Sabbath because observing was the only thing you could do on the Sabbath! Frankly, that's what its purpose was—a foreshadowing of our eternal rest in God. If we have truly entered into that rest in our souls, our minds, our emotions, the only thing we can *do* is observe. That is what the rest is all about. Look at all the things on the Sabbath you can't do! Virtually the only option on the Sabbath was that everyone spend the day observing their life, their family, their surroundings, their God. That's it! We have entered into this rest, the rest of Christ, without a doubt.

Paul paints us a picture when he talks about "the life that I now live I live by the faith *of* the son of God who loved me and gave himself for me." Paul said, "For I am dead and my life is hid with Christ in God." It demonstrates his constant adherence to the absence of himself from this life and literally standing in that place of simply being an observer. "I live by the faith *of* the son of God" I think it's an indication of simply being an observer. What else can you do when you have been removed from the equation except be the observer? Paul was an observer of his own life. He said, "I don't do what I want to do, and I *do* what I don't want to do!" He was just stating his contradictions he needed to come to peace with. Now he is at peace with that. He asks who would deliver him? His answer? "Thanks be to God, it is our Lord Jesus Christ.

The vantage point of the observer is very powerful. You can extrapolate this all the way back to God himself being the observer of his own creation. Genesis says God saw his creation and said it was good. He observed all of this. He saw the daylight and the dark and said it's good. So, the position of the observer connects God to us. Now there is no separation between the two. When we see Jesus observing his life, we know that we are now in Christ and we and God are one. Then we can see the logic that being the observer is our role as well, in unison.

We are to observe this life. Jesus and God and We are ONE. Ultimately that's what God is—The Observer. Therefore, we being ONE, this is our most powerful role.

Here's a thing to consider. I've focused on the fact the observer is the most powerful position to be in. Now think about Paul saying the gospel is the power of God. He said, "For I am not ashamed of the gospel because it is the power of God unto salvation." I don't know everything about that power. However, I do know that the power of God leads us to salvation.

So what does the power of God produce in our lives? What does the saving of the soul achieve? Does it heal our bodies, our financial shortage? No, the greatest salvation I've experienced so far is to be taken from every other position, the guilty AND the judge. Just think if you were just removed from those two positions—being condemned and being the judge—if you are taken out of just those two positions, you will realize life is about to take a new direction.

When I taught in churches and auditoriums around the globe about us being freed from sin, people in the audience lost the position of the condemned. They all flocked to the front after the meeting and asked me, "What do we do now?" "We don't judge; we're not guilty; what do we do now?" And I had no answer. I'd be silent to this question because I felt the answer was so profound it did not need me getting involved.

If I have a perception of what that answer might be at this point, it's that the gospel has removed us from all these other positions to empower us. It is the power of God in our lives to put us in the position of the observer. It is the most powerful position you can be in.

The courtroom dynamic demonstrates that beautifully. The defense rests. The prosecution rests. So, now *you* certainly can rest!

When people are in that observer position in a crisis, they are no longer tormented with the pain normally associated with mental and emotional disturbances. They don't experience the tragedy. Everybody around them experiences the tragedy more than those to whom it is actually happening. I can tell you from the experiences of myself and many others, that the power of God leads you to this observer position.

I've been observing this effect even in my best friend Chris.

My friendship with Chris has spanned over 17 years now. I started sharing the gospel with him almost 17 years ago in my living room. Chris went home after about an hour and a half of me listening to him and me sharing grace and peace with him. Unbeknownst to me, he went home and diligently looked up everything in the Bible I was telling him about. Some days later I got a call from him and he proceeded to tell me it is impossible for there to be any such thing as sin. I had not even allowed myself to venture into that territory. And here was somebody, a young Catholic boy, who had heard about grace and peace for the first time, and he was discovering the fact that if this is true, there can't be any such thing as sin! His life has been really amazing to watch progress.

Here in the last year, he's bowled over by what has happened to him. He's amazed by how he reacts and acts toward all kinds of things now. He tells me the people who work for him, all of his relationships, everybody that's watching him over the years are saying, "What's happened to you? You don't react the way you used to." Mostly, Chris just smiles and goes on. He doesn't have a whole lot to tell anybody. I think what we're seeing in Chris and others is bringing us to a point of understanding where we can even put our finger on a little bit of what a saved soul looks like. A saved soul is beginning to look a whole lot like an observer. A saved soul is looking a whole lot like a witness. A saved soul is one who can view the situation almost as though it is not he or she experiencing it. They are able to speak with the wisdom of observing without the impact or the persuasion that comes when you are experiencing and so emotionally invested in the outcome no matter which side you're on. A saved soul doesn't take things so personally.

It's often said, when describing a dispute, "There is their side, then there is the other side, and then there's the truth." Well, the truth is what the observer gets to see. It's not his side or her side and the truth. The truth is what the observer sees. By participating as the observer, he actually gets to see the truth of the situation. Why? The observer is not afraid to be wrong. He's not afraid to be proven wrong. He's not afraid to learn something new. He's not afraid to say "I never knew that." He's not afraid to be corrected. None of these things are a problem for the observer.

When you take on a role of responsibility in these things, the judge, the accused, whatever, you have your defenses up. But there is something about this position of the observer so powerful you don't have defenses and therefore you can see a much broader scope of the situation. These things are nothing to attain to. These things will be produced in your heart and will come to your sense of consciousness as you continue to stay with the gospel and let it do its work.

If there is anything "supernatural," this is it. Truly, it is not logical or scientifically verifiable that the consistent, persistent repetition of the story of Christ and what it produced for the entire human race, including you, should have such a powerful and dramatic impact on the human soul. But I'm here to tell you, it does. It will. If there is anything left we can honestly describe as a miracle, the saving of one's soul, the stabilizing of one's intellect, mind, emotions, and will is that one thing.

Letting the gospel do its work is a very powerful way of describing this, because you don't have to work the gospel. The gospel and the heart were designed to be together forever. The heart without the gospel is like missing a vital organ—the most important vital organ. But God has created a new heart and has given that heart the perfect helpmeet or companion and has forever deemed that these two should be "one" and never be parted. "What God has joined let no man put asunder." That is what we are trying to communicate. We're trying to help people to not put asunder the gospel that God himself has given us as a companion. It's what he's given this new creation, this brand new heart, and says "Now I have not only created you but I have created a companion for you." God created man in the Garden and then said "It is not good for man to be alone." Therefore, God created a companion for him. God recreated all of us, though male and female, we are all as one in Christ. It stands to reason that God would also give that new creation a companion.

What God has joined together let no man put asunder. This is the stand for the defense of the gospel that has been my life's commitment. Sadly, there are forces in this world that function solely to tell lies to separate the heart from the truth.

On one of our radio shows we talked about the whole issue of the devil. If there is a devil, what would its goal be? I don't know if "the devil" is a term describing an individual or a frame of mind. It's irrelevant because whatever it is, it is defeated and it remains so even in our minds as long as we stay out from under the law.

The number one force opposing the gospel is the one out there trying to get us separated, to cause a divorce of the soul from the gospel. The only goal of that force would be to cause you to fall back into a "state of fornication" with the law. You can't fornicate with the law, religion, legalism, performance, none of that. This fornication is not something that is going to help the health of the relationship of the gospel, your companion to this new creation, to your heart, to all of us collectively in one identity including God himself. The gospel is very much like a companion that has been form-fitted to the human heart and is constantly going to be there with us. We inhibit its effectiveness when we fornicate.

There are so many types and shadows of fornication we have been given that illustrate why we should not step into this adultery against this companion. The only way you can offend the grace of God, if the grace of God is indeed that companion, is to "fall in bed" with the law. If anything is true to this analogy, you don't want to offend the gospel. It's not that the gospel is going to get angry and leave. It's that the offence will keep you from seeing, understanding and experiencing this perfect union.

You don't have a bad heart needing a good gospel. You don't have a good heart needing a bad religion. You have a perfect heart that is in need of a perfect gospel. And the good news is the perfect heart has been created by God, and it's been given a perfect gospel. With the gospel, the heart grows. It expands. It includes. It understands. It thrives. It loves. It continues to embrace more. It understands all things. It embraces all things. It holds nothing against anybody. It is a cup which overflows to the saving of the soul!

This is a union of love, an absolutely perfect love between the perfect new creation, that brand new perfect heart God has given the entire human race, with this perfect gospel. The only thing keeping them apart from a practical standpoint is religion. There is no religion that is going to allow the union of the gospel to the heart to be released to "procreate." The gospel and the heart go together. The only thing that alienates the heart from the gospel is legalism. It is the only devil out there. The only Satan you will ever have to deal with is legalism! It's the only thing that's ever going to try to divide because nothing else has such a vested interest in dividing your heart from the gospel.

Don't sell your life short or prostitute your life to a lower form of existence on this planet. Your heart was made for the gospel. The gospel was made for your heart. Let them lie together. Let them come together. Let them feed together. Let them grow together. Let them be one. Let them sing you a love song. I hear the gospel in so many beautiful songs in popular *secular* culture. I see the gospel in movies and all the arts.

The arts are called "arts" because they are gifts. Any gift is inexorably attached to the gospel. That's why when you see people freely, without the influence of religion, expressing their artistic gift; it is always, always going to preach the gospel to us. The sad thing is seeing people's gifts tangled up in legalism and seeing the mess that comes out of that.

We have a society where when a gift begins to express the freedom of the gospel, you know the gift and the gospel are in union together. So, I get much more excited about a song that comes along, or a play, or a poem, even from artists who have absolutely no inclination about the gospel. I watched *The Lion King* and could see the gospel all the way through it. *Dead Poets' Society,* one of my all-time favorite movies, is just saturated with the gospel from beginning to end with no attempt by it to be "spiritual" whatsoever.

Paul said even nature itself could help us to understand these things if we just watched. So, the gospel, far from being a foreign power to the heart, is in fact, its natural element. The gospel is the only thing that matches the heart perfectly. The knowledge of the gospel is natural to the heart upon conception into this life. It's kind of like somebody describing meeting the love of their life! It is just letting these words come in and letting the brain begin to exercise itself in the truth of the gospel away from legalism. Finding the way of the heart frees the soul. Finding the way of the heart is joy unspeakable. The way of allowing the heart to grow is full of glory. Finding out about your own heart, this is the salvation of your soul. What a powerful way to exist on this planet! And to quote the great late Karen Carpenter, "We have only just begun!"

If I were to compare this to the discovery of the New World, I would not say our ships have even landed on the shore yet of the new territory. Still, an incredible revolution *is* underway nonetheless! We *can* see the shore! I'm just glad to be on the boat and to be a part of the group of people who are willing to stake their lives on something not just for their own benefit but for the benefit of everyone else who is here and will come after.

I entreat you to embrace the gospel exactly where you are.

Reject the thought you need to change *anything!* You're not a broken image that needs to be repaired. You are ONE. You and God are ONE. Pertaining to God, you must cease thinking you have to change. And, please for the sake of your own heart and your mind and your soul, you *must* let the gospel embrace you where you are unequivocally, without hesitation and without reservation.

I guarantee you the gospel is not going to stand back and wait to see whether or not you are at a certain place in life or growing spiritually or in prayer before the gospel embraces you. The gospel embraces you exactly where you are. Where you are in the gospel is where you are. It's not where you ought to be. It is where you are.

Don't move. Please, don't move. Just let the gospel embrace you. Right here, right now.

Edwards Brothers Malloy
Thorofare, NJ USA
August 31, 2012